'A vivid and sensual record...Deakin plunges us time and again into icy, galvanizing currents, emerging on the knife edge between aching and glowing'
Adam Thorpe, *The Good Book Guide*

'Deakin's evocation of place is superb'
Robert McCrum, *Observer*

'The chapters unfold like a warm tide...Roger Deakin is an immensely likeable waterbaby'
Sara Wheeler, *Daily Telegraph*

'A triumph of topographical and naturalist writing...to weave environmental and cultural concerns so deftly together in this enchanting and original travel book is a real achievement'
Ken Worple, *Independent*

'This is a literal *retour aux sources*, a search for refreshment. It works'
Adam Nicholson, *Times Literary Supplement*

'Evocative, funny, thoughtful and inspiring, this deserves to become a classic of travel writing to stand alongside such individual memoirs as Bruce Chatwin's *In Patagonia* and Patrick Leigh Fermor's *A Time of Gifts*'
Wiltshire Times

'It is the casual inclusion of esoteric detail, wittily expressed, that makes this book so engaging, along with Deakin's mastery of the arresting image'
Dublin Sunday Tribune

'The richness of *Waterlog* must give it the widest possible appeal'
Oldie

ROGER DEAKIN

Waterlog

A swimmer's journey through Britain

WITH ILLUSTRATIONS BY
David Holmes

VINTAGE BOOKS
London

IN MEMORY OF MY MOTHER AND FATHER
AND FOR MY SON, RUFUS

Published by Vintage 2000

27

Copyright © Roger Deakin 1999
Illustrations copyright © David Holmes 1999

First published in Great Britain in 1999 by Chatto & Windus

Vintage
Random House, 20 Vauxhall Bridge Road,
London SW1V 2SA

www.vintage-books.co.uk

Addresses for companies within The Random House Group Limited
can be found at: www.randomhouse.co.uk/offices.htm

The Random House Group Limited Reg. No. 954009

A CIP catalogue record for this book
is available from the British Library

ISBN 9780099282556

Penguin Random House is committed to a sustainable future for
our business, our readers and our planet. This book is made from
Forest Stewardship Council® certified paper.

Printed and bound in Great Britain by Clays Ltd, St Ives plc

CONTENTS

This Summer I went swimming
this summer I might have drowned,
but I held my breath
and I kicked my feet
and I moved my arms around
moved my arms around.

LOUDON WAINWRIGHT III, 'SWIMMING SONG'

Who would not be affected to see a cleere and sweet River in
the morning, grow a kennell of muddy land water by noone,
and condemned to the saltness of the sea by night?

JOHN DONNE, 'DEVOTIONS XVIII'

I

The Moat

THE WARM RAIN tumbled from the gutter in one of those midsummer downpours as I hastened across the lawn behind my house in Suffolk and took shelter in the moat. Breast-stroking up and down the thirty yards of clear, green water, I nosed along, eyes just at water level. The frog's-eye view of rain on the moat was magnificent. Rain calms water, it freshens it, sinks all the floating pollen, dead bumblebees and other flotsam. Each raindrop exploded in a momentary, bouncing fountain that turned into a bubble and burst. The best moments were when the storm intensified, drowning birdsong, and a haze rose off the water as though the moat itself were rising to meet the lowering sky. Then the rain eased and the reflected heavens were full of tiny dancers: water sprites springing up on tiptoe like bright pins over the surface. It was raining water sprites.

It was at the height of this drenching in the summer of 1996 that the notion of a long swim through Britain began to form itself. I wanted to follow the rain on its meanderings about our land to rejoin the sea, to break out of the frustration of a lifetime doing lengths, of endlessly turning back on myself like a tiger pacing its cage. I began to dream of secret swimming holes and a journey of discovery through what William Morris, in the title to one of his romances, called *The Water of the Wondrous Isles*. My inspiration was John Cheever's classic short story 'The Swimmer', in which the hero, Ned Merrill, decides to swim the eight miles home from a party on Long Island via a series of his neighbours' swimming pools.

One sentence in the story stood out and worked on my imagination: 'He seemed to see, with a cartographer's eye, that string of swimming pools, that quasi-subterranean stream that curved across the county.'

I was living by myself, feeling sad at the end of a long love, and, as a freelance film-maker and writer, more or less free to commit myself to a journey if I wanted to. My son, Rufus, was also on an adventure Down Under, working in restaurants and surfing in Byron Bay, and I missed him. At least I could join him in spirit in the water. Like the endless cycle of the rain, I would begin and end the journey in my moat, setting out in spring and swimming through the year. I would keep a log of impressions and events as I went.

My earliest memory of serious swimming is of being woken very early on holiday mornings with my grandparents in Kenilworth by a sudden rain of pebbles at my bedroom window aimed by my Uncle Laddie, who was a local swimming champion and had his own key to the outdoor pool. My cousins and I were reared on mythic tales of his exploits – in races, on high boards, or swimming far out to sea – so it felt an honour to swim with him. Long before the lifeguards arrived, we would unlock the wooden gate and set the straight, black, refracted lines on the bottom of the green pool snaking and shimmying. It was usually icy, but the magic of being first in is what I remember. 'We had the place to ourselves,' we would say with satisfaction afterwards over breakfast. Our communion with the water was all the more delightful for being free of charge. It was my first taste of unofficial swimming.

Years later, driven mad by the heat one sultry summer night, a party of us clambered over the low fence of the old open-air pool at Diss in Norfolk. We joined other silent, informal swimmers who had somehow stolen in, hurdling the dormant turnstiles, and now loomed past us in the water only to disappear again into the darkness like characters from *Under Milk Wood*. Such indelible swims are like dreams, and have the same profound effect on the mind and spirit. In the night sea at Walberswick I have seen bodies fiery with phosphorescent plankton striking through the neon waves like dragons.

2

The more I thought about it, the more obsessed I became with the idea of a swimming journey. I started to dream ever more exclusively of water. Swimming and dreaming were becoming indistinguishable. I grew convinced that following water, flowing with it, would be a way of getting under the skin of things, of learning something new. I might learn about myself, too. In water, all possibilities seemed infinitely extended. Free of the tyranny of gravity and the weight of the atmosphere, I found myself in the wide-eyed condition described by the Australian poet Les Murray when he said: 'I am only interested in everything.' The enterprise began to feel like some medieval quest. When Merlin turns the future King Arthur into a fish as part of his education in *The Sword in the Stone*, T. H. White says, 'He could do what men always wanted to do, that is, fly. There is practically no difference between flying in the water and flying in the air . . . It was like the dreams people have.'

When you swim, you feel your body for what it mostly is – water – and it begins to move with the water around it. No wonder we feel such sympathy for beached whales; we are beached at birth ourselves. To swim is to experience how it was before you were born. Once in the water, you are immersed in an intensely private world as you were in the womb. These amniotic waters are both utterly safe and yet terrifying, for at birth anything could go wrong, and you are assailed by all kinds of unknown forces over which you have no control. This may account for the anxieties every swimmer experiences from time to time in deep water. A swallow dive off the high board into the void is an image that brings together all the contradictions of birth. The swimmer experiences the terror and the bliss of being born.

So swimming is a rite of passage, a crossing of boundaries: the line of the shore, the bank of the river, the edge of the pool, the surface itself. When you enter the water, something like metamorphosis happens. Leaving behind the land, you go through the looking-glass surface and enter a new world, in which survival, not ambition or desire, is the dominant aim. The lifeguards at the pool or the beach remind you of the thin line between waving and drowning. You see and experience things when you're swimming in a way that is completely different from any other. You are *in* nature, part and parcel of it, in a far more complete and intense way than on dry land, and your sense of the present is overwhelming. In wild water you are on equal terms with the animal world around you: in every sense, on the same level. As a swimmer, I can go right up to a frog in the water and it will show more curiosity than fear. The damselflies and dragonflies that crowd the surface of the moat pointedly ignore me, just taking off for a moment to allow me to go by, then landing again in my wake.

Natural water has always held the magical power to cure. Somehow or other, it transmits its own self-regenerating powers to the swimmer. I can dive in with a long face and what feels like a terminal case of depression, and come out a whistling idiot. There is a feeling of absolute freedom and wildness that comes with the sheer liberation of nakedness as well as weightlessness in natural water, and it leads to a deep bond with the bathing-place.

Most of us live in a world where more and more places and things are signposted, labelled, and officially 'interpreted'. There is something about all this that is turning the reality of things into virtual reality. It is the reason why walking, cycling and swimming will always be subversive activities. They allow us to regain a sense of what is old and wild in these islands, by getting off the beaten track and breaking free of the official version of things. A swimming journey would give me access to that part of our world which, like darkness, mist, woods or high mountains, still retains most mystery. It would afford me a different perspective on the rest of land-locked humanity.

My moat, where the journey first suggested itself, and really began, is fed by a vigorous spring eleven feet down, and purified by an entirely natural filtration system far superior to even the most advanced of swimming-pool technology. It is sustained by the plant and animal life you will find in any unpolluted fresh-water pond left to its own devices and given plenty of sunlight. There seems to have been a period, from the later Middle Ages until the seventeenth century, when moats became as fashionable in Suffolk as private pools are today. There are over thirty of them within a four-mile radius of the church in the nearby village of Cotton. Moats are now considered by historians like Oliver Rackham to have functioned as much as status symbols as anything else for the yeoman farmers who dug them. Mine was probably excavated when the house was built in the sixteenth century, and runs along the front and back of the house but not the sides. It had no defensive function except as a stock barrier. It would have yielded useful clay for building and formed a substantial reservoir, but it was certainly never intended for swimming. Its banks plunge straight down and it has no shallow end. At one end, where you climb in or out by a submerged wooden cart-ladder I have staked to the bank, a big willow presides, its pale fibrous roots waving in the water like sea anemones.

The moat is where I have bathed for years, swimming breaststroke for preference. I am no champion, just a competent swimmer with a fair amount of stamina. Part of my intention in setting out on the journey was not to perform any spectacular feats, but to try and learn something of the mystery D. H. Lawrence noticed in his poem 'The Third Thing':

Water is H_2O, hydrogen two parts, oxygen one,
But there is also a third thing, that makes it water
And nobody knows what that is.

Cheever describes being in the water, for Ned Merrill, as 'less a pleasure, it seemed, than the resumption of a natural condition'. My intention was to revert to a similarly feral state. For the best part of a year, the water would become my natural habitat. Otters sometimes set off across country in search of new territory, fresh water, covering as much as twelve miles in a night. I suppose there is part of all of us that envies the otter, the dolphin and the whale, our mammal cousins who are so much better adapted to water than we are, and seem to get so much more enjoyment from life than we do. If I could learn even a fraction of whatever they know, the journey would be richly repaid.

Packing, the night before I left, I felt something of the same apprehension and exhilaration as I imagine the otter might feel about going off into the blue. But, as with Ned Merrill in 'The Swimmer', my impulse to set off was simple enough at heart: 'The day was beautiful and it seemed to him that a long swim might enlarge and celebrate its beauty.'

2

I-SPY AT THE SEASIDE

Scilly Isles, 23 April

ST MARY'S ROAD and Tresco Flats could easily be somewhere in the East End of London, but they are the names of some of the treacherous waters that have wrecked so many ships on the islands and rocks of the Scillies. I had sailed over from Penzance on the *Scillonian* to St Mary's harbour, and was now bound for the quiet island of Bryher in an open boat with an engine like a rolling kettledrum. We chugged through the calm water of Appletree Bay in the spring sunshine, past the islands of Samson and Tresco, to land at a makeshift planked jetty known as 'Anneka's Quay' after Anneka Rice, who built it (with a little help from the Parachute Regiment) for one of those television programmes in which she performed the impossible before breakfast. Half a dozen of us disembarked along the sandy boardwalk on to the beach path, where I met the postmistress with her red bicycle waiting to hand over the mail. She directed me to a B&B, and in less than twenty minutes I had a room overlooking the bay and was on my way for a swim.

Having crossed the island in a quarter of an hour's walk, I followed a rim of doughnut rocks to the white sands of Great Popplestones Bay. Apart from a solitary sun-worshipper out of sight at the far end of the bay, I was alone. It was still April, and the swimming season could hardly be said to have begun; hence my migration to the reputedly balmy climate of these islands, 'bathed in the warm Gulf Stream', as they put it in the brochure. So far, so good. This was my first sea swim, so I thought I had better grasp the nettle of a skin baptism. I stripped off and ran naked into the water, screaming inwardly with the sudden agony of it. It was scaldingly cold, and the icy water kept on tearing pain through me until I got moving and swam a few frantic strokes as children do on their first visit to the deep end, then scrambled out breathless with cold; a mad moment of masochism. So much for the fabled caress of the gentle Gulf Stream. I climbed straight into my wetsuit and swam comfortably out again into the amazing clear water in a flat calm, crossed the little bay, marvelling at the brightness of everything, and swam back again. The sand was white and fine, and shone up through the water. Small dead crabs floated amongst the thin line of shredded bladderwrack and tiny shells oscillating up the beach. The silence was disturbed only by nature's bagpipes, the incessant gulls. I climbed out onto rocks that glinted gold with quartz and mica, stripped off the wetsuit, and lay down to dry in the sun. Spread out next to me, it looked like another sunbather.

The black rubber Bibendum travelled about with me like my shadow. I knew from the outset that I would have to confront the Wetsuit Question and concede that if I were to swim in all seasons and every variety of open water, I would need to wear one from time to time. So I had myself measured for a tailor-made suit by two friends one night in their kitchen in Suffolk. I stood in my swimming trunks before the fire after dinner while they measured me with a cloth tape from the sewing drawer. The wetsuit couturier had sent a list of the required measurements that could hardly have been more thorough had I been going into space: 'base of throat to top of leg', 'neck to shoulder edge', 'centre back to base of neck', and so on, down to the ankle circumference. When we had finished, someone discovered that the tape had shrunk an inch-and-a-quarter, so we had to re-calculate everything. But the suit fitted like a banana skin when it arrived.

The problem about wearing a wetsuit is sensory deprivation; it is a species of whole-body condom. Of course, there are people who like rubber. They enjoy the feel of it; they may even find it aesthetically pleasing. But there is no getting away from the fact that a wetsuit is an anaesthetic to prevent you experiencing the full force of your physical encounter with cold water, and in that sense it is against nature and something of a killjoy. On the other hand, I tell myself each time I struggle into the rubber, not a drop of water ever actually reaches the skin of the otter. Its outer fur traps air in an insulating layer very like a wetsuit, and the inner fur is so fine and tight together that the water never penetrates it. So if otters are allowed what amounts to a drysuit, I reckoned I could permit myself the occasional, judicious use of the wetsuit to bolster my chances of survival. It can make a long swim in cold water bearable, even comfortable, but it cannot approach the sensuality of swimming in your own skin.

At a triathlon meeting nearly everyone wears a wetsuit, and I always find the best place to witness these events is at the point where the contestants come out of the water and hurry comically towards their bikes, peeling themselves out of wet rubber as they go. It is easy to pull a muscle in the Houdini contortions sometimes necessary to escape from your suit. But some of the most useful equipment for the wild swimmer can be a pair of wetsuit boots and gloves. It is your hands and feet that will drive you out of the water before anything else.

More or less alone on the wild side of this innocent island, I felt myself slipping fast into a 'Coral Island' state of mind. There was exploring to be done. I set off past the Great Pool, a shallow fresh-water tarn outside the modest Hell Bay Hotel, the only hotel on the island, climbed Gweal Hill and found a ruined Bronze-age chambered tomb, then aimed for the shore at Stinking Porth. A pigtailed islander was repairing a low-slung cottage by the bay, and the last washing line in England was proudly flying the family underwear in the breeze. I walked along the top of the shoreline on well-sprung sea pinks. Banks of rocks and earth protected the island along this Atlantic coast, planted by the islanders with agapanthus. Its tough, adventurous roots bind the earth and rocks together and when it flowers in summer it must create a magnificent pale blue hedge along the sea. It was the first of many plants I encountered growing wild on Bryher that I was used to seeing inside conservatories. I snapped, crackled and popped along the line of dried bladderwrack that probably gave

Stinking Porth its name, humming to myself and getting lost in a pleasant daze of walking-blues rhythm. I was stopped in my tracks by a dead porpoise at my feet, tangled in seaweed and oil, baring the hundreds of little saw-teeth serrating its jaw as it began to decompose; the petite, elegant tail curled by the sun as though flipping out of its bonds of black kelp. The greatest excitement of living on islands like these must be the sheer variety and constant surprise of what gets washed up on your local beach or rocks. For one woman, out strolling on the Porth Hellick beach on St Mary's on 22 October 1707, the surprise was Sir Cloudesley Shovel, Admiral of the Fleet, whose flagship, HMS *Association*, was wrecked on the Gilstone Rock along with three other ships, and two thousand men were lost. Sir Cloudesley was miraculously still just alive, so she promptly murdered him for his emerald rings.

Spotting the porpoise took me back into the world of the *News Chronicle I-SPY* books, especially No. 1 in the series, *I-SPY at the Seaside*. I still have my original collection of I-SPY books, carefully concealed in a secret dossier, improvised from a cigar box, labelled: 'Private and Confidential – *I-SPY* Tribe'. I became an active Redskin around the age of seven, and the details of my sightings are carefully filled in with pencil. 'Going to the sea', says the introduction, 'is always exciting. But it's simply wizard when you are an I-SPY. Such a lot of things to look for – such fun putting them in your record! It's thrilling to see your score mount up.'

Back at the *News Chronicle* Wigwam in London, Big Chief I-SPY awarded points for each entry in your record book. For the rarer things you scored more than for those which were easily spotted. It is interesting to compare how rare or common things were perceived to be in the 1950s, compared to our present-day perceptions. In my *I-SPY Birds*, I find that the linnet and the song thrush score a mere twenty points, level pegging with the starling and the house sparrow. Both birds have suffered big declines in population over the last twenty-five years, and would probably rate more points now. In *I-SPY in the Country*, a grass snake scored a surprisingly low twelve, not much more than a frog, toad or scarecrow at ten, and less than a cattle grid at fifteen. An otter scored a mere twenty, at the same level as a road sign saying, DANGER THIS ROAD IS SUBJECT TO FLOODING, and only marginally more than a thatched pigsty at fifteen. (I have searched high and low for a thatched pigsty and I still haven't seen one.) One of the highest-scoring sightings in *I-SPY at the Seaside* was, in fact, the porpoise or dolphin. Both scored a princely forty, and it was time to open the Tizer if you saw one. The dolphin, according to *I-SPY*, is 'a very fast swimmer, and can move through the water quicker than you can scoot along the road on your cycle'. According to the book, I saw my first porpoise swimming in a school off Portrush on 20/4/54. I spotted my lugworm on 17/9/53 at Eastbourne.

Big Chief I-SPY always ended his messages to us Redskins with the coded message 'Odhu/ntinggo'. If you're a Paleface, I'm afraid you'll have to work it out for yourself. I wish I could help, with my copy of *I-SPY Secret Codes*, but it is Private and Confidential and 'Redskins are enjoined to keep this book in a safe and secret place.'

Masses of wild flowers grew everywhere in this Bronze-age landscape of ancient tracks, hedges, stone walls and tiny bulb fields, nearly all of which were now abandoned, grazed or cut for hay. None of them was more than a half or quarter of an acre and they were full of celandines, bluebells, wild garlic, violets and daisies, as well as leftover daffodils. The islands' traditional flower-growing economy was killed off mainly by the Dutch, who now cultivate everything under glass all the year round. Instead, there is tourism, and the wild flowers abound. Sea cabbage and rock campions line the shore, and pennywort grows from the stone walls. A pair of cows in a paddock munched at their plastic bucket beside five hundred lobster pots and an old Rayburn cooker. The blackbirds were trusting and unafraid.

Down at the southern end of the island I swam in Rushy Bay, a delightful sheltered sandy cove which looks across to Samson. It was completely deserted and I crossed from one side of the bay to the other. The intensity of the sky, the white sand, and the rocks that stood up everywhere out of the sea, had a dream-like quality reminiscent of Salvador Dali. Further out, puffs of light breeze squiffed the sea into little

Tintin wavelets with kiss-curl tops. Someone had been here earlier; I found a number of elaborate sand and pebble mazes, one with the caption written with a stick: 'A Scilly Maze'. They too had a distinctly Bronze-age look to them. As I swam out, I pondered the mazes, and a theory John Fowles proposes in the book *Islands* that a pebble maze across the water on St Agnes was originally constructed by Viking visitors, or even a Phoenician sailor two and a half thousand years ago. Such ancient mazes are quite common in Scandinavia, but their ritual significance is a mystery. Fowles thinks it may have been connected with the grave, and escape into reincarnation. He also thinks Shakespeare imagined the maze-like *Tempest* in the Scillies. Drifting ashore again over the seaweed and sand, I wondered how many shipwrecked sailors had landed here, alive or drowned. If there were mermaids anywhere in the world, they must be here.

I walked back past another maze – of tall hedges of escallonia, senecio and pittosporum, a New Zealand immigrant that does well here in the frost-free conditions and provides belts of shelter from the Atlantic storms for the flower crops. Back in the Fraggle Rock Café for dinner, Les, the proprietor, said she and a gang of her friends originally came to Bryher to live twenty years ago as hippies. They weren't the first. In AD 387, a couple of early Christian bishops called Instantius and Tibericus came to the Scillies and founded a cult of free love well away from the hurly burly of the Dark Ages.

Bryher has a wonderfully relaxed approach to tourism, with little children's stalls outside some of the low garden walls offering painted stones or big pink and purple sea urchin shells for sale for pence left in a Tupperware box. There is an all-pervading sense of a Whole Earth Catalogue culture of improvisation and mixed economics. I recognised it straight away and warmed to it. It reminded me of a time, not long ago, when money was not the main topic of conversation. The Bryher lobster pots, I noticed, are built on a foundation of a steel boot-scraper doormat, with a tented framework of half-inch blue alkathene water-pipe covered in netting, and a funnel entrance improvised from a plastic flowerpot.

The looting of wrecks continues to be an important component of the island economy. There are people who can get you almost anything, depending on the nature of the latest cargo to be washed ashore or upended on the rocks. The current treasure trove was a container ship called *Cita*, wrecked off St Mary's and something of a floating department store for the jubilant islanders. Suddenly every household had a brand-new car battery, plastic toothbrush-holder (a choice of yellow, pink or blue), new stainless-steel sink, several bottles of Jack Daniel's, and a mahogany front door. This information suddenly made sense of the abundance of mahogany front doors lying about in front gardens, slightly frayed at the corners from their adventures at sea, some already installed incongruously in cottage doorways, garden sheds and extension conservatories. All of this, of course, was in strict contravention of the Merchant Shipping Act 1995, Part ix, Section 236, which obliges you to report any cargo you find from a wrecked vessel to the Receiver of Wreck. Forms for the purpose are available from Falmouth, just a two-day journey away on the ferry.

The delight of Bryher is that nowhere on an island a mile and a half long is more than half an hour's walk away. I went over Shipman Head Down to the cliffs above Hell Bay to watch the Atlantic sunset. There were convenient plump cushions of sea pinks on every ledge, and I watched the rocks gradually surfacing like bared teeth as the tide fell. I find sunset more dramatic than dawn because you know the spectacle is going to improve as it reaches a climax. The sun dropped like a billiard ball over the rim of the known world in due splendour, and I was watching from the front row.

I was piped awake early by the oystercatchers next morning, and set off along one of the sandy island paths to Green Bay, facing east towards the island of Tresco. It is more sheltered here, and there were boats pulled up on chocks for repair, and a boatbuilder's shed. Around it, near the shore, was a dazzling semi-natural colony of plants that must have originated in the tropical gardens at Tresco: dark blue aechium (which can grow nearly a foot a week), bright yellow aeolium, banks of blue agapanthus, and creeping masses of the colourful succulent osteospermum.

I went down to the beach for a swim in the Bronze-age fields. The Scilly Isles are the last outcrop of a ridge of volcanic granite that forms the backbone of Cornwall and they were, until about 4,000 years ago, the high points of one big island called Ennor. But the melting of the polar ice caps that began after the last Ice Age meant that Ennor's lowland valleys and fields were gradually submerged by the rising sea.

I donned the wetsuit, mask and snorkel, and swam out into the shallow sandy bay. It was high tide and about thirty yards off the shore I looked down at a pair of stone walls meeting at a right angle, and a circle of stones that must once have been a sheep pen. With seaweed hedges growing from the stones, these are the patterns and remains of the patchwork of old fields that once stretched all the way across the valley to Tresco. They are really just a continuation of the remaining field boundaries on shore. This may be why some stretches of water around the Scillies still have names from Before the Flood that are literally outlandish, like Garden of the Maiden Bower, or Appletree Bay.

As I swam back and forth across the bay, face-down in the clear salt water, searching out the diagonals of more old field walls, lulled by the rhythm of my own breathing amplified in the snorkel, I felt myself sinking deeper into the unconscious world of the sea, deeper into history. I was going back 4,000 years, soaring above the ancient landscape like some slow bird, and it reminded me how like the sea a field can be; how, on a windy day, silver waves run through young corn, and how a combine harvester can move through barley like an ungainly sailing vessel. I imagined ploughmen with seagulls in their wake tilling these fields, and their first flooding by a spring-tide storm, the crops ruined and the earth poisoned by the salt. The relation between the remaining fields and these that were submerged is an intimate one. Much of the island topsoil is composed of centuries of seaweed, forked into carts at low tide and flung about as a mulch. The molluscs, of course, were all quite at home on the stones of the sunken walls, and the winkles could have been so many land snails.

I was struggling out of the wetsuit on the beach when I noticed a bumblebee fly straight out over the sea towards

Tresco. Three more took the same line of flight and I tracked them well out along the three-quarter-mile journey to the next island. Tresco has some famous gardens which would be highly attractive to bees, but Bryher was hardly short of flowers. Was this, I wondered, some ancient flight path used by bees 4,000 years ago and somehow imprinted in the collective bee memory? Or had some ambitious forager scented flowers on Tresco and blazed the trail? Along the tide-mark were thousands of the most beautiful miniature shells, all much the same snail design but coloured russet, orange, peach, white, speckled, grey and silver. Each of them might have represented one of the drowned sailors whose spirits crowd the seabed of the Scillies.

Next afternoon I boarded the *Scillonian* and rode the Atlantic swell back to Penzance. A party of men with deep tans, pony-tails and expensive manly footwear with miles of bootlace, dotted themselves about the deck, bagging all the suntraps, and sat with their backs to the funnel or a life-raft, eyes shut, heads back, wearing beatific expressions. (They were met later at Penzance by waving women in jodhpurs and Range Rovers.) I sat against my rucksack, gazed down the snowy wake, and entered my own reverie.

One of my most vivid images from childhood is of the six Pullman camping coaches silhouetted against the sea at dawn, seen through the window of the night-sleeper from Paddington to Penzance. To stay in one of them, with the beach on the doorstep, would have been my idea of the perfect holiday. We never did, and I had always meant to take a closer look at these chocolate-pudding objects of desire in their faded brown, cream and gold livery. Back on the mainland, this is where I bent my steps the following morning, with breakfast Thermos flask, currant bun, newspaper and swimming kit. The coaches were still there, now shockingly dilapidated, halfway along the beach from Penzance by the old, disused Marazion station, and looking across to St Michael's Mount. The railway companies had the excellent idea during the 1930s of putting their old rolling stock to good use by converting it to accommodation as camping coaches, and shunting them into sidings in the countryside or at the seaside all over Britain.

The brown and cream was flaking, and the ornate gold-leaf circus signwriting of the names the Pullman company gave to each carriage was only just discernible: *Mimosa*, *Alicante*, *Flora*, *Calais*, *Juno* and *Aurora*. The range of the associations told you how well-travelled these retired old ladies were. They belonged to an era when holidays in France or the Mediterranean were the province of the well-to-do; when travel was a dignified affair involving porters, trunks, and station-masters with fob watches. Ordinary folk didn't even dream of travelling to such places for their holidays. The Cornish Riviera was heaven enough for them and the Pullman camping coaches must have looked like luxury, even if the reality was more spartan. They had water and electricity laid on, and you entered your coach via a roofed balcony at one end with a rail to hang out the towels after your early-morning dip. Ironically, it was the railways, and these Pullman coaches, which helped pioneer access to the very Mediterranean resorts that were eventually to seduce the British away from their native swimming holes and to the decadent delights of tepid bathing. Buckets and spades went out of fashion. Water-skis, windsurfers and wetsuits took their place.

I stood on a wheel and climbed up the rusting iron chassis of *Alicante*. The vandals had long ago won the struggle for access and it was heartbreaking to see the beauty and craftsmanship that had been all but destroyed by neglect and wanton spite. Oval bevelled mirrors in the living room all smashed, panelling and light fittings torn off, and carriage windows, with their rounded corners, boarded up with ugly chipboard. I walked through the tiny kitchen, oblong living room, and down a corridor past two little bedrooms, the bathroom and WC. Floor level was almost five feet off the ground. The standards of craft and the materials used in the railway carriage works in Derby or Hexham were unusually high. Some of the ceilings had been ripped to reveal that the boarded carriage roofs were supported on curving vaults of solid oak.

I walked along the water's edge in my wetsuit to the town beach in Marazion where I swam the half-mile across the shallow sandy bay to St Michael's Mount. My course lay to the west of the submerged causeway, into the mouth of the little harbour, where I paused in the sunshine by a row of cottages. The place was almost deserted, but I had no interest whatever in exploring it, because every inch was already so obviously too much explored. It bore all the hallmarks of the tourist industry: signposts to absolutely everything, and signs outside the pub that tell you what kind of coffee they serve. The romance of a fabled island castle has mostly evaporated in the usual ironic ways. It is attractive because of its air of splendid isolation, but instead of repelling all boarders, it beckons them like a siren. It was once the main harbour in Mount's Bay before Penzance and Newlyn established themselves, and its extinct Benedictine monastery attracted a different kind of pilgrim. If I lived on an island, I would want it to be a full-time affair with no causeway and all the romance of inaccessibility. I can recommend swimming there and back as one way of restoring some sense of adventure to your visit.

Back in the deserted railway siding, I sat on the balcony at one end of *Alicante* and poured out my tea. Perhaps all this destruction was simply what Robert Frost called 'a brute tribute of respect to beauty'. These six coaches by the sparkling sea had always had something of Xanadu about them for me – always fired my imagination. Now I felt somehow robbed, as though romance itself were at a standstill. There was something practical and egalitarian about letting such symbols of the life of the Orient Express or Golden Arrow to working people for their holidays on the humble Cornish Riviera, like renting Chatsworth or Cliveden room by room. These carriages had travelled Europe, all the way to Istanbul and back. They were exciting and glamorous as well as lovely, and for a fortnight's holiday you could call one home. Now all they stood for was the singular poverty of imagination that could let them rot and rust to extinction.

3
LORDS OF THE FLY

Hampshire, 6 May

THE MOMENT I arrived in Stockbridge I scented water. And when I switched off the engine, I heard it. Arriving by car seemed all wrong. I should have been tethering a horse, or handing him over to an ostler. The place has an air of faded gentility, dominated by the rambling Grosvenor Hotel halfway along a main street that must be at least thirty yards wide, like a scene out of the Wild West. Before the 1832 Reform Act, this modest village returned two members of parliament, who had of course paid for the privilege. It was a classic rotten borough. There's an old Georgian rectory with two enormous magnolias either side of the front door, and the most beautiful country garage in all England. It still sells petrol from the original pumps. With perfect timing, a Morris Minor pulled up just as I was admiring the festive red-white-and-blue painted doors and a balcony festooned with geraniums to match, growing in suspended tyres.

The village is a riot of small rivers, a rural Venice. Half a dozen different streams, all purporting to be the authentic Test, flow under the wide main street and emerge to gossip through the hinterland of gardens, paddocks, smallholdings, toolsheds, old stables and outhouses behind the facade of shops and cottages. The gurgling of fast-flowing water is everywhere, and mallards wander the streets at will, like sacred cattle in India. Their ducklings are regularly swept away on the rapids, so there is always the poignant dialogue of orphans and bereaved mothers to strike anguish into the heart of the passing traveller.

How marvellous to find a place that values, uses and enjoys its river like this, instead of tucking it away out of sight, corseted in a concrete pipe. Stockbridge has made the most of the Test in a hundred different ways. And everywhere there are trout, as there are cats in the night streets of Istanbul. Renowned as the finest chalk stream in the world, the Test is a fly-fishing Mecca, home of the august Houghton Fishing Club. The fishing rights along these hallowed banks quietly change hands at over £1 million a mile and a day's sport on the Test can cost as much as £800. If they caught me swimming in their river, these people might cheerfully have me for breakfast, poached, with a little tartar sauce. But there are no greater connoisseurs of fine fresh water than our native brown trout, and I was determined to share with them the delights of the Houghton Club waters.

Five minutes out of the village down a waterside path, I was alone in the meadows on the brink of a wide, cold-water swimming hole, scene of the noisy reunion of the wandering offspring of Mother Test. Slightly to my surprise, there were no fishermen about, so I hurled myself straight in. The water made me gasp. The colder it is the better trout like it, because water's oxygen content rises as the temperature drops. (This is why there is such a superabundance of marine life in the oceans nearest the poles.) I crossed a gravelly bend, swimming across the current into the confluence, a pool screened with bullrushes along the far bank. Some early swallows swooped low over the water. Squadrons of shadowy trout darted against the pale, stony bed creating bow-waves as they sped away. I turned and glided downstream, brushed by fronds of water crowfoot that gave cover to the trout as well as to the nymphs of the mayflies that would soon emerge to seduce them. No wonder trout love the Test. It is fast, startlingly clear, and alternates between riffling shallows and deeper pools. The bottom is chalky gravel with the odd worn brick. And there's plenty of cover.

Long Pre-Raphaelite tresses of water buttercup belly-danced in the current. I anchored myself on the weed, buoyed by the racing stream, then swam two hundred yards downstream to a peaty bay where the cattle come to drink. One side was kept clear of trees and vegetation to give a clear run to the rods, with all the cover on the opposite bank. A romantic-looking couple in their sixties passed by through the meadow and we exchanged a polite 'good afternoon'. They did their best to look unsurprised. Growing acclimatised, or numbed, I swam on, expecting at any moment to encounter a fly-fisherman knee-deep in waders, wondering what on earth I would say if I did.

The Houghton Fishing Club has its headquarters at the Grosvenor Hotel in Stockbridge, not, as you might imagine, in the village of Houghton a few miles downstream. Such are the oblique ways of English exclusivity. Houghton Club membership, which normally numbers between a dozen and sixteen, is by invitation only, as I was succinctly informed in a one-line reply when I later wrote asking if I could join. With its dining marquee pitched in Tent Meadow by the river and its annual springtide feasts to celebrate the first rising of the mayfly and the grannom (another species of trout fly which rises in April), the club in its early days was an arcadian affair. It was founded by the Rev. Canon F. Beadon in June 1822 as an offshoot of the original Longstock Fishing Club a few miles upstream, so it can claim to be the second oldest club in the country. The annual membership subscription at that time was £10. From the beginning, the twelve members of the club, all disciples of Izaak Walton, made it a custom amongst themselves to record their activities, observations and thoughts in a club journal, the 'Chronicles', kept at the Grosvenor Hotel where the Houghtonians would come down by stage coach, and later by train, to stay. When Walton published *The Compleat Angler* nearly two hundred years earlier, in 1653, he gave it a sub-title, 'The Contemplative Man's Recreation'. The 'Chronicles of the Houghton Fishing Club' captures the same thoughtful, playful, holiday mood of generous sociability, full of song and verse, engendered by the river.

The Grosvenor was the club headquarters from the beginning. The anglers eventually bought the place lock, stock and barrel in 1918, and it is still full of stuffed fish in glass cases, sporting prints of every description, and dry flies mounted in frames: the Detached Badger, Red Quill, Gilbey's Extractor, Blue Winged Olive and the Houghton Ruby. The convivial, Pickwickian spirit of this all-male 'Fellowship of Anglers' is well described by one of its founder members, Edward Barnard, in an early entry in the chronicles:

> For let it be here recorded, that in this Club the good example of Izaak Walton, our Patron Saint, has been so invariably followed that no jealousy, no envying, no strife, no bickering has ever existed. The wish of an individual, whether expressed or implied, has been the Law of all; the happiness of each other has been the compass by which all have steered; no angry word, no selfish feeling has ever betrayed itself in our enviable circle. Every successive Meeting has been the means of uniting more firmly, if possible, that friendship and good fellowship which has manifested itself from the beginning; which it has been the object of all to encourage; which it has been the unalloyed satisfaction of all to have experienced, and which, with hearts so constituted, must remain unshaken. Our Society may be dissolved by circumstances over which we have no control, but the Friendship which our Meeting has established, and the remembrance of the many happy hours passed in the company of each other, can only terminate with our lives.

The club had no rules but two customs; one, that no fish was to be killed under a pound, the other, 'that no member was to fish before the 1st January nor after the 31st December in any year – Leap Year not excepted'. The Houghtonians were eccentric to a fault, often facing bleak, unsuccessful seasons when hardly a trout was landed, with equanimity and good humour. The journal vividly conveys the literary atmosphere of wit and raillery that prevailed, combined with an obsession with the minutiae of the craft of fly-fishing and a genuine love of natural history. On 2 June 1860 a hurricane wrecks the club's dinner tent, yet on the same day someone records 'six white water lilies in bloom in ditch at bottom of marsh', and the members continue their interminable debate about whether or not to allow the handsome grayling to mingle with the trout in the club waters and be fished. (There were two schools of thought; the first that grayling made excellent sport and good eating versus the second, that grayling diminished the numbers of trout by preying on spawn and competing greedily for food.)

These Lords of the Fly recorded their catch as diligently as any train-spotters, so that when the time came to celebrate their centenary with a dinner at Claridges on 7 June 1922, Lord Buxton was able to quote the exact number and weight of fish caught during the one hundred years the club had been in existence: 37,045 fish weighing just over 31½ tons, of which 30,483 were trout and 6,562 were grayling. The trout averaged 1 pound 15 ounces and the grayling 1 pound 12 ounces.

All the members took a special, vested interest in 'the Natural History of Fish and the Insects on which they feed', recording in the journal the dates of the first spring appearance on the Test of certain birds and insects over more than a century; the swallow, sand martin, house martin, swift, cuckoo, mole cricket, glow-worm, and three of the most important local trout flies, the grannom, mayfly and caperer. The anglers often fished well into the evening or even stayed up all night dozing before the embers of the fire in the parlour of the Boot Inn at Houghton in their efforts to catch the opportunity of a rising of their quarry in the hour before dawn. In less auspicious conditions they would while away their days and evenings by writing verse, sketching or painting, performing conjuring tricks, or devising new ways to enjoy their catch: 'A small pike wrapped in wet paper and placed for twelve minutes in the hot wood-ashes at the Boot, which proved most excellent when brought to table.'

Mostly, though, they debated the rise of the fly, the meta-morphosis of water-breathing larvae into air-breathing insects that can excite the wary trout to a moment's indiscretion that may end on the angler's hook. The club's two main meetings, with feasts in the dining tent, centred round the rise of the grannom fly in April and that of the mayfly towards the end of May. In the days of the post-chaise it was important to the anglers, who were men of substance to whom time was valuable, to predict each rise accurately and time their departure from London economically so as to avoid having to drum their fingers in the Grosvenor Hotel reading *The Minor Tactics of the Chalk Stream* by Skues, or glancing through *The Fly Fisher and the Trout's Point of View* by Col. E. W. Harding whilst awaiting the pleasure of *Ephemera danica*.

Writing in the journal on 17 April 1830 in 'a state of uncertainty' about the rising of the fly in dull windy weather, Edward Barnard makes 'such observations as would enable me, at a distance from the rivers Itchen and Test, to judge of the precise period at which the first rise of the Mayfly would take place in these rivers'. Barnard was the grandson and namesake of a famous Provost of Eton, and was dubbed 'Piscator' when he was at the school, he was such an obsessive disciple of Izaak Walton's art. The flowering of the common tulip in London gardens was Barnard's first clue, combined with the full blooming of the whitethorn, elder and guelder rose and the coming into full seed of the common hedge garlic. Final confirmation of the imminent emergence of the Hampshire mayfly would be the full flowering of the double red peony in Islington or Chelsea. The birth of this unpredictable insect could come as early as it did on 18 May 1848 or as late as 11 June 1855.

The club's obsession with the metamorphosis of *Ephemera danica* led not only to the feast they held in their tent called simply 'the Mayfly' but to some elaborate prose in the club journal: 'It is a marked characteristic of certain creatures – vertebrate as well as invertebrate – to pullulate in abnormal numbers at irregular intervals on the stimulus of some favourable concatenation of physical conditions whereof the nature has hitherto evaded recognition.' As the Houghtonians raised their glasses at the mayfly feast to 'The Rising Generation', there was much animated exchange of fishing stories and natural history notes, often spiced by Barnard's 'keen perception of the ludicrous': how Colonel Wigram saw a rat swimming, cast at him, hooked him by the near right foot and landed him; how an immense and elusive trout was landed on 29 July 1859 by James Faithful, one of the keepers, on a hook baited with the intestines of a moorhen; how, in the same month, the marsh helleborine bloomed in Machine Meadow; how an eel, spotted all over with yellow, was caught and pronounced by the British Museum to be a semi-albino, and another, creamy pink with a bright yellow dorsal fin, was captured by the village sweep on 14 July 1886; how, when the village street was first tarred, and it rained, the mayfly mistook it for the river and laid eggs on its glistening surface; how a 6-pound pike landed by Mr Warburton on 18 July 1853 was found to contain in its stomach a 1-pound pike, a water vole, and a live crayfish 'which swam away merrily when restored to the water'.

In 1854 nine otters were killed in the club waters; year in, year out, the journal dispassionately records the keepers' steady war against them. For some reason, probably habit, their weight was always meticulously recorded: 'Fine dog otter, 21 lbs. Female 16 lbs. Another male, 23 lbs'. Sometimes they were trapped but not killed, perhaps let go elsewhere for the benefit of the hounds. Now there are no otters at all in the Test.

When the north wind blew and the members were confined indoors the club turned into a literary salon. They wrote songs, composed heroic couplets by the yard, and jotted Latin verse in the journal. They lampooned each other – and affectionately patronised their river keepers, Faithful and Harris, for their rich dialect: '7th May 1862. Faithful *loquitur* – "Yes, them's dace; slender little 'umbugs! They slips through the two-inch mesh like nothink. The roach is the worst, though; they be nasty, guggling things." Elsewhere, another of the Stockbridge men is quoted observing, 'It ha' been a cluttersome sort of a night, and I don't like they whirlipuffs this morning, they never does fishing no good. Besides I heard the eels smack last night – that's never no good sign.' Here and there a keeper's letter, with its phonetic spelling, finds its way into the journal as an occasion of further well-bred hilarity: 'June 1830. SIR, I Rite To in Farmyu that this Last Weicke wee Have Been Trubeld very Much with Porchars and wee Watch them very Narely on Sunday mourning A Bout 7 o Cloack.'

*

The cosy *Wind in the Willows* flavour of the Houghton Chronicles is enhanced by the members' close familiarity with their stretch of water. Every least feature of this landscape has a name. I was now moving further downstream, swimming where it became deep enough, wading or paddling through the frequent shallows, amazed at the abundance of trout. The local names I recalled from the chronicles were so potently redolent of familiarity that they wrought in me an acute awareness that I did not belong here, that I was an interloper. Yet I was also half-enchanted by the world evoked in the journal. Boot Island, the Broken Trunk, Cooper's Mead, Town Water, Sheep Bridge, Tanner's Trunk, Goff's Shallow, Bossington Mill were all as baffling to me as the nicknames for people and places at school when you first arrive. For all its natural attractions, there was no getting away from the fact that this river was a highly exclusive club, artificially managed for the benefit of a fortunate few.

After perhaps ten minutes' communion with the naiads of the Test, I glided out of the main stream into another shallow peat-lined inlet perforated by the hooves of cattle, who had chewed off the tops of the reeds. I arose less elegantly than the mayfly out of nine inches of water and looked around the deserted water meadow. Still no sign of trout rods. I hurried, shivering, back to my towel along a well-worn footpath, picking my way through the cowpats that were always regarded as a good omen by the original Houghton anglers.

The chronicles record several involuntary dips. On 3 June 1869

General Dixon, not satisfied with matutinal ablutions, took a mid-day bath in the open river; but, in the interests of morality, he kept his clothes on. Mrs Flowers took an active part in his rescue, and it is proposed that the Club should present her with a medal, for preserving to his country and the Club so inestimable a life, as also for the merit of landing by far the heaviest object that was ever taken out of the river.

Village bathing had always been popular on the Test. It even has its own bard, Frank Cleverly, who has lived all his life at King's Sombourne, six miles away. His collection of poems about village life around the little winterbourne there is ironically entitled *Deep Flowed the Som*. As boys, the poet and his friends used to make regular expeditions to bathe in the Test, clutching the bars of soap their mothers made them take with them.

Lillie's, where I had tea and hot chocolate after my swim, burying my face in the steaming cup, takes its name from Lillie Langtry, who used to stay here with the Prince of Wales a hundred years ago when Stockbridge was a racing town and there was a popular racecourse a mile away up on Danebury Hill. I tried to imagine paparazzi of the time lugging plate cameras into position for a snap. Racing must have appealed to Lillie's instinct for drama because she owned her own racing stable at Newmarket and was in the habit of coming down for Stockbridge Week with her beau. She scored some famous successes with her horses. I took it as a good omen when I discovered that 'Merman' was one of them. He won the Ascot Gold Cup, Jockey Club Cup and Goodwood Cup in a single season.

Warmed up and inwardly glowing, I set off to explore the shops. Near the post office there was a fast-flowing village pond where water surged from under the street, rotating ducks like bath-time toys in its vortex. Two-pound trout slipstreamed their own shadows. In the window of John Robinson, High Class Family Butcher, were three stuffed ferrets, two partridges and three fancy pheasants. Also a grey squirrel, likewise stuffed, atop the spice rack, and a cricket bat, bearing the painted legend 'Robinsons X1 v. Broadway X1'. Mr Robinson achieved national fame as a champion of individual liberty when he boldly refused to stop selling beef on the bone to his customers and advertised the fact in this same shop window. A discreet notice mentioned that Mr Robinson is also a 'Private Barbecue Specialist'.

Further along the street was Stockbridge's sumptuous village delicatessen, 'For Goodness' Sake', offering its own venison pie, four-fruit marmalade, gooseberry preserve and 'Millionaire's Ham'. 'Today's Special Offers' were Sevruga caviar slashed from £49.50 to £45.00 and potted lobster down from £2.65 to £2.30. A notice on the door said: 'Please knock loud and long and I will be over in about <u>one</u> minute.' I knocked loud and long. About one minute later an amiable man in tweeds and rude health from living on all these good things popped over to serve me. I carried off various preserves unique to Stockbridge but somehow resisted the Sevruga.

Just across the road I discovered a delightful tray of old books and knick-knacks outside a little cottage. I thumbed through a book on practical girl-guide techniques, such as the construction of an airing rack out of hazel poles, or the baking of 'bush bread' by poking a green stick through a ball of dough and placing it over the hot embers of a camp fire. There was a useful chapter for road protesters on tree houses and rope ladders, and a section on the study of spiders. Guides were invited to make a collection of cobwebs or even to sit and watch them being spun, like Robert the Bruce did in prison. There was even a cobweb-spotter's form to fill in, under the headings: 'First thread fixed', 'Spokes complete', 'Weaving begun', and 'Weaving completed'. I bought this useful volume, together with a pair of eggcups.

Shopping in Stockbridge felt a bit like being Alice in Wonderland. There were no people, just little hand-written messages everywhere bearing instructions. I fully expected to go into the pub and find a 'Drink Me' notice on the bar. The sign by the books and eggcups read: '50p an item. Money through letterbox of Mole Cottage. In aid of street children of Guatemala.' Clearly there wasn't a problem with the street children of Stockbridge.

The following morning, ten miles to the east in Winchester, I ran into a swarm of reporters outside the Crown Court for the opening of the re-trial of Bruce Grobbelaar, Hans Segers and John Fashanu on charges of fixing the results of football matches for the benefit of some Far-Eastern betting syndicates. Photographers milled about, waiting for Grobbelaar and Co. to arrive. There was excitement in the air, and I couldn't resist slipping into the gallery of Court 3 with the assorted hacks covering the story. At least twelve wigs busied themselves around the court, as well as numbers of clerks, and

I mused on the cost of it all. The first trial had collapsed because the jury couldn't reach a verdict. They had found the evidence incomprehensible. Addressing the jury, the judge referred with relish to 'the vast files of papers which are available to us all'. Counsel for the prosecution told them: 'Parts of the story are, dare I say it, quite exciting. Others are extremely turgid.' You could say that again. The interesting bits were the bizarre details about the business lives of these footballers. Fashanu's company, Fash Enterprises, had its offices at Warm Seas House, St John's Wood. Grobbelaar's company was the Mondoro Wildlife Corporation Ltd., Mondoro being, the court was helpfully informed, the Shona word meaning 'Lion God'. Nothing like this ever happened in swimming, I naively thought at the time. The furore over the allegedly doped-to-the-gills Chinese team at the Australian games was yet to come. So were similar accusations against the Irish Olympic champion swimmer Michelle Smith and her trainer-husband Erik de Bruin.

I soon adjourned to René's Patisserie for breakfast, and followed that with a reconnaissance of the main object of my visit, the Itchen, one of William Cobbett's favourite rivers. Cobbett loved every inch of the Itchen Valley, from the source at Ropley Dean near Alresford all the way to the sea at Southampton. 'This Vale of Itchen', he writes in *Rural Rides*, 'is worthy of particular attention. There are few spots in England more fertile or more pleasant; and none, I believe, more healthy.' Even by Cobbett's time, Winchester was 'a mere nothing to what it once was' – a place of residence for the Kings of England. But it still has King Arthur's round table in the Guildhall next door to the court where the three errant footballers stood trial. And it still has the Winchester College water meadows, where Izaak Walton must have fished in his later years while staying with his daughter Anne. He died in Winchester in 1683. When I asked my way to the meadows in a bookshop, the proprietor said: 'Let's step outside and I can direct you with more gusto.'

I approached the river through narrow streets lined with college houses and SILENCE – EXAMS notices. The teachers all seemed to live in some splendour, in period town houses like

Mill Cottage, approached through a small latched gate and a white wrought-iron footbridge across a mill-race. Roses over the door, a tortoiseshell cat curled by the milk-bottles, and the morning paper half in the letterbox completed the picture. The banks of the little stream, a branch of the Itchen, were decorated at intervals with PRIVATE – NO ACCESS notices. In another of these houses, almost next door to the college porters' lodge, an advertisement on a postcard in the window caught my eye: STONE HOUSE DATING FROM 11TH C. IN CRESPIANO NEAR FIVIZZANO, LA LUNIGIANA, MASSA CARRARA, ITALY. 9–12 ROOMS, 3 FLOORS. 100,000,000 LIRE = £36,000 ETC. This contrasted with another window card I had noticed earlier up in the town: A WHITE HOM MADE TEDDY BEAR WITH WHITE TROUSERS £6.50.

The pathos of this affected me all day. This was a city of such contrasts; the bishop in his palace, the footballers investing huge sums in their offshore enterprises, a gardener in a 'Madness' T-shirt circling on an Atco mower round a mulberry in the college grounds, the invisible students at their exams, the teddy-bear maker coaxing the tailored white trousers over the chubby legs.

Approaching the Itchen along College Walk, I came eventually to the water meadows and two or three piebald horses grazing by the river. I vaulted a low fence, steadying myself on a PRIVATE FISHING notice, and crossed the meadow to a convenient willow, where I changed into bathing trunks and a pair of wetsuit boots for the return journey from my swim, and sank my rucksack and clothes into a patch of nettles. At the chalky, gravel bank I confirmed Cobbett's observation, made on 9 November 1822, that: 'The water in the Itchen is, they say, *famed* for its *clearness*.' I plunged into the river, which was three to four feet deep, with here and there a shallow, sandy bank cushioned by water crowfoot. The current was fast enough to make it slow going if I turned and struck out upstream. But I rode downstream with the river in a leisurely breaststroke, keeping my eyes open for whatever might be round the next bend. I was rewarded with the sight of a water vole crossing over and disappearing into the reed-bed on the far bank. The river swung round in a long arc through the water meadows, and very sweet it was too. Here and there I saw the dark forms of trout, and minnows hung in the sandy riffles. This was very fine swimming, and I continued downstream towards the places once known as Milkhole and Dalmatia, where the Winchester College boys used to swim. The Itchen is fed at intervals by natural springs, which is why there are watercress beds along the valley. At Gunner's Hole, a fabled bathing pool further upstream which I intended to explore in due course, the springs are said to create dangerous undercurrents from time to time, and in the early part of this century a boy was drowned there. What the college now calls 'proper swimming' only began in 1969 when an indoor pool was built.

Breaststroking softly through this famously clear water I was soon dreaming of the strawberry garden at the family seat of the Ogles at Martyr Worthy upstream, thus described by Cobbett:

> A beautiful *strawberry garden*, capable of being *watered* by a branch of the Itchen which comes close by it, and which is, I suppose, brought there on purpose. *Just by,* on the greensward, under the shade of very fine trees, is an *alcove*, wherein to sit to eat the strawberries, coming from the little garden just mentioned, and met by bowls of cream coming from a little *milk-house,* shaded by another clump a little lower down the stream. What delight! What a terrestrial paradise!

I had climbed out of the river and was strolling back through the lovely water meadows still far away in my daydream, milkmaids plying me with laden bowls of fresh strawberries and cream, when a *shout* rudely intruded on my pink and brown study: 'Do you realise this is private property?' The horses looked up for a moment and resumed their grazing. I decided to ignore the two irate figures on the fenced footpath and pressed on with all dignity in my bathing trunks towards the hidden clothes in the nettle patch. It crossed my mind to make my escape across the water, but then I thought of Cobbett and what he would have done, and that settled it. I was going to stand up for my rights as a free swimmer.

I got changed as languidly as possible, then casually leap-frogged the fence and sauntered off along the path, whistling softly to myself, as an Englishman is entitled to do. 'Excuse me,' came a voice, 'does that fence mean anything to you?' This was unmistakable school talk, and I turned round to confront two figures straight out of Dickens; a short and portly porter with a beard and Alsatian, and a gangling figure on a bike with binoculars, strawberry-pink with ire, the College River Keeper. I introduced myself and enquired the cause of their disquiet. They said the river was the property of the college, and full of trout for the pleasure of the Old Wykehamists who sometimes fish there. It was definitely not for swimming in by *hoi polloi.*

'But the ladies in the public library told me the whole of Winchester used to swim in the river here right up to the 1970s,' I said.

'That's just the problem,' they replied. 'A few years ago we had six hundred people coming from the town, swimming in the river, eroding the banks and leaving litter behind.'

It sounded like paradise to me.

'But surely,' I said sweetly, 'we should all have access to swim in our rivers just as we should be free to walk in our own countryside. Don't they belong to all of us?'

The River Keeper practically fell off his bike. The porter flushed a deeper strawberry and allowed the Alsatian a little closer to my person. They both looked pityingly at me.

'There's plenty of coast and sea not far away if you want to swim,' ventured the porter.

At this point things suddenly turned nasty. They accused me of scaring away the trout and the porter muttered about calling the police. I said stoutly, and perhaps unwisely, that if I frightened away the fish, which I doubted, perhaps I was doing them a good turn, since if they stayed they would only be murdered by the Old Wykehamists. I told them I swim in the Waveney all the time in Suffolk in a place where bathers and anglers have co-existed happily for at least a century. And anyway, I said, why not designate one stretch of river for bathing and another for the Old Wykehamist fly-fishermen?

'We couldn't possibly do that because the water quality is too dodgy,' said the porter. 'Upstream of here they spray pesticides on the watercress beds and there's a sewage works discharging what should be clean water, but isn't always, into the river.'

I quoted Cobbett to them on the famously clear water. They laughed. There was no sign of the police, but the porter urged me to go away immediately and have a shower with plenty of hot water and soap to wash off all the pollutants in the river. People had been getting skin rashes, he said. Wishful thinking on his part, I fancied.

'But if the water is so evil and polluted, why aren't the trout all dead?' I asked. 'And why have you fenced in this footpath in a straight line miles away from the river instead of letting people enjoy winding along the lovely banks? Isn't that a bit mean?'

'I'm not wasting any more time with this,' he said, and flounced off, the Alsatian casting hungry looks over its shoulder.

The episode raised some serious issues about swimming in the wild, if you can call Winchester wild. I reflected again on Cobbett, and how upset he was at the hanging of two men in Winchester in the spring of 1822 for resisting the game-keepers of Mr Assheton-Smith at nearby Tidworth. What they did amounted to little more than I had just done, yet I had not, in the end, been marched, dripping, up the hill to join Grobbelaar and Co. in the dock. Things were changing in Winchester, but only slowly. The truth was, I had enjoyed my row with the water bailiffs very much. I already felt invigorated after a really first-class swim, and now I felt even better after a terrific set-to. But it seemed sad, and a real loss to the city, that the college no longer allowed swimmers in the river, or picnickers on the water meadows. I was left feeling very much like the otter, 'trapped but not detained', by one of the Houghton Club keepers in December 1853.

The matter of ownership of a river is fairly simple. Where a river runs through private land, the riparian owner also owns the river itself. On the question of access, the key legislation is the 1968 Countryside Act, which deliberately defined riverside and woodland as 'open country' in addition to the 'mountain, moor, heathland, cliff, downland and foreshore' originally listed in the 1949 National Parks and Access to the Countryside Act. 'Riverside' includes the river as well as the banks in the definition of the Act. So whenever politicians mention 'open country' they are talking about rivers and their banks, as well as all those other kinds of countryside such as mountains and moorland. And when the Labour Party Policy Commission on the Environment promised, in July 1994, 'Labour's commitment to the environment will be backed up with legally enforceable environmental rights: a right of access to common land, open country, mountain and moorland,' they meant rivers and river banks too.

On the very same day as my Winchester fracas, Chris Smith, the Secretary of State for National Heritage, had been saying: 'I look forward, as Heritage Secretary, to working in partnership with the Ramblers' Association to secure access to open country, mountain and moorland for the ordinary people of Britain. Let's make a "right to roam" a reality!' So how about the right to swim? That so many of our rivers should be inaccessible to all but a tiny minority who can afford to pay for fishing 'rights' is surely unjust? I say 'rights' to point up the paradox, that something that *was* once a natural right has been expropriated and turned into a commodity. Fishing rights are only valuable because individuals have eliminated a public benefit – access to their rivers – to create an artificial private gain. The right to walk freely along river banks or to bathe in rivers, should no more be bought and sold than the right to walk up mountains or to swim in the sea from our beaches. At the moment, only where a river is navigable do you have rights of access along its banks.

In a recent survey of public opinion, the Countryside Commission discovered that one in three of all the walks people take in Britain involves water, or waterside, as a valued feature. In April 1967, a government official drawing up the 1968 Countryside Act observed:

We have received a considerable volume of representations that the present arrangements for securing public access and providing a right of public passage on waterways is inadequate. In our opinion the solution lies in extending the powers to make access agreements or orders to rivers and canals and their banks ... and we would propose therefore to extend the definition of open country to include these categories.

The flaw in the 1968 Countryside Act turned out to be that it relied on giving local authorities powers, but not *duties*, to create more access to rivers and their banks. Making voluntary agreements with private landowners could still work, if only the local authorities put more energy into it, and if only the landowners didn't have such enormous vested interest in the lucrative fishery. The government now says it will 'seek more access by voluntary means to riverside, woodland and other countryside as appropriate'. There is plenty of scope for such schemes: if all the river banks in Buckinghamshire were opened for public access, it would double the total length of footpaths in that county. Riverside access is extremely popular. Perhaps we should learn from New Zealand, where they have renewed a law originally enacted by a colonial governor at the request of Queen Victoria. 'The Queen's Chain' gives a twenty-two-yard strip of public access along the bank of every river in the land. Across the Channel in Normandy and Brittany, too, people have unlimited access to the rivers.

The Environment Agency, meanwhile, is being influenced by the powerful vested interests of the riparian owners into confusing the natural value of chalk rivers like the Itchen and the Test with their commercial value. It is allowing them to be managed exclusively for the benefit of trout fishery along much of their length. What were once richly varied wild trout rivers have been allowed to become highly manipulated leisure enterprises capable of delivering a more or less guaranteed catch of four or five fish to the people, often tourists, who can pay to fish there. Trout fisheries also persecute the pike, culling coarse fish by electro-fishing, even removing such essentials to the ecology of natural chalk streams as brook lampreys and bullheads. Besides all this, they cut and remove the weed that would otherwise naturally hold up the flow and maintain the depth of water, as well as harbouring the invertebrates that provide vital food in the rivers' ecosystems. On one short stretch of the Test above Whitchurch, the owner deploys over sixty different traps for stoats and weasels along the banks, which tend to be manicured of their natural cover with strimmers to accommodate the fastidious new breed of angler. What is at stake is the very resource that, left alone, would create and sustain the wild trout: the natural chalk stream.

Crayfish were once so abundant in the Itchen that when the river keepers cleared gratings and sluices along Winchester College water meadows, there would be dozens of them amongst the weed. But a few years ago the fish farms upstream introduced the American crayfish. The new arrivals carried a fatal disease, the crayfish plague, to which they, but not our native species, had developed immunity. The result has been the near-extinction of the wild crayfish from the Itchen. They are now reduced to a few isolated populations in side-streams or backwaters, having been replaced by their American cousins.

Now that the coast was clear again, I sauntered along the footpath across St Stephen's Mead, in search of the once-popular college bathing hole, Gunner's Hole. It was called after the Rev. H. Gunner, one of the college chaplains. There used to be a wide arc of changing sheds following the curve of the river bank, thatched huts on an island, and a system of sluices to regulate the natural flow of the water. Gunner's Hole was about a hundred yards long and twelve yards wide, and the stretch of river was dredged of mud and concreted along its banks towards the end of the nineteenth century. It even had a handrail around the area of 'a high diving erection with four stages and two springboards', as the *Public Schools' Handbook* called it in 1900, continuing enthusiastically: 'Gunner's Hole is now second to none as a bathing place in England. Here, under the shade of the limes, are the best features of a swimming bath and a river rolled into one.'

Sure enough, Gunner's Hole was still there, secluded under the shade of enormous plane trees and poplars, one or two now tumbled over the water. Its motionless surface was entirely covered by a classic duckweed lawn, the fabled disguise of Creeping Jenny, a monster of nursery folklore who would suck children under if they went too close, closing innocently over them to hide all trace of their fate. The massive concrete walls of the pool were in surprisingly good condition, and, on the basis that stolen fruit always tastes sweetest, I climbed through the concrete river inlet sluice to drop in silently at the deep end. Sinking through the opaque green cloak was like breaking the ice. I laboured down the hundred yards of the pool, mowing a path in the lawn which closed behind me as I went. Moorhens scampered off, half-flying over the billiard-baize green. The water beneath was still deep, but no longer the ten feet it used to be below the diving boards. It had silted up to between five and seven feet. Reaching down, I felt soft mud and ancient fallen branches, and sensed giant pike and eels.

Breaststroking back like a fly in soup, I reflected that Gunner's Hole must have been where one of the legendary sea-swimmers of our times evolved his style. Sir James Lighthill was amongst the great mathematical scientists of the century. He became Lucasian Professor of Mathematics at Cambridge, and later Provost of University College, London. From Winchester he won a scholarship to Trinity College, Cambridge at the age of fifteen, and became a fellow at twenty-one. Lighthill was pre-eminent in the field of wave theory and fluid dynamics, and studied and analysed the pattern of the fierce currents that run round the Channel Islands. He was a strong swimmer, and put his knowledge to the test by becoming one of the first to swim the eighteen miles round Sark in 1973. By careful homework, Lighthill calculated the best course and timing to take advantage of the swirling, ferocious tides and currents. In ensuing years he returned and swam round the island five times. On his sixth island tour, in July 1998, aged seventy-four, he swam all day and was close to completing his nine-hour voyage when he ran into some rough seas. He was seen to stop swimming and died close to the shore. As was his custom, he was alone and had no boat with him. He regarded swimming as 'a most pleasant way to see the scenery', and swam on his back to conserve energy, describing his style as 'a two-arm, two-leg backstroke, thrusting with the arms and legs alternately'. I imagined the young Lighthill swimming up and down Gunner's Hole on summer evenings, perfecting his stroke, observing the complexities of the swimming style of the stickleback, and calculating distances.

There was no longer any sign of the diving boards or the changing sheds, still marked on the 1953 Ordnance Survey map, but when I swam back to the concrete inlet I caught hold of a bit of the original handrail and climbed over into the fresh, fast water of the main river. In a metaphor for its history, Gunner's Hole used to carry the main stream, and is now a backwater. Dropping into a pool above the main sluice that controls the river level, I shed duckweed in a green confetti ribbon that went licking away on the stream. Standing chest deep, pinioned to the slippery wooden sluice gates whose grain stood out like corduroy, I imagined a future without fish farms or watercress beds, when the river could flow as sweetly as ever it did in Cobbett's day, and there could be bathing again in Gunner's Hole.

4
A PEOPLE'S RIVER

Cambridge, 12 May
I ARRIVED IN CAMBRIDGE in the morning, in magnificent warm sunshine, frustrated, now, that I had agreed to attend a meeting there first. I had driven up from Winchester via London, where I spent a few days seeing friends, buying maps, and searching for goggles that wouldn't pinch the bridge of my nose. In the meeting, my thoughts drifted back to the Scillies as overhead projectors whirred, and artspeak and acronyms droned on. It felt interminable, especially as we were tantalisingly close to the Mill Pool, so I could actually hear the river crashing through the weir from where I sat. It is at this weir, above the Silver Street Bridge, that the Cam begins. All the river upstream of here to Grantchester is the Granta, and above Byron's Pool it is still the same chameleon river but it is the Rhee.

The moment the meeting was over, I bolted like a schoolboy and nipped straight along the towpath across Coe Fen to the old Sheep's Green bathing sheds, birthplace and headquarters of the Granta Swimming Club. I spent three years at the university here, so the city and the river are full of memories, including swims from the men's bathing sheds, which are still there, but padlocked and abandoned beside the iron foot-bridge, built over the river in 1910. The women's bathing place was on the opposite bank, a hundred yards upstream in a beautiful walled garden. It had a changing house for bathers, which now stands half-ruined without a roof, and an enchanting view upriver to Robinson Crusoe's Island.

I crossed the bridge and went into the walled garden, still a lovely place but oddly neglected in a city with a taste for fine buildings, even little ones. An old japonica grew up the wall, and a pair of yews stood on the lawn. Most impressive of all was the neo-classic summer house, a stone temple of Venus that looked out across the river. I could see where the diving boards and ladders were once bolted into the concrete quay. I changed in the swimmers' temple, and looked out through its balcony window into the clear tributary it overhangs. A magnificent foot-long perch, the dandy of the stream, swam lazily through the shallows. Someone, perhaps a swimmer, had etched an epigram into the stone: SUMMER '77 WOZ HEAVEN. I went in off the quay and swam upstream towards Grantchester. The river was deep, cool and inscrutable. In the 1950s, the Granta was still so clear here you could see a sandy bed twelve feet down. I swam against the gentle current, past the old willows the river swimmers used to dive off, round Robinson Crusoe's Island, where Dolby's boathouse once stood in the twenties, and past the island site of an even earlier, more secluded women's bathing place, long extinct. It was on the Snobs' Stream, a leat which branches off the main river here, past the island, and runs down to Newnham Mill by the Granta Pool. Bathers used to reach it via a chain-link ferry that plied from a landing-stage beside the walled garden, and mothers would often take small children. I ventured down Snobs' Stream, but it was now weedy and overgrown. This was where everybody in Cambridge still learnt to swim long after they opened the hundred-yard outdoor pool at Jesus Green in May 1924. You had to be able to swim across it before Charlie Driver, the custodian of the bathing sheds, would allow you into the main river.

I swam upstream towards Paradise Island, where bathers used to camp and picnic with canoes. The Granta felt soft and lazy after the lively Hampshire trout rivers. Then I turned and swam downstream under the bridge and past the men's bathing place, where there were once diving boards and ladders. The men's springboard used to have a 'run-up' that stretched right across the lawn of the bathing enclosure, so you could dive and hit the water halfway across the river.

Forty yards further on there used to be another board, at a deep place they called 'Aunt Sally'.

The men's bathing place was an unofficial academy of swimming, and Charlie Driver presided over it from 1903 until he retired in 1937. He was a fine gymnast, high-diver and ornamental swimmer, and used to put on displays at the annual gala on the river. Charlie was short, dark and handsome, with curly hair and a black moustache. He saved a good many bathers from drowning, and he was always ready to teach people to swallow-dive off the high-board, or to demonstrate the techniques of ornamental swimming: the propeller, the torpedo, the submarine, the spinning wheel or the water-top. One of his young apprentices in 1910 was Jack Overhill, who became the most celebrated river-swimmer in Cambridge and founded the Granta Swimming Club in 1934.

Jack Overhill swam in the Granta every day for sixty-two years. He began swimming all through the year when he was eighteen and continued until his wife, Jess, died when he was eighty. He died in 1989 aged eighty-six. He would break the ice to swim in winter, sometimes cheered on by the skaters, and was always a mainstay of the Granta Christmas Day swim, which attracted fifty-two swimmers in 1934. The tradition was to swim a friendly 50-yard Christmas handicap, but it was occasionally shortened to 35 yards if conditions were too rigorous, as in 1921, when the air temperature was 16 degrees fahrenheit and the water 35 degrees. There were only two entrants for the race that year, Billy Swann and Jack Overhill. Billy Swann got out after 20 yards because it was too cold. Jack was ahead anyway, and won.

Jack Overhill left school at fourteen and began life as a shoemaker like his father. He wrote thirty-three novels, and left a remarkable record of the day-to-day lives of ordinary swimmers in the river at Cambridge in some of his diaries and unpublished work. Under the good-humoured tutelage of Charlie Driver, the young Jack's swimming and diving gradually improved. He swam in the flooded Grantchester meadows with his friends, practised high-diving off the top bedrail on to his bed, and was delighted when his heavyweight friend Boss Benton finally fulfilled his ambition to break the springboard by performing a 'Naughty Boy', a running dive in which the diver bounced his bottom on the board before entering the water. He was one of the self-styled New Town Water Rats, who almost lived at Sheep's Green in the summer. He won his first swimming trophies in July 1919, at the age of sixteen, in the Cambridge Peace Celebration sports on Midsummer Common. His friend Archie Clee thrilled the crowd on that occasion with a daring dive off Victoria Bridge into shallow water.

The Cambridge University swimming team, the 'Tadpoles', swam in the Granta further upstream from Sheep's Green towards Grantchester Meadows, and in 1924 Jack Overhill, swimming for the Cambridge Amateurs, just missed beating J. T. A. Temple, the university champion. Jack was one of the first people in Cambridge to swim the six-beat crawl. One evening in 1920 he was standing on the iron footbridge by the bathing sheds when a man in a red bathing costume came downstream and passed under the bridge, swimming a stroke he had never seen. He drew parallel with a racing punt, kept level with it for a while, then pulled away to one of the ladders and walked off to change. Jack was amazed. Most people at that time either swam the trudgeon, a kind of crawl with a scissor-leg kick, the breaststroke, or the original backstroke, with a frog-leg kick and both arms windmilled in unison. But this swimmer was *kicking his legs up and down, like someone walking backwards*. The bathing sheds were on fire with inspiration. This was the crawl, and the disciple swimming it was Jack Lavender, a Cambridge man who had learnt the new style in London, where he swam for the Civil Service.

The crawl! Stories about it were beginning to appear in *Chums* and *The Boys' Friend Library*. In one, a boy called 'The Dud' pretends he can't swim, then amazes his friends by winning a race swimming the crawl. In another, a boy-swimmer called 'Fish' Fanshaw raises 'a water-spout' with his feet as he does the hundred yards in seventy seconds. Overhill taught himself the crawl from an illustrated article in an encyclopaedia, although Jack Lavender did come down one Sunday to hold a master-class, demonstrating the crawl as he

41

lay across a chair. After that, the river went quiet for weeks as swimmers practised the six-beat crawl, muttering to themselves the varied rhythm of its leg-kicks: 'Major, minor, minor, Major, minor, minor'.

But the honours for the most impressive swim in the Cam still belong to Tom Ford. In 1936, when he was fifteen, he swam upstream against a headwind and fast-running stream from Baitsbite Lock to Jesus Lock, a distance of 3½ miles, in 2 hours, 22 minutes, 11 seconds. That same season he swam 5 miles in a race from Kew to Putney in just under 1 hour and 10 minutes.

The Sheep's Green swimmers would go in for other river fixtures too: the Ely Mile, where they dived in off barges, and the Prickwillow Gala, where a makeshift board was nailed to the underside of the bridge for the diving competition. One year it gave way under a diver. Anything up to sixty swimmers used to line up on punts ready to plunge into the Silver Street Mill Pool for the start of the annual Swim Through Cambridge in July. Competitors would swim down the Backs, where the sheer walls of the colleges rising straight from the water make it impossible to land for much of the way. Just as you were feeling the cold at Magdalen Bridge, you would swim past the outflow of the old electricity power station on the right bank, and the water would turn miraculously warm. The swim ended at Jesus Green, and was eventually abandoned in the early sixties because of the polluted state of the river. In earlier years, the river water had been so clear that Charlie Driver would often put a glass of it on the table in the pavilion at the bathing sheds and extol its purity.

Getting out of the river without ladders when I arrived back at the walled garden could have been difficult, but I swam round into the entrance of the tributary that flowed in by the stone temple. It felt suddenly much colder, as though it were springwater from underground, and it was very clear. I came out up a brick step into the garden, changed, and walked out along the footpath towards Grantchester Meadows. The path was rutted by bike tyres and fringed with meadowsweet and rushes. I passed the Pembroke College water meadows, which used to be flooded in winter for ice-skating at night, and still have the lamp-posts that held the floodlights.

The meadows were full of buttercups and the smell of wet grass. I went up to Grantchester, ignoring Byron's Pool because it is now ruined as a swimming hole by an ugly concrete weir and the constant drone of the M11 a few hundred yards away. Byron and Rupert Brooke, who both loved this place and swam naked here, would hardly recognise it. Brooke used to canoe up from King's College as an undergraduate, and later moved into the village. The nymphs, like T. S. Eliot's in *The Waste Land*, are departed, and have left no addresses. I entered the river instead from just below the village, at a bend where there's a gently shelving beach of gravel and bits of old brick. From here, I drifted downriver all through the meadows, by pollard willows in a row down the far bank, overtaken by the occasional punt. Tractors worked the flat fields and lovers walked in the meadows or lay together on the bank. Here and there I met friendly anglers in muddy bays between the rushes. I glided on in the still green water, brushed by the rubbery stems and pads of lilies. It is now a general characteristic of lowland rivers that there is too much fertiliser leaching off the land, and too much waterweed. Sunset was coming up, and reflections trembled on the willow trunks. Moorhens jerked along the mudbanks on luminous green legs, their red bills and jet-black feathers vivid in the evening light. Fats Waller could have written 'Your Feet's Too Big' to moorhens, with the line 'Your pedal extremities are simply colossal.' They walk like little girls at parties in their mothers' high heels. I love them *because* their feet's too big.

On a magnificent May evening, I seemed to be the only swimmer in this much-swum stretch of river. Jack Overhill and his Granta Swimming Club friends used to stroll through these meadows wearing only trunks in the sunshine, following the winding banks, diving in where it looked inviting at Otter Corner or Deadman's Bend, and drying in the sun. They used to swim the two and a quarter miles from Grantchester Mill to Silver Street in an annual event that began, at Jack's suggestion, in 1934. There were 33 entrants for that first swim, won in 56 minutes, 42 seconds, and the swimmers had to walk most of the first 200 yards from Grantchester mill-pool through the shallows. Jack Overhill's son, also Jack, used to perform 50-foot swallow dives from the top of a tree at a point in the meadows where the river was 20 feet deep. The fifteen-year-old had learned to swim across the river at three, and had his picture in the *Daily Express* and the *Cambridge Chronicle*, standing next to eighty-year-old George Mason, vice-president of the swimming club and the oldest swimmer in Cambridge.

In the imaginary company of Jack Overhill and his roving band of wild swimmers, I strolled back through the meadows in my swimming trunks to where I had left my rucksack beside a pair of obliging anglers. I changed and retraced my steps into Grantchester, entering the village past a lovely ancient walnut tree by the road, much hacked-about and pruned, but still going strong. Rupert Brooke probably never dreamed that the village pub, the Red Lion, would one day be renamed after him, but the new sign went up in 1975. There's now a strong case for a further re-christening to the Lord Archer since the novelist moved into the village.

The chief delight of Grantchester is its long, low retaining walls: the buttressed, yellow Cambridge brick churchyard wall, and the farmyard wall around the long bend in the village street by the Orchard Tearooms. The way the road and the walls meander through the village perfectly echoes the river and its associations. Jack Overhill knew James Nutter, whose family had worked Grantchester Mill for three generations. He in turn knew Rupert Brooke when he lived in the village after graduating before the First World War and used to meet him as he arrived on summer mornings at the pool. Nutter would already have had his swim, and Brooke would generally be on an old bicycle, and dressed only in shirt and trousers. James's brother Edward thought Brooke snooty, so he blocked up the path from the mill to Byron's Pool to stop him using it. Brooke simply crept through a hole in the hedge further down the road.

The big mill-pool is still a satisfying place to swim, if

shallower than it used to be. A dozen of us once came here as students in punts one summer night at dusk and swam in the pool, on and on into the night. Now it was deserted, and I circled its chill eddy just once, like some ritual dance, joined by my absent, long-lost friends, and the ghosts of Rose Macaulay and Virginia Woolf, who each swam alone with Rupert Brooke in Byron's Pool, and of Jack Overhill and his band of roaming bathers. Byron's lines seemed to echo down from his pool just up the river:

> So we'll go no more a-roving
> So late into the night,
> Though the heart be still as loving,
> And the moon be still as bright.

Next morning I had a late breakfast in one of my favourite places in the world: the University Library in Cambridge. Whatever you think of Sir Giles Gilbert Scott's heavy-duty design for the outside of the building, it is surely impossible not to be enthralled once you step inside and begin to wander about its labyrinths like Charlie in the chocolate factory. I often walk and climb for miles in there, up and down its austere corridors and steep staircases, following esoteric clues scribbled on scraps of paper in the librarians' special code. I love the questing spirit of the place. Even better is the serendipity of searching the shelves for the book you think you need and discovering an even more interesting volume perched cheek-by-jowl beside it.

   This is what happened that morning. I had gone into the library intending to go straight to the Map Room in my continual search for esoteric swims, when I called into the Periodicals Room to look something up on the way, and chanced on an early back-number of *Nature in Cambridge-shire*. Thumbing through it at random, my eye lit on an article entitled 'The Search for Moor Barns Bath'. Two Cambridge botanists had gone out into a field near Madingley, two miles from where I was sitting, in search of the wet-loving plants that were recorded by naturalists in the eighteenth and nineteenth centuries growing around a lost open-air bath fed by springs. The bath itself had eluded them. Writing his account of Madingley in *Parochial Antiquities of Cambridgeshire* in 1781, William Cole said: 'I cannot finish this account of Madingley without mentioning the famous Bath of that Parish, about a mile from the Church on the Side nearest Cambridge, it being much frequented by the Students of Cambridge, and others, for their Health; it is generally thought to be one of the coldest in England.' No doubt the presence of springs, and much splashing about by students gasping with the cold, created ideal conditions for the forty-seven plant species recorded growing round the bath at one time or another since 1727. The same springs were said also to supply an unusually pure and cold well, known as Aristotle's Well, at which Samuel Pepys records slaking his thirst on a walk out of Cambridge with his fellow undergraduates during the hot summer of 1653.

The story had a *Raiders of the Lost Ark* flavour to it that appealed to the boy detective in me. Here was a real life Holy Grail. I went to the Map Room and asked one of the librarians for Moor Barns Farm. She soon produced two maps, dated 1849 and 1886. I unfolded the beautiful things on one of the enormous billiard-table desks. The bath and the springs beside it were shown on the earlier map but not on the later one. Aristotle's Well appeared on both, as well as some farm buildings, a stream, and 'Gallyon's Field', with a good deal of wet ground. There was also a moat, and a wood, the Moor Barns Grove, where the bath and springs were originally located.

I had to go and look straight away, so I hurried out of the library and walked over towards Madingley, shivering inwardly as I tried to imagine the Coldest Bath in England. The road ran alongside the Moor Barns Grove, then I turned off down the footpath to Girton. I heard the spring before I saw it, hidden in brambles and nettles down the steep bank of a ditch. Parting the brambles with my boot and treading down the undergrowth I could see the bottom of a clear chalky stream, spring water gushing from an old rusty pipe. It burst out all around it too, with such enthusiasm and brightness that I had to go down there and taste it straight away. It was icy and delicious.

This was exciting. I had certainly found the spring that fed the Moor Barns Bath, part of the same complex of powerful springs that should also rise up in the woods above to supply Aristotle's Well. I went back uphill, following the Moor Barns Grove, now reduced to a strip of spinney only ten yards wide, but originally a much wider band of wood around Gallyon's Field. The spinney was unusual for having a dense undergrowth of snowberry bushes, probably planted as game cover. I found myself in the right angle of woodland where the cold bath and springs were shown on the earlier map of Gallyon's Field, a piece of land about as wet as George Hamilton IV's handkerchief: it had clearly resisted all attempts at drainage. It had ended up as a clay pigeon shooting school, now derelict. Surely a remnant of the bath was here somewhere? Had it been completely destroyed when part of the wood was grubbed up some time around 1860, or was it just covered up? There were springs here all right; water oozed up everywhere.

Tramping around the wood's edge and the field, I couldn't help noticing that the place was thick with cuckoo pint, a plant that loves the wet. It is one of my favourite wild plants. John Cowper Powys, who was obsessed with the magic of bathing and water all his life, liked it too. This was his most 'poetical' flower, 'always growing where the dews are heaviest and where the streams are over-brimming their banks. Born of chilly dawns in wild, wet places, cuckoo flowers are the coldest, chastest, least luxurious, most hyperborean, most pale, most gothic, most Ophelia-like of all our island flowers.' There were bluebells too, and a lot of celandines.

The man I really needed was the Cambridge archaeologist and dowser T. C. Lethbridge. He was the figure at the centre of the Gogmagog Affair, an archaeological controversy that eventually drove him from Cambridge in frustration and despair in 1952. At Wandlebury Ring on the summit of the Gogmagog Hills to the south of Cambridge, Lethbridge believed there must be a giant figure of Gog embossed on the hill with chalk like the Cerne Abbas giant. He dowsed, and he used an iron bar, driven into the turf, to prospect for the hidden chalk outline he thought was there. In fact, what he claimed to have found were traces of the giant chalk figures of a woman on horseback with a sword-waving warrior on one side of her, a sun-god on the other, and the moon behind her. Although there was certainly an Iron-age settlement up there, the Cambridge academe discounted Lethbridge's work as unscientific, and he eventually left the city, taking his dowsing rods and pendulums to Devon. Lethbridge dowsed on, and wrote that he had perfected his craft to the point where his pendulum could detect truffles in a nearby wood, or distinguish between sling stones that had been used in battle and identical-looking stones gathered from a beach.

I crossed the field towards an interesting rectangular depression some fifteen feet by twenty-five. A striking bank of cowslips rose up one side, and still more cuckoo pint. It was almost on the same level as the old moat I had seen on the map, now dry. Was this the site of the bath? If so, it must have been a delightful place to bathe, although the picture that came to my mind, of goose-pimpled undergraduates, naked, purple and prancing with numbed extremities, rather spoilt the romance.

Crossing the field again, with my pencilled map in hand, I found Aristotle's Well straight away. Just below it was another rectangular area of very wet ground full of willow herb. Could this too have been a bath, fed by the same spring as Aristotle's Well? The well itself was an ancient brick structure like a buried egg. I shifted the heavy hexagonal concrete lid the farmer must have made for it, threw myself flat on my belly, and looked inside. Again, perfectly clear water flowed from a pipe in the brick into a pool some four or five feet deep. I had never seen a well this shape before. As I lay admiring its secret beauty I wouldn't have been in the least surprised to have discovered a water nymph at my shoulder. I couldn't reach the surface to taste the springwater, but it looked and smelt good, and it felt cold all right. It was satisfying to discover a neglected fragment of history in such an unremarkable field.

The air was heavy with St Mark's flies; shiny, black, and about a half-inch long, feeding on cow-parsley flowers. They are top-heavy insects, with a thorax like an old Dragon Rapide biplane and a body that tapers to nothing. Their flight is jerky and uncertain. They kept taking off like Blériot on a maiden flight, dropping out of the sky quite suddenly, only to catch themselves, as if on an invisible safety net, and set some new and equally aimless course. Their larvae live on the roots of wet grasses, and they must all have emerged at the same moment without any clear idea about the direction their lives should take. Truly a fly for our times.

Cold bathing remained popular all through the seventeenth and eighteenth centuries, and four Cambridge colleges had their own cold baths: Peterhouse, Pembroke, Emmanuel and Christ's. It is hard to imagine modern undergraduates hiking out here for an icy dip or a drink at a spring. The idea that the baths in the Moor Barns thicket could have been 'the coldest in England' sounds very much like the sort of advertising claim that would be made for a spa, or a similar commercial enterprise. It has the ring of untruth. Was someone charging admission to these baths? Well into the nineteenth century, resorts such as Scarborough advertised the coldness of their bathing as a major attraction. And they were quite right in claiming that cold bathing was good for people.

Back in the Map Room after my unscheduled detour, I returned to my original purpose of discovering the most natural course across the country for the continuation of my journey. In his book *Maps and Dreams*, the anthropologist Hugh Brody describes how the Inuit of British Columbia dream the route of each new hunting expedition, experiencing in their dream the very animal or fish they will hunt and kill, and even drawing a map on a piece of paper before setting off. In Sam Shepard's play *Geography of a Horse Dreamer*, Cody dreams the winners of the horse and dog races. And the Aboriginal songlines, as well as following the footprints of the totemic ancestors, wind invisibly about the continent connecting waterholes. My journey too would have as much to do with the geography of my mind as with that of this country. In some ways my desire to seek out and join up stories, memories and my own physical experience of swimming in watery places throughout the land had little to do with the official kind of maps. If I had a totemic ancestor, it was the otter, or the eel, swimmers who often cross country by land, following their own instinctive maps. Yet I was still drawn to do much of my dreaming in the Map Room, browsing for hours over Ordnance Survey maps of varying scales. Somehow I found the sheer presence of the maps inspiring; the delicate accretion of the detail of our landscape all around me. Much of this country was still *terra incognita* to me. I would often begin with the 1-inch map, progressing to the greater detail of the 2½-inch, the 6-inch, and even the great 25-inches-to-the-mile series made in the second half of the nineteenth century.

I studied the nautical charts that show tides and currents too. I was specially interested in the Hebridean island of Jura, where George Orwell lived, and the fearsome whirlpool that lurks in the Gulf of Corryvreckan off the wild northern coast, making it almost impossible to navigate. I pored over the six-inch map, staring at the single word 'whirlpool' marked in the almost mile-wide straits that separate Jura from the rugged, uninhabited island of Scarba. I calculated the exact distance across at the narrowest point: 1,466 yards. Practically speaking, the distance was meaningless, because the tidal currents would carry a swimmer well off the course of a straight line. I felt sure that, in the right conditions and at the right moment in the complex pattern of the tides, I had a sporting chance of pulling off the Corryvreckan swim. I knew, at any rate, that I would have to go up there and try.

I deciphered the contours and the 6-point type on neatly-folded sheets, gazing into spots of turquoise that were tarns, or thin veins of blue that rooted into hills and sometimes bore promising words like 'waterfall'. The wilder the terrain, the harder it was to unravel the thick brown tangle of contours into an imagined landscape such as Dartmoor, with its rivers tumbling off the high ground in every direction. I connected the blue marks on these maps mentally, imagining possibilities, not planning a route as a military man would, but feeling my way towards the places that most aroused my curiosity, more like a prospector. One map I singled out was that of the Rhinog Mountains in Wales, a big sweep of wild, trackless country I had visited once before with my son. Strung out below the ridge was a series of enticing tarns, and the paper was marble-veined with rivers and streams.

I had requested the map of the Fens too, which I now spread out on the big desk. Water was spilt all over it in trickles of blue, some sinuous, continually doubling back on themselves, others the dead straight lines and grids of the Dutch engineers who pioneered so much of the drainage. You could swim halfway round the world in these fens. Here and there a road tried to find its way through the maze of blue lines, but this was clearly, uncompromisingly, a vascular system of water. Roads in the Fens had come as something of an afterthought, as fen people moved about by barge or boat or on foot along wattle duckboards until well within living memory, and many just stayed put. At the centre stood the Isle of Ely on the Great Ouse. The long sink of the Ouse Washes ran in a confident diagonal across the unfolded sheet.

I scarcely heard the buzz from the tea room next door that filtered through the massive Egyptian catacomb wall. I was already swimming with the eels on Adventurer's Fen, trying to decide whether to go up Burwell Lode or Reach Lode, whether I might manage to cross the Great Ouse below Denver Sluice, and wondering where exactly it was that fen people were baptised in the River Lark at Isleham. Could I swim along the Crooked Drain at Stuntney, I wondered, or the Black Drain on Hilgay Fen? I was using the map, in fact, not to find my way but to get lost; to lose myself in the landscape. Wherever I eventually wandered and swam would be my own non-conformist map of our land. After a day's armchair-swimming, I set out the next afternoon for the real thing: the Fens themselves.

5

SWIMMING WITH EELS

The Fens, 14 May
THE APPROACH TO Ely is always dramatic. The city and its
cathedral loom at first faintly through the blue haze of the
Fens, distinguishable as a whiter shade of pale. As you draw
closer the whole island shimmers like a mirage or a UFO that
has just landed, and as the cathedral spire comes into focus,
the place seems poised to take off again. Even the moated
allotments, with their lowly huts like outside privies, derive an
air of grandeur from their own row of boundary poplars
reaching for the heavens and striping them with long
shadows. This is a holy island no less striking than Mont St
Michel, and no less holy, set off by the graphic flat horizon,
rising out of the deep brown earth beneath a sea-blue sky. It
dominates the most mysterious landscape in Britain, full of
water and odd corners that can still be hard to reach, let alone
find. As Daniel Defoe put it when he surveyed the Fens from
a safe distance at the top of the Gogmagog Hills in 1724: 'All
the water of the middle part of England that does not run into
the Thames or the Trent, comes down into these fens.'

I was on my way over to join Sid Merry, the last eel trapper
in a city where the monks once paid their tithes to the
cathedral with 30,000 eels a year. Sid Merry was born by the
waters of Babylon, an island separated from the city by the
Great Ouse, opposite the slipway by the Ship Inn. Cut off
from the rest of the city, and often flooded, it must have been
christened by some wit in one of the monasteries or at the
cathedral. The Merrys' house on Babylon is now long gone,

like the other seven that once stood there, but Sid still owns the land. He grows vegetables on it and keeps ducks and geese in pens surrounded by fences of eel-netting. A variety of old boats in various states of repair stand around propped up by wooden stilts.

We boarded his punt from a wooden landing-stage. I sat on an upturned crate feeling curious and apprehensive at the prospect of meeting my totemic ancestors. Sid untied several keep-nets full of puzzled-looking eels that hung underneath the boat and attached them to the landing-stage. The light was softening, and by the time our evening's work was done, it would be dark. Sid goes out every day just before dusk to lay his eel-traps in the river, and the lines of complex nets and hoops, weights and steel chain lay in neat piles like laundry in the bottom of the boat. Everything had a distinctive whiff of mud, water-mint and fish. As we went down the wide, lazy river the only sound was the punt's outboard engine and the slapping of the bow-waves against the banks.

Sid is a wiry, weather-beaten man of medium build who knows the Great Ouse as well as anyone. He and his father used to trap eels in baskets or eel-hives. 'They would sink naturally to the bottom once they were soaked enough. What we'd do was get a little tobacco tin and prick holes in it and fill it full of worms, and the eels would go in the basket after it.'

Like many people who lived by the water, Sid and his dad also used to put out a night line for eels. It would be about thirty yards long with a dozen hooks baited with small fish, sparrows; anything dead and preferably rotting. They would throw it out last thing at night and harvest the eels off it before first light. Eels will try anything to avoid the light, and will tangle the lines if left until daybreak. There was always a market for eels in the Fens. People would sell them in buckets and baskets in Ely market until just a few years ago. But unless you sold out, you were left with eels on your hands, because you can only sell them alive. Once killed, an eel must be cooked straight away, and in warm weather they will die within five minutes of leaving the water.

Sid steered the boat off the river into a narrow channel that leads under a railway bridge whose bricks are scored by the passage of barges from the old clay-pits, now themselves sheets of reedy open water. The cargoes of clay were for mending and building the raised banks of the fenland rivers and dykes. We slid past a great crested grebe on her floating nest and Sid began laying the nets straight off the stern along the edge of the reed-bed. This is where the eels would go to feed at night. A kind of anchor went in first, followed by a length of chain, and then the 'leader' nets that guide the unsuspecting creatures towards the mouths of the traps, which each have a series of funnels and chambers along the lines of a lobster pot. Sid laid twenty nets in two rows but didn't seem to mark their position. Why? 'Because I don't want to lose them to anyone. I just say, "All right, there's a tree there, or a bunch of nettles," and make a mental note.' As we chugged back in the sunset, and the eels began their night-life below us, Sid mapped the shape of his year.

All winter he makes new traps in his attic and in the workshop at the end of his garden from yards of special sheep-netting. He starts trapping in April when the weather warms up. An eel trapper likes a sultry night with a reasonable flow on the river. The flow spurs the eels to move about and hunt for food. He keeps going all summer until September, when the silvers go away. Silvers are the mature eels that are ready to make the fabled journey across the Atlantic to the Sargasso Sea where they breed. Eels emerge from the Fens in three distinct runs to the sea in September, October and November, and they usually go on the new moon. The rougher the river the better they like it. They are caught in wing-nets, stretched right across the river. You see them dimly sometimes, swimming in processions about three feet down, always in midstream. Eels are clearly in close touch with the moon, moving with it like the tides and shunning the sun. It is no wonder, when you consider that they spend the first three years of their lives as elvers drifting on the ocean currents towards our shores. They are sea creatures living inland.

The elvers arrive in May, after hitch-hiking along the Gulf Stream from the Sargasso, preyed upon by just about every living creature in the Atlantic. They swim up the river at night in dark brown shoals like tadpoles, although nowhere near so many now as there used to be. They are still caught in big landing nets on the Severn where they fetch prices that are inflated by their recent scarcity, and are sent off to the gourmets of France and Japan.

I spent that night in Freckenham, dreaming of my mother teaching me to swim, cradling my head as I kicked my legs in the water. I returned through the Fens in mist at a quarter to six next morning to meet Sid and collect the night's catch. His friend John was on board too, also dressed in yellow oilskin trousers but lacking the old tweed fishing hat Sid seemed to live in. John's job was to help haul in the tackle and untie the netting at the bottom end of each trap to release the eels.

As we approached last night's reed-bed, Sid's eye was on whatever subtle landmarks he had chosen to help him locate the row of sunken traps. He throttled down the engine and John swung a grappling iron over the side, waited for it to sink, then heaved. 'I think it's the nets,' he said. 'I hope it's not a body.' In came the chain, then the first of the traps with the dark brown glistening shapes and flashes of white belly. Nothing could be more streamlined or agile than this. An eel's head, with its eyes set close together and high in the skull, and the sharp snout, bears a remarkable similarity to Concorde. Nothing could be so outlandish. An eel is so mottled and green and varnished in mucus it could be an uprooted plant, a mandrake root come to life.

John untied each trap at the bottom and tipped the creatures deftly into the plastic tub, where they subsided into a glutinous tangle, making little kissing sounds. Their electric energy was astonishing. They reared straight up in the tub on the tips of their tails like snakes, waving their little heads about looking for a way out, swaying like puppets, naked as bedsprings. Every now and again an eel spilled on to the bottom of the boat and slithered in reverse, then forward, curling itself into a question mark as if to say: 'What the hell is going on here?' I noticed they picked it up with a towel, or a pair of kinked tongs, and Sid explained: 'You keep your fingers away from them. If they did happen to get hold of you,

you'd know about it. The trouble is they suck everything in, and the teeth go inwards and . . .' He pursed his lips and made a sucking sound. 'I did get nabbed once; they got this finger. But I got it out. Same as pike, you've got to be careful.' Sid sorted the eels as they came in, flicking the smaller ones back. Some nets had as many as half a dozen eels in them. John had to keep disentangling young 3- or 4-inch bream out of the leader nets. 'No ruff,' he says, 'thank God.' Ruff are horrible little spiky fish that get tangled in the net like bits of thistle.

It was a respectable catch: about 25 pounds altogether. Sid's biggest eel to date weighed 7¼ pounds and measured nearly 4 feet. It was not as big as the 10 eels he saw recently that had come out of the lake at Holkham Hall in north Norfolk when they drained and dredged it. They weighed between 8 and 12 pounds and were up to 6 feet long. Nobody seems to know why some eels get the urge to breed and become silvers and others just stay where they are and grow. Some, like the Holkham eels, may just find themselves cut off from the sea. Sid says they're usually between 10 and 20 when they go back to the sea, weighing between 1 and 4 pounds. They grow about an inch a year, so the 7-pounder he caught was probably a 45- or 50-year-old. Once they have gone back to spawn in the Sargasso, the silvers never return. Like spawning salmon, they simply die.

On the way back Sid spoke of his best-ever catch. 'It was May Day – the first Spring Bank Holiday on a May Day – and I was down here at the clay pits in a place I had netted several times before. That night I just thought "I'll drop them here again." There was a row of willow trees all along the bank with their roots in the water, and I know what had happened. The fish had gone in the previous day, because it was a nice day, and spawned. The eels had followed them in at night, but they couldn't get at the spawn because they hit the nets first. I got 285 pounds out of 10 nets; about 250 eels, probably more.'

He said the best conditions for catching eels would often be rough weather. 'We used to say a good thunderstorm would get them started.' Eels will travel overland during rain. Sid remembered a thunderstorm one afternoon about the time the silvers were making their way back towards the sea. They came out of a pond and across a field on Highflyer's Farm just outside Ely, but the storm didn't last long and the sun came out. Sid had the farmer on the telephone asking him why there were dead eels all over his field and where on earth did they come from.

I asked what eels eat. 'Everything,' said Sid airily. 'Fish, fish spawn, worms, frogs, snails, all rubbish, bodies, anything. They'll eat one another. They're proper scavengers.'

'Bodies?'

'Oh yes. When people drown themselves, if you pull the bodies out you pull eels out with 'em.'

Sid knew what he was talking about, too.

'There used to be a pub down here called the Ship. They would come out of the pub and walk straight into the bloomin' river.'

Sid and his brothers and sisters all swam in the Great Ouse as children. 'Father used to have a long pole and put a bit of rope round your waist and that was how we learnt. There was what we called the Ely Bathing Place near the station. It had a nice gravel bottom and you could nearly walk right across the river. There was an old crane there we used to swing off by the bonding house wharf. We would swim off the slipway, and by the Black Horse at Littleport. People have had their feet bit by pike. They can be vicious, especially if they're hungry and you happen to go by kicking your feet. They're out in a flash.'

Sid's grandfather, James, was famous for his life-saving on the Ouse. He was a crane driver on the Great Eastern Railway wharf in the days when most people still travelled around the Fens by water. At a civic ceremony in Ely in 1906, Mr Merry was presented with a variety of elaborate gifts that included a walnut chiffonier, a dining table, a 'purse of gold' and a framed testimonial inscribed: 'Presented to Mr James Merry by his fellow citizens as a token of their appreciation of the bravery shown by him in rescuing twenty people from the River Ouse during a period of twenty years.' He had been 'received with much cheering', and said in his modest reply that 'the rescues he had effected were only what any ordinary

Englishman would have done had they been placed in the same circumstances'.

Back at the landing-stage on Babylon, Sid poured the eels out of the tub into a plastic fish-tray in the punt and began sorting them by size with the tongs. The bigger ones went into a keep-net under the boat with others reserved for a 'special customer'. The rest went into another net, also stored in the cool shadow of the punt, to await the weekly visit of Bill, the wholesale merchant. He would take the eels back to London, jelly them, and sell them on. With added gelatine.

Sid is a purist when it comes to jellying. 'The actual jelly's in the skin. A lot of people do wrong and they'll skin an eel, but I never skin mine. All the goodness is in that liquor, and it will set like a jelly. Bring them to the boil, let them simmer ten to twenty minutes according to size, and stick a couple of shallots in too. If you're having them stewed, make some white sauce and have them hot. They're very good fried in butter with shallots and a glass of white wine, or dipped in batter and fried at my brother's fish shop.' As a man who eats an awful lot of eels, Sid should know.

It was still only breakfast time when I left Sid and went off to swim in Adventurer's Fen in a pool at the junction of Burwell Lode and Reach Lode. (A lode in the Fens is a small river, between five and twenty yards wide.) I went in across a raft of reeds and subsided rather than dived into the half-clear green water. It was surprisingly shallow: only three to five feet, with a soft, black, mud bottom. Reach Lode and Burwell Lode stretched away from the confluence in straight lines for as far as I could see, like two enormous swimming pools, banked and raised some twenty feet above the surrounding fen. Floating at this level, I felt half-suspended in the reflected sky and very remote from anywhere.

I swam down the middle of the wide stillness of Burwell Lode to where it joins Wicken Lode, and, further on, the River Cam. I had a powerful sense of eels in the reeds and in the invisible mire below. Divers who go down in the Fens see holes in the river bottom where big eels lie up, growing their annual inch and waiting for nightfall. A fish rose before me in a lazy flick. The morning was already warm, with little white clouds bringing the sun in and out, and the shallow water felt mild enough too, in spite of a breeze that combed the surface in flurries. I breaststroked a few hundred yards along the deserted lode and began to appreciate the sense of space. The banks, contoured and softened by reeds, didn't look nearly so uniformly straight once I was in the water. A marsh harrier came over, its quiet, loping wings darkening the sky for a moment.

The rich, black silty earth along the banks of the Cam around here has been farmed by the same families for years. Because the river was the main artery of transport, the farmhouses and buildings were all sited along its banks. Two miles away, I had met a family who have farmed at the remote junction of Swaffham Lode and the Cam for over a hundred years, and have always swum in the river. In summer they have ten or twelve children swimming from the farm, and building elaborate carpeted rope walks as diving platforms in the trees. Thirty years ago, the whole village used to come out to the farm to picnic and swim in the river in summer. At harvest time, the farmers, farm workers and children would all be covered in the black peaty dust off the land at the end of each day. They would each be given a piece of soap to take into the river as they bathed, washing off the grime, larking about, and sending bubbles of lather floating off down the river. Even the grandmother, who was over eighty, used to swim in the Cam in a hat with her pearls and glasses on. Alver Badcock and his River Board gang would come along on a barge once a year to dredge the lode, with their own hut and stove on board. As recently as the 1960s, the sugar beet was taken away from the farm on barges, which would line up in a row to be loaded with thirty tons each.

As I turned off to swim under a wooden bridge and up Wicken Lode, the sound of warblers was everywhere in the green clouds of sallow bushes on the opposite bank. A water pump was audible somewhere in the distance, a reminder of the energy-intensive measures which the draining of the Fens has made necessary. Like any other unnatural system of land management, it doesn't quite add up. The Fens today will work only with the massive invisible input of electricity to run the pumps that keep the system working.

The water in the lode was becoming brilliantly clear – 'gin clear' as they say here. The banks were thick with reeds. Roach were clearly visible under the lily pads. It was obvious that I was swimming beside a nature reserve, but since Wicken Lode is open to navigation, and, more to the point, none of the wild life seemed to be taking the slightest notice of me, I could see no objection to this. I could certainly think of no objection to the delicious water except W. C. Fields's famous quibble about what fish do in it. I swam right up to a frog, which eyed me, but didn't dive or even blink. As every member of the Special Boat Unit knows, you are pretty well hidden when you swim, and aquatic animals are relatively unconcerned about you once you too are submerged. You have become, after all, one of them.

Just then, a group of birdwatchers appeared in the top of a wooden tower hide on the other bank and began scanning the fen with binoculars. Was this a search party? The moment was suddenly reminiscent of a scene in Geoffrey Household's *Rogue Male*, in which the fugitive hero, half-dead from torture and in need of clothes, purloins the trousers of four bathers off a river bank and hides from them in the water, then steals downstream with his soggy raft of breeches. A group of us, sharing a Paddington flat in the sixties, used to know the book almost by heart and derived from it a coded cult language. One of our inventions was the verb 'to quive', meaning to move by stealth, covertly, as when stalking a wild animal, or up to no good. It derives from the name of the anonymous hero's ruthless and relentless pursuer, Major Quive-Smith, a master of tactics and field-craft who runs our man to ground in a hidden Dorset lane, like a wild animal.

I *quived* silently into the reeds and floated there up to my nose like a crocodile until they had gone, taking a good deal of boyish pleasure from their failure to notice me. The moment it becomes a subversive activity, swimming is that much more interesting. I swam upriver to a crystal pool where the New River flows in to join the lode and there is a mooring. Why was the water so very clear? I had two theories: first, that this was water pumped up from underground by the Environment Agency to prevent Wicken Fen from drying out and losing its essential character as a wet fen; and second, that it was springwater from around Snailwell, which is also the source of that quintessential fenland river, the Snail. Perhaps, because the fen is managed in such a benign way, with no agricultural chemicals, this was just how water could be anywhere, if we would only look after it with more care.

I scrambled out with the help of the reeds but still managed to daub myself in a woad of black silt, so that I had to face the walk back along the bank in my swimming trunks, looking like some neolithic erstwhile inhabitant. I passed a digger, fortunately unmanned, that had unearthed a huge tree of bog oak six feet down in the peat. This remnant of the ancient woods that grew here over 4,000 years ago was now almost pure black, with the peat that preserved it still fresh. Such trees were not necessarily oak; they may have been pine or yew and were often very tall, eventually killed by rising water levels and felled by storms. A boat came along the lode; some sort of pleasure launch. But the couple on board in yachting caps just waved a cheery hallo as though quite accustomed to meeting half-naked tribesmen at large in the Fens.

Now fully clothed, I returned through the village of Wicken where the churchyard headstones sang a requiem of fenland names: Dorcas Bishop, Jabez Taylor, Violet Bailey, Albert Delph, Sophia Kettle, Joseph Tebbitt, Joshua Hatch, Steadman Aspland. I also met Mr and Mrs Bullman in the best bungalow front garden in England. They had built a model village complete with a working water mill, pub, village hall, manor house, cottage hospital, fish and chip shop, church, vicarage, barn, chapel, forge, fire station, hotel, bakery, butcher, post office, florist, hairdresser, various cottages with outside privies, a station, signalbox and railway. There was even a car-boot sale and a tourist information centre. Only one thing was missing: a swimming pool. Still, there is something generous and public-spirited about a beautiful front garden. It is quite different from the back garden, which is a private pleasure. Occasionally in a city you will see from the

61

top of a bus a bright waterfall of windowbox flowers down the front of a house or flat in an otherwise dull street. The Bullmans' garden was like the spontaneous gestures of welcome you encounter when you travel in the Arabian countryside, bringing the pleasure of surprise to passing strangers.

That night I met Ernie Hall playing darts in the Three Tuns at Welney, where three grey and white cats curled up in the window, and a washing line on the river bank danced with long johns, flowered frocks and pairs of woollen gloves. He told me how, after work on hot days, he and his friends used to dive off the bridge there into the muddy Hundred Foot Drain, swim down on the ebb-tide to the Crown, three miles away, sink three pints while the tide turned, then swim back up on the rising tide to Bank Farm, where he lived. 'Nobody worried,' he said. 'There was no law against it.' Bank Farm lies just below the massive bank of the Hundred Foot Drain, some twenty feet below the surface of the river. 'We used to drink that water in the Hundred Foot,' said Ernie, sipping his pint thoughtfully. 'There was nothing else to drink. We used to siphon it out and take turns to do the pumping. It was bloody hard work.' They would stand the water overnight to let the silt settle, decant it, and boil it. They had water butts too, so not a drop of rain was ever wasted. 'If you ever drink rainwater you'll never drink nothing else.'

When it froze they would take to their skates and travel the dykes and rivers like roads for miles all over the Fens. A favourite would be to skate from Littleport for three miles up the Great Ouse to Brandon Creek, where it meets the Little Ouse, for a drink at the Ship. On a Sunday afternoon at Welney in cold weather there would be 2,000 people skating on the Ouse Washes, and even more for the Fenland Skating Championships on Bury Fen if it froze hard enough. Welney has produced more first-class skaters than any other fenland village, breeding whole families of champions.

I was struck by the fierce loyalty amongst these people. Everyone in the Three Tuns agreed with Ernie when he said they were all salt of the earth in the Fens and would 'give you a sack of potatoes as soon as look at you'. Once you got beyond Cambridge, however, 'They wouldn't give you the drippings off the end of their nose.' They were still talking about a dog otter that had been found killed on the road at Welney three weeks before, and they all remembered the last coypu captured in the river there. It weighed 35 pounds and was probably eaten by the lock keeper upstream at Earith, who used to trap the amiable rodents for the stewing pot.

Another of the fenmen, Don Dewsbury, described standing on the banks of the big Hundred Foot Drain in stormy weather and feeling the banks shaking with the sheer weight of water. He had worked for the Great Ouse River Board for fifty years, and was once on a barge in the river with his friend Budgie from Soham when the banks burst and they were washed through on a great wave of brown surf and beached in the middle of a potato field. Mick Willets, who lives by the sluice at Denver, said he once picked potatoes from aboard a punt on a farm at Willingham with his auntie during the 1947 floods.

Each village would have its own favourite natural lido. Across the Fens in Cottenham, the people would walk north along a track over Smithey Fen to swim where the sandy bank slopes gently into the Old West River. Pop Day was one of the swimmers, and he had seen as many as a hundred bathing there together and basking on the banks. He undid his shirt buttons to show me the scar he got from diving into the river over the hedge at Stretton Pumping Station and cutting his chest open on the shallow gravel. He said most of his friends still have scars from diving accidents in the river. Kamikaze running dives from the far side of the hedge were a favourite sport. No fen boy was truly initiated without a set of scars from the lacerating thorns or unknown hazards under the surface. At that time there was a lot more traffic on the water, and the swimmers would splash people in the boats, holding on to the gunwales, and getting into trouble.

Pop learnt to swim in the Old West River, by the steam-powered Stretham Pumping Station. He and his friends clung on to an old oil drum, gradually learning to let go and keep swimming. Later, they graduated to underwater swimming, and bets and dares. But the favourite bathing hole in that part of the Fens was near Wilburton where the Old West River runs past Australia Farm, so called because it was so remote. Just as everyone on the Fens seemed to go by their nickname – 'Fish', 'Turkey', 'Boxer', 'Scadger', 'Pop' – so did fens, farms, dykes and rivers. Names from the colonies or remote wars were often used to denote a far-away field or farm. Hence Sebastopol Farm, or Botany Bay, where the Twelve Foot Drain joins the Little Ouse at one end of Stallode Wash, miles from anywhere.

The River Lark was known as Jordan, because people came from all over the Fens to be baptised by total immersion in its waters at Isleham. The Fens have always been strongly non-conformist and are well provided with Baptist chapels. Isleham has two, the High Street Baptist Chapel and the Zoar Chapel, as well as its original church, and people were baptised in the river here from at least as early as 1812 until the early seventies. In search of the original baptism places on the river, I went down Sun Street next morning, along Waterside to Fen Bank and called in at the best source of local knowledge in any village: the allotments. The day was again fine and warm, and the allotmenteers were all out pottering in the quiet, purposeful way of these places, in and out of their sheds with watering cans. Oh yes, they said, people used to come past on their way to be baptised. 'We used to have a laugh when the tall ones went by,' said one of them, 'because the vicar was a short bloke and we'd say, "He'll never get his head under." ' The gardeners pointed out three places on the river: one by the old ferry; another by the new bridge, where there was a hole in the river bed, since filled in; and the third, eventually more popular, a watering and bathing hole on a bend in the river known as 'the Horse Pond'.

I breaststroked three hundred yards down to it from just below the bridge, navigating the occasional weed-jam, in water no more than four or five feet deep with a velvet silty bed that sent shivers through me when I put my feet down on it. There I found a deep pool and a gently shelving beach, now muddy but with a firm, sandy foundation. It was a drinking place for cattle in the riverside meadow and a roost for swans.

Mrs Jenny Davis, the last person to be baptised in the river at Isleham, had sent me some photographs of the ceremony. In one, the minister and his assistant stand waist-deep and fully-clothed in the Horse Pond, with Mrs Davis dressed in white between them. In the other they duck her under completely before helping her to 'go up out of the water'. There are fewer trees in the photos than there are now. Willows grow fast. Baptism is wonderfully pagan, and there's nothing half-hearted about going through the full works in a river. It takes nothing away from the symbolic re-enactment of Christ's death, burial and resurrection and the washing away of sin, to say that the ritual is really grafted on to something much older and pre-Christian. It clearly harks back to a time when the rivers themselves were deities, as they certainly still are in India, where people hop in and out of the Ganges at every opportunity. At the sacred ghat at Hardwar, one of the seven great places of pilgrimage for Hindu India, two million people are said to have bathed in the river on 13 April 1962 at the Dikhanti fair to celebrate the birthday of Ganga. I stood up to my waist in the Horse Pond, pushed my toes into the mud, and tried to imagine such a scene in Isleham. It would give the allotment holders something to talk about.

Feeling baptised by the naiads of the Lark, I swam back upstream to the bridge and scrambled out up the steep muddy bank clutching at handfuls of tough ryegrass. The other side of a breathtakingly secular concrete weir, through meadows full of sacred cows, a stone beside the old chain-ferry landing-stage commemorates the baptism of the Rev. Charles Spurgeon, 'The Prince of Preachers', on 3 May 1850. Spurgeon was a fifteen-year-old Newmarket schoolboy then, but went on to be ordained and to preach to Baptist congregations that reached 12,000 and packed the Surrey Gardens Music Hall in London.

The Isleham Baptists stopped immersing people in the Lark in 1972 because they thought it had become too polluted. It didn't feel at all bad when I swam at Isleham, and appeared even better when I plunged in an hour later further upstream in a delightful deep pool beside an old hump-backed bridge above the mill at Icklingham. But the water is not as clear as it was when the allotment gardeners of Isleham were young and learnt to swim in it, each pushing a floating log by way of water-wings. They remembered the river as sparkling and transparent, with a clearly visible gravel bottom instead of the caked black mud I still wore on my calves.

With the Lark water scarcely dry on me, I rang the Environment Agency to enquire whether the river was still polluted, or whether it might once again be safe to be baptised in the river. I was told that my question was 'multifunctional' and could not therefore be answered over the telephone. It was, apparently, a far more complex question than I naively realised and would involve the expenditure of staff time in more than one department, for which I would have to be prepared to pay. I explained that I was not a scientist, just an ordinary member of the public, and really only sought a simple yes or no answer. Mr X told me to write in to the Customer Services Department, refused point blank to give me his name, and rang off before I could utter so much as a multifunctional word.

I did write in, and received a reply free of charge informing me that:

> All rivers which contain sewage effluent, however well treated, will contain E. Coli and coliforms or worse, and the Agency would therefore discourage you from immersing people in the river. There is also a risk, albeit slight, of 'Leptospirosis' or Weil's disease. This is caused by a bacterium which is carried in the urine of domestic and wild animals, particularly rats.

Apart from the flattering misapprehension that *I* was to be doing the baptising, the letter showed very little faith in the ability of either the agency or the Lord to provide. Somewhere along the way, we seem to have left behind T. S. Eliot's conception of the river as 'a brown god'.

The Lark was full of God's creatures in the far-off pre-Environmental Agency days, but they all met their maker in one of the worst incidents of industrial pollution in recent years in the late 1980s. The sugar factory at Bury St Edmunds leaked some of the highly toxic effluent from the treatment of sugar beet into the Lark. Nothing is more polluting than sugar, which deoxygenates water by promoting the massive growth of bacteria. As the poisoned water went downstream it killed everything. The river has since recovered, and I saw plenty of fish, but the question remains (although the answer could cost you), could it happen again?

Lorry drivers on their CB radios on the A14 call Bury St Edmunds 'Sugar City'. Driving by, it would be easy to imagine the sugar factory as a giant conspiracy against the nation's health, financed by a mafia of dentists and heart surgeons. It looks its most satanic at night, when clouds of evil-smelling white smoke and steam billow like candyfloss out of a forest of steel chimneys and hi-tech ducting, floodlit in lurid pink and orange. Half-hidden and fortified behind high-wire fences and ramparts of earth, the place looks like a missile launching site. In winter, when the sugar beet season is in full swing, there is even a system of deodorant mist sprays around the perimeter fence perfuming the evil-smelling air. You can always tell something untoward is going on in a place when you see large numbers of trees being planted. All round the factory a gleaming new spinney conceals vast lagoons full of rotting beet sludge. Wild clematis picturesquely clambers up the chain-link barricades, and rabbits innocently graze the verge. Just as this pot pourri of perfume and stench assails the puzzled nostrils of the traveller, a sign comes into view beside the road: WELCOME TO BURY ST EDMUNDS, BRITAIN'S FLORAL TOWN.

Across the A14 from the sugar factory, I stood outside the Bury St Edmunds Tesco. Here, the Lark had been treated with something less than reverence as it flowed through the vast forecourt car park. Pure Spring Water may be highly valued on the shelves inside, but outside, the real thing was ignored. This was a world of tarmac, four-wheel drives, storm drains, smooth, black engineering bricks and steel safety rails. The hapless Lark, which once meandered gently through water meadows here, had been neatly packaged in an outsized concrete canyon. No water vole would dream of venturing here, nor otter, purple loosestrife or figwort. The water was impossibly remote and fenced. If this were a zoo, they could safely keep crocodiles in it. Even after torrential rain, the infant river could hardly be more than a far-off six-inch trickle, yet it was treated like a monster, a flash flood waiting to happen. Tesco, who like Nature to behave herself, had originally wanted to conceal the stream altogether inside a concrete pipe – a drain – and were forced into this dubious compromise by the Environment Agency.

In Japan, Morocco or the Isleham allotments, running water is a joy, and always presents the architect or gardener with an opportunity for celebration; the chance to make something beautiful. Water bubbles in a maze of miniature streams and sluices through the village orchards of the Ameln Valley in the Anti Atlas mountains, dances down rivulets across the hot plain from the Atlas to fill the ornamental lakes in the Marrakesh botanical gardens, or swirls down makeshift gutters off the Isleham shed roofs into allotment water butts, where it is highly prized. As I had returned past the Isleham allotments with my wet togs, the allotmenteers ministered peacefully to their cabbages, decanting the holy butt-water from their cans with appreciation, if not reverence. By contrast, in a prosperous and sainted English town, I witnessed the public humiliation of the Jordan of the Fens. By the Bury St Edmunds Tesco I sat down and wept.

6

At Swim-Two-Birds

Suffolk, 16 May

I WAS LESS THAN an hour's drive from the moat, and I had been missing the dramatic changes that occur in it literally from day to day in spring. It is constantly repainting and renewing itself. Swimming somewhere familiar is quite as addictive as a familiar walk, or bike ride, or sleeping in your own bed. So I returned home that night, and went straight across the lawn behind the house to the moat, lying very black and still, reflecting a cloud-filled sky, with the half moon floating near the willow tree. All that disturbed the surface was the slight wave as a moorhen dived and crossed underwater to the shadow of the hedge, where it surfaced for a moment, then hid, submerged. The wing-beats of a pair of mallards whistled as they circled the field, making repeated low runs over the water, uncertain whether it was safe to land, muttering uneasily. The choirs of toads whose song had filled the air at the end of March were silent now, and the wild orgy of beasts with two backs, or even three, floating about the margins, bloated and tangled in skeins of their own glutinous spawn, had subsided. I took the torch to two old aquariums by the bank, where I put some of the spawn for protection, and saw tadpoles stirring when I tapped the glass. Shining into the moat, its beam caught dozens of newts swimming underwater. I leant down by the cart-ladder and fished out the thermometer on its bit of string: sixty-one degrees. I would swim in the morning.

I fell asleep within a minute of hitting the pillow, dreaming of a time before the Fens were drained, when the villages were all islands, and people lived there like the Marsh Arabs in the days of Wilfred Thesiger. In the middle of the night I was woken up, as ever, by the cock pheasant that roosts not fifteen feet from my bedroom window in a tangled rambling rose on a wigwam of hazel poles. At precisely four o'clock, he suddenly chortles loudly, then ruffles his feathers self-importantly like a man who has had his say at a public meeting. Then, just as I am going back to sleep, he does it again, this time from the lawn, where he paces like a school-master, muttering to himself. Sometimes I wish someone would shoot him, but immediately repent because we are such close neighbours.

To my delight and relief, I awoke later to the thrumming of wing-beats in the chimney that heralds the arrival of the swallows – my swallows – from Africa. The sound was deep and breathy, and vibrated through the wood-framed house, and through me. When I bathed in the moat, the birds were already busy dibbling clay from along its margins for nest improvements. They feed off the moat too, skimming over me on a regular flight path as I swim, snapping their beaks audibly as they swoop and hawk for insects, some just emerging from their larval stage in the water. They seem to be engrossed in an endless conversation with one another, arriving later and later from their migration each year, so I fret about them anxiously. I always note the day in my diary and it is usually somewhere between the 19th and 27th April. They had returned while I was away. The moment they arrive, they will fly in and inspect the chimney where they nest. It acts as a bass organ pipe, and amplifies their tiny wing-beats to a rumbling that can sound like a passing lorry. Such an emphatic affirmation of spring is always welcome, but in these days of diminishing returns in the world of migrant birds it is also a terrific relief to know that the last of the free spirits have survived another season. Their little colony of mud nests, looking like a Dogon village in Africa (where I imagine them spending their winters), has been there for ever and must have been kilned almost to earthenware by my winter log fires. Bits fall off from time to time, like fragments of Easter egg, and when I see the birds getting mud from the moat, I think of the original Tudor builders, who did just the same when they made the house.

Rain in the night had made the moat wonderfully fresh and clear. I walked across the wet lawn and went down step by wooden step into the inviting water, because I didn't want to disturb the insect, mollusc and amphibian city, already far into the rhythms of its day, by diving. The submerged jungle of Canadian pond weed was beginning to thicken and encroach from the banks towards my central swimming lane. Only a strand or two wrapped round your arm or neck interrupts the rhythm as you flick it off. It would have to be pruned.

At the end of my first two chilly lengths, a frog leapt off the bank almost straight into my face, and others watched me from the water. That they are far outnumbered now by the toads is due, I think, to predation of their tadpoles by the newts, which much prefer the young of frogs to those of toads. There is no native creature quite so exotic or splendid as the male great crested newt, or eft, as country people called them, in full display. They are the jesters of the moat, with their bright orange, spotted bellies and outrageous zig-zag crests, like something out of a Vivienne Westwood show. I hung submerged, in the mask and snorkel, and watched these pond-dragons coming up for air, then slowly sinking back into the deep water, crests waving like seaweed. They are so well adapted to the underwater life, I have to remind myself that they only come to the moat for six or seven months from February to July or August, to reproduce. Then they return to land, where you may not notice them unless you're a gardener. You dig them up with the potatoes. They hide like bookmarks between old, vertically stacked roof-tiles, or entomb themselves in dusty crevices in the brick-pile. Sometimes they even turn up mysteriously in the kitchen in the autumn. They look a lot happier in the water.

The voles had been busy, too. As a swimmer, you notice details, with your child's-eye view of the world three inches above the surface, and the voles had made new holes at water level, just too small to take a tennis ball. But the most spectacular change I noticed, as I breaststroked up and down, was the explosion of birdsong all round the moat. Two rival blackcaps were doing their best to outsing each other across the water in a fiercely inventive contest reminiscent of the duelling banjos in John Boorman's *Deliverance*. And all the wood pigeons in Suffolk, who seemed to know there is sanctuary in the trees along the banks, were cooing their hearts out.

One of these birds was so busy eating just-opening ash buds from a branch overhanging the water, that she took no notice of me as I swam up beneath her. I noticed later that she had a nest in the willow. Why pigeons are so keen on ash buds I don't know, but they will take the greatest risks to get them, teetering on the ends of twigs and reaching far out into the void to peck at them. They couldn't do such acrobatics on other trees because the twigs would snap. Ash is more supple and keeps springing back. Each time it whipped, the pigeon almost lost balance, then spread her wings and dipped her tail wildly, and clung on. A little fusillade of raindrops plummeted from the branch and splashed all round me. The ash was far behind all the other trees in leaf; it is always the last, except for the mulberry, so its buds are full of the very first and freshest of the sap. For the ancient Norse people, this tree, Ygdrasil, was the tree of life. So it follows that its sap is the very stuff of procreation, the essence a pigeon will do anything to taste as she prepares to nest and lay.

Country people have, or had, little phrases birds are supposed to say, and the wood pigeon's song is usually interpreted as 'Take two cows, Taffy', or 'Joe's toe bleeds, Betty'. It is no different from Charlie Parker playing 'Salt Peanuts', except that pigeons seem to have difficulty remembering how their song goes. They usually manage to get through the first line, but suddenly break off halfway through the second. Then another pigeon starts up somewhere else, like a prompt, and away they all go again. The blackcaps, meanwhile, made my swim a delight with song of such liquid beauty and complexity that it rivalled even the nightingale. It would be hard to imagine two more contrasting birds, yet they worked well together musically; the pigeons providing a base line, and the blackcaps extemporising insanely higher up the scale. I felt like George III, who was serenaded by a chamber orchestra when he bathed in the sea at Weymouth. It certainly beat Phil Collins over the PA at the swimming pool.

The sun had come out, and with it the damselflies. They appeared from nowhere, right on cue, like a corps de ballet sweeping across the stage. Their dance was accompanied by a new song: the sudden squeaking, oozing, dripping chorus of a flock of starlings darkening the hawthorn hedge in the field. They sounded like some great Victorian cotton-mill, with all the engines, shuttles, fly-wheels and belts trundling at full tilt, squeaking, jolting, rattling and clattering. Afterwards, I sat wrapped in my towel observing the tadpoles doing lengths in their aquarium. Then I decanted them gently into the little bay where the pigeons drink, wished them luck, and watched them disappear into the weed.

7

TIDERIPS AND MOONBEAMS

Norfolk, 12 June
I SET OFF EARLY in a glowing dawn and drove on empty
roads to the Norfolk coast, where I had arranged to meet
Dudley, an old swimming and sailing companion. I could
think of no better prospect than to enhance the day with
bathing, walking and conversation on one of the best beaches
I know. The journey through the rolling countryside of north
Norfolk always feels to me like crossing over into another
land, another state of mind. It is close to home, yet remote.
The sudden lightness of being there, with such endless miles
of level space, feels like a holiday, even for a few hours. Time
passes slowly when you are a dot on the horizon. There is no
anti-depressant quite like sea-swimming, and Holkham is
where I usually go when I'm feeling sad. Striking out into the
enormous expanse of cold sea, over the vast sands, I immerse
myself like the fox ridding himself of his fleas. I leave my
devils on the waves. North Norfolk is one of those places
where the weather never seems to bear any relation to the
forecasts. The whole of Britain can be covered in cloud, yet as
you approach the coast up here, it is braided with a magic
band of blue. The Royal Family must have known a thing or
two when they chose Sandringham as a country cottage.

You arrive at Holkham beach as you would at Glynde-
bourne, Epidaurus or Newmarket races; there is a sense of
occasion, as befits a visit to one of our most impressive
stretches of wild coastline. Opposite the entrance to the
Holkham estate you turn into a dramatic wide boulevard of

poplars called Lady Anne's Walk and pay the Viscount Coke's amiable gatekeepers a modest sum to park. We felt we should be showing our passports. Even at this hour there were a couple of parked horseboxes with the ramps down, and a few Volvos with 'A dog is for life not just for Christmas' stickers in the back. This elegant cul-de-sac leads half a mile across the grazing marshes to a narrow gap in the Holkham Meals, the strip of mixed pine and holm-oak wood that runs along the dunes west to Burnham Overy Staithe and east to Wells.

Dudley and I set off barefoot over the sandy boardwalk through the wooded dunes and emerged blinking from the shade into the great gleaming theatre of Holkham Bay. A majestic sweep of dunes delineates an endless beach where, at low tide, the sea is only a distant whispering line of white. In the middle of all this are a couple of piratical sand islands that get cut off by the tide and are popular with lovers and picnic parties. Further west towards Burnham the dunes rise into a whale-back ridge reminiscent of the Malverns. There used to be the rusty hulk of an early Austin almost completely buried in the sand, but now I suppose it has sunk for ever, or dissolved. Coming along below the dunes was a string of twenty racehorses and their lads, returning to the horseboxes. It is the sort of thing you expect to see in Ireland, but there are often hoof-prints in the Holkham sand, and you can gallop for miles beside the sea.

We made for the surf across the almost deserted beach and half-waded, half-walked into the sun towards Scolt Head and Burnham Overy Staithe. One of the great joys of Holkham beach is to swim in the lagoons that appear in the sands as the tide goes out. Most are only just deep enough for a wallow, but some are up to four feet deep in places. They can be very warm, and I once stepped on a Dover sole in one. Miles from anywhere, we came upon a waterhole that was especially long and deep, and splashed about in it like two desert travellers in an oasis. Watching the little waves criss-crossing and buffeting each other, Dudley remembered how, as a boy learning to sail in Canada, he would study why this or that current behaved the way it did, or why there was a deep channel in the sand here but not there. Standing knee-deep in the sea and feeling it tug this way and that before we plunged out into deeper water, we agreed that these are indeed serious questions. Swimming into the sun, we struck out against the current. Our coast is being altered by the sea at every tide, and every storm, and nowhere more than here on the east coast. Back there on the beach I had searched for a whale jaw the size of an armchair that was stuck fast in the sand last winter, but was buried now, or washed away. Holkham is compulsive beach-combing. Razor shells are strewn everywhere like bones in a Mad Max film, and the delicate, finely perforated shells of sea urchins are beached like tattooed bums or paper masks.

Three miles on, by the entrance to Burnham Harbour, opposite Scolt Head Island, the channel buzzed with dinghies going in and out. Boats were pulled up on the beaches, and families picnicked in the dunes. I swam alone across to the island and back, dodging the Lasers and Enterprises. I felt the vigorous tug of the tide, and crossed the channel diagonally. If Nelson ever bathed, this would surely have been one of his haunts, close to his native Burnham Thorpe. But it was the policy of the navy to discourage and even forbid sailors to swim. Traditionally, few fishermen were swimmers either, the idea being that if you are going to drown in a shipwreck it is better not to prolong the agony.

We followed the path through Overy Marsh towards Burnham, passing two houseboats moored under Gun Hill. One was based on Noah's original drawings for the ark, with a single window facing west across the marsh. It bore a notice: 'This ark is used by a local artist as a simple working space. You are welcome to see inside when he is here. The only item of value inside is the Vieuw.' From the spelling, we deduced that Noah was Dutch. I could think of worse places to be stranded in the Flood.

A butterfly went past over the sea lavender. I said it was a swallowtail. Dudley thought it was a cabbage white. 'That's the difference between us,' he said. I kept my eyes firmly on the sandy path ahead, hoping to find a lizard out sunbathing. Dudley would probably think it was a stick, but I would know it was a lizard. We were, after all, in one of English Nature's prime reserves. There have been attempts to reintroduce the sand lizard here, but they have an uncooperative way of eating their own young. These dunes are also home to the natterjack toad, who likes to dig himself as much as a foot into the sand in the daytime, emerging at night to roam the flotsam line of the beach, hungrily rummaging the dead seaweed for the *Assiette de Fruits de Mer* of small creatures it contains.

Swimming into Burnham Overy Staithe on the mud-warmed rising tide, we entered a time warp. Sailing people sat about amongst the dinghies with picnic baskets and those Acme Thermos flasks finished in pale green Hammerite that weigh about the same as a milk churn. A woman in rust canvas shorts and plimsolls, with masses of fair curls like Titty in *Swallows and Amazons*, was fishing lifejackets out of a Land-Rover Discovery. She told us that the channel through which we had just swum was known affectionately to the locals as Dead Man's Pool. They have a way with metaphor in Burnham, always seeing in the New Year round a bonfire of old boats.

A friend who has spent her springs and summers in Burnham Overy Staithe all her life, once told me, 'I can trace the creeks in the lines of my own hand.' We walked back towards Holkham, navigating through waves of sea lavender on the saltmarsh mud, crazed and frosted with salt, until we reached the dunes again and ascended Gun Hill, where I spotted a common lizard sunbathing obligingly before a clump of marram grass. The view into the hazy distance of this great sweep of utterly wild coast silenced us both for some time. Three miles inland we could make out the elegant wooded landscaping of Holkham Park, with its landmark obelisk and the fine house well sheltered from the sea, looking out instead over a lake. Holm oaks are the distinctive local tree here, planted all over the estate by the pioneering agriculturalist Coke in the eighteenth century. According to one of the Holkham Hall gardeners, the trees first arrived as acorns in a consignment of china from Italy. They had been used as a kind of eighteenth-century bubblewrap, and Coke told his men to fill their pockets with acorns in the mornings and plant them all round the estate. Until Thomas Coke built Holkham Hall in the middle of the eighteenth century, there had been almost no trees here at all, but, as the historian David Dymond discovered, no fewer than 2,123,090 trees were planted on about 720 acres of the park in the twenty years from 1781. It is interesting that although the holm oaks and Scots pines, all planted by Coke, form a useful evergreen screen against the cold winds blowing in across the North Sea straight from the Ural Mountains of Russia, they also hide it from view. It is only relatively recently that we have come to regard a view of the sea as a thing of beauty. For our ancestors, the sea was to be feared and shunned from sight. When Humphry Repton designed Sheringham Hall, or 'Bower', further along this coast, in 1812, he positioned it facing east of south, away from the sea, only three-quarters of a mile away. He thought that 'A view of the sea . . . ought not to be the first consideration.'

A little further on, we were greeted by a sign, courtesy of English Nature, informing us that 'Naturists are requested to keep to the beach. Naturism is not permitted in the woods, or outside designated areas within the dunes.' Curious about the 'designated areas', Dudley and I headed straight off in search of them.

There is nothing quite so good as the feeling of hot sand sifting between your toes as you walk along the tops of dunes. We followed an undulating ridge path through a deserted, silent dunescape. Surely there was nobody about? By and by we came to a little village of driftwood windbreaks built around the natural declivities in the dunes. Still no sign of life. There were stacked-up red, yellow and blue plastic fish trays signalling a desire for privacy and goodness knows what else. Then, one by one, heads began appearing over the parapets of what the poet Kit Wright has described as 'lust bowls'. Just as suddenly, the heads bobbed out of sight again and the silence continued. It was like the Somme at midday. We were surrounded by dozens of humans in this superheated warren and they had all gone to ground. Nonetheless we felt observed. It was an odd feeling, which we readily exchanged for the freedom of the beach below. 'They're obviously much engrossed in their books,' observed my companion.

Hastening away in the general direction of the distant sea, we encountered another of English Nature's notices: MEMBERS OF THE PUBLIC ARE WARNED THAT THIS PART OF THE BEACH IS UNDER USE BY NATURISTS. The telling use of the words 'warned' and 'under use' made it quite clear that in the well-dressed offices of English Nature a naturist would be regarded with the same degree of alarm as an unexploded mine. Looking back from the beach towards the Somme as casually as we could, naked figures could be seen rising up from time to time out of the bunkers for surveillance purposes. It was like a scene from *Watership Down*. The Unclothed Ones were mostly male and very white, but a few varied in hue from underdone to deep Greek Island tan. Every now and again, in ones or twos, they would make the long trek across the beach to cool off in the sea. There was a distinctly erotic air to the place that somehow lent a restless, urban feeling to the wild and beautiful dunes, and put them out of bounds.

The noticeboards and the frisson of nudity about the dunes bespoke the continuing British confusion about bodies. Well into the nineteenth century, to go swimming was to go naked, especially in the wild. I have a print of a photograph, taken at the bathing-lake in Victoria Park, Hackney, in 1899, in which not a single one of literally hundreds of boys bathing is wearing a stitch, and there is not a girl in sight. Until halfway through the eighteenth century, people still swam in the sea principally for their health, but during the next fifty years they came to the beaches more and more for pleasure. The elaborate bathing machine was simply a recognition by the Victorians of the erotic potentialities underlying sea-bathing. Mention of the seaside was often the occasion for a nudge and a wink. The characteristically English obsession with swimming costumes and near-nudity was the *raison d'être* of McGill's seaside postcards. You find it in the heavy-handed humour of a letter, dated 1930, to the *Swimming Times*, on behalf of 'The Slowbutsure Breast Stroke Swimming Club of Wobbleham Village, Little Loweringham'. It is there, too, in the Amateur Swimming Association's edict, in the same year, that costumes 'must be non-transparent, shall be one piece, devoid of open-work, and reach within three-and-a-half inches from the base of the neck, back and front. In the leg portion, the costume shall be cut in a straight line round the circumference of each leg.' Even as recently as the 1997 World Championships in Australia, when Steve Zellen lost his trunks as he dived in at the start of a race and swam on, he was disqualified. (Arguing his case before the judges, he said he would have stopped had it been a backstroke event.)

English Nature's warnings alerting people to the possibility that a naturist might pass within their field of vision shared something of the comical quality, it seemed to me, of the Vatican's precautions, described in this cutting from the *Telegraph* I found recently on a friend's study wall:

VATICAN OBLIGES SHY SWAMI

Special arrangements of unusual rigour have had to be made at the Vatican over the weekend for the Papal audience of Pramukh Swami, an Indian spiritual leader, who has not seen a woman for 46 years. In order that he should not break this rule inadvertently in the Vatican of all places, women, including nuns, were kept away from the route as the 63-year-old Hindu monk was brought to the Papal palace and ushered into the Papal presence on Saturday. The sect's leader is accompanied by nine other monks and by a group of laymen whose special task it is to warn him in good time of the approach of a woman and then guide him with his eyes shut.

It was getting really warm, and, not to be outdone, we stripped off to wade and swim alternately in the general direction of Wells, accompanied by a posse of oystercatchers and several sandpipers, who scampered after invisible delicacies with desperate urgency as the tide went out, uttering little cries of discovery. We again felt the fierce undertow that runs along this coast, and the sea bottom was full of sudden dips and channels. Bathing off this beach, you feel the literal meaning behind Larkin's line about misery in 'This Be the Verse': 'It deepens like a coastal shelf.' I thought of the two children, brother and sister, who had drowned a few miles away, at Holme-next-the-Sea a year or so earlier. The family had been picnicking on the wide beach and the children had wandered off to play or paddle in the far-off sea. Their parents suddenly realised they had lost sight of them and began the increasingly desperate search. In line with contemporary fears about paedophiles, much of the anxiety and police attention focused on the possibility of abduction, at the expense of what some might consider the far more obvious danger: the sea. Nobody will ever know what actually happened that day, but it is likely that the children paddled innocently into the warm, inviting shallows, only to stumble into one of those sudden troughs in the sand and find themselves in deep water, clutched by the riptide. In the space of two weeks they were to be carried thirty-four miles round the coast to the beach at Sheringham by the same powerful sea current that sweeps south down the whole east coast of this island, bringing ever more pebbles to the great shingle bank at Blakeney Point.

There were places where the current tugging at our legs almost stopped us wading, and where swimming would not have been a good idea. Whenever we swam, we noticed how much we drifted. Like the currents, waves behave differently all along this beach, and we came to a place where people were vigorously body-surfing into the shallows. I thought of Byron, who 'wantoned' in the breakers in Italy at Lerici. We threw ourselves into the naked buoyant tumbling, and gloried in the abandonment in wave after wave, happy as the bathing pigs of Kythnos we had once discovered.

We had been sailing across the Aegean in a small wooden sloop, heading for the harbour at the northern end of Kythnos, but were blown so far off course by the Meltemi that we almost missed the island altogether. Having just managed to claw our way around its southern tip into the shelter of a providential cove, we rode out an anxious night and awoke to rosy-fingered dawn and a perfect sandy bay. There was not a soul in sight. But the beach was not empty. In the shade of a tin shelter on driftwood stilts, occasionally strolling into the sea for a dip and a roll in the shallows, lolled a dozen ample sows. I hope those pigs still have the beach to themselves.

Heading back for tea at Holkham Hall, we followed the tracks of a pram which had been wheeled a mile across the sands. Amongst the big limes and oaks in the park there were roe deer and sheep, and on the higher fields, an abundance of partridges and hares. The estate is not normally artificially stocked with partridges, so their success must be ascribed to the habitat. There has always been plenty of shooting on these Norfolk estates, but there are miles of good hedges too, the crucial factor for the breeding partridge. I had come across a copy of *The Shooting Man's Bedside Book* by 'BB' staying with some country friends. Holkham featured strongly in the chapter on record bags. It may not make ideal bedside reading for all of us, but on 19 December 1877 a shooting party of eleven killed 1,215 hares, and on 7 November 1905 a party of eight shot 1,671 partridge. It was a neighbouring estate, however, that took the prize for the Record Mixed Bag. At the end of a single day's shooting at Stanford on 31 January 1889, Lord Walsingham's party staggered in with an assortment of pheasants, partridges, red-legged partridges, mallard, gadwall, pochard, goldeneye, teal, swans, cygnet, woodcock, snipe, jack snipe, wood pigeon, herons, coots, moorhens, hares, rabbits, otter, pike and rat. A rare tribute to the biodiversity of north Norfolk.

Henry Williamson, the author of *Tarka the Otter*, loved the abundance and variety of living creatures in this countryside, and for seven years he lived and farmed five miles along the coast at Stiffkey. When Dudley returned home after tea, this is where I went, pitching my tent in a field that was once part of a wartime RAF camp, overlooking thousands of acres of wild saltmarsh, and Cabbage Creek. It is easy to get lost in this watery maze, and find yourself marooned on a rising tide.

From 1937, Williamson farmed 235 acres here, struggling to bring the derelict farmland back into good heart at Old Hall Farm. He recorded his day-to-day adventures in *The Story of a Norfolk Farm*, and in a regular column in the *Evening Standard* which ran all through 1944 and '45, under the title 'A Breath of Country Air'. He always left writing the column until the last possible moment, and his two little boys would be waiting in the kitchen, re-tying the laces of their plimsolls ready for the sprint up Stiffkey street to the post van at half past four. The poet of *Tarka* bathed with his children in the warm water of the marsh pools, often by moonlight, after as much as twelve hours' prickly work in the harvest fields.

At dimmit-light, or dimsey, as they called twilight on Tarka's River Taw in Devon (where Williamson lived before and after Stiffkey), I went out over Stiffkey Marshes and swam in the Stiffkey Freshes. A deep pink moon rose up over Blakeney Point, whose bleached pebbles shone from across the water. Although I couldn't see them, I knew there were seals not far away on its outer beaches. A line of small boats rode at their moorings out in Blakeney harbour.

I felt the tide running in as I entered the sea. It advanced at astonishing speed, gaining three or four feet each minute, spilling over the almost level muddy sands in a rolling three-mile meniscus that stretched unbroken all the way west to Wells. The water was warming itself as it inched up the wandering guts and channels where the sun had beaten all day. It was calmed by the sheltering arm of the great shingle bank opposite. I floated out into the freshes, the water beyond the marsh, through bands of seaweed, letting myself drift with the tide along the strand towards the mouth of the Stiffkey River, where there were houseboats, half-hidden in the winding creeks, shuttered, silent and dark against the moon. I listened to the sea percolating into the marsh, sliding up every little meandering mud canyon, between the glidders and uvvers – the mud banks – trickling about the mycelium of creeks, gently rocking the glistening samphire. Even the tiniest channels in the mud or sand mimicked the patterns and movement of a great river.

As I bathed, I imagined Williamson, now an otter himself, swimming at dusk with nine children in one of the marsh pools, with the reflected wing-tip lights and the roar of the warplanes returning to the airfield behind Stiffkey. Then the air would be quiet again, as it was now, except for the cries and splashings of the children, and the marsh birds. The girls' clothes, draped over sea lavender, might well have included blouses or aprons of a fine red cotton, then the fashion in Stiffkey, because the 'mashes' were a popular children's hunting-ground for the much-prized scraps of the red drogue parachute targets, which were towed to and fro all day by aeroplanes, while gunners practised, filling the wide sky with black puffs of smoke.

When Williamson died, it was Ted Hughes who delivered the memorial address at the service of thanksgiving in St Martin-in-the-Fields. Hughes had found and read *Tarka* at the age of eleven and counted it one of the great pieces of good fortune in his life. For the next year he read little else. 'It entered into me,' he said, 'and gave shape and words to my world as no book ever has done since. I recognised even then, I suppose, that it is something of a holy book, a soul-book, written with the life-blood of an unusual poet.' Hughes regarded Williamson as 'one of the truest English poets of his generation', although he never published a word of verse. *Tarka* had taken four years to write, and went through seventeen drafts. Williamson rewrote Chapter Eleven, which begins at the source of five rivers up on Dartmoor, thirty-seven times. He described the writing of those paragraphs to Hughes as 'chipping every word off the breastbone'. The two men became friends when Hughes, not much over thirty, and still spellbound by the magical book, found himself living in the middle of Devon on the Taw not far from where Williamson, now in his sixties and also still under Tarka's spell, was working in a hut on a patch of land he had bought with the prize-money his book had won him long ago. (He had sold the Norfolk farm by the end of 1945, his dreams unrealised.)

I have always admired Williamson, not only for the beauty and ice-clear accuracy of his writing, but for the moral basis of his vision, which sprang from the natural world and his passionate concern to take care of it. In this, he was far ahead of most of his contemporaries. Hughes described Williamson at that service of mourning as 'a North American Indian dreamer among Englishmen'.

When I came out of the water, my shadow fell twenty feet

along the shell-strewn shoreline. The moon was rising towards a thin band of mackerel cloud, and terns, duck and wading birds called to one another all over the marsh. Nothing much had changed since Williamson was here, driving his grey Ferguson tractor in a mackintosh tied up with baling twine, building his wooden tide-doors to keep the river from flooding his fields, and trapping eels in his ditches.

8

BORROW & THOREAU

North Wales, 14 June
I WENT TO WALES because the place is stiff with magic,
because the Rhinog Mountains are something like a wilderness where I would be free to wander like pipesmoke in a
billiard room, and with the kind of apparently random
purpose with which the laughing water dashes through the
heather, rocks and peat. I went there to be a long way from
all the powerful stimuli Wordsworth said prevented us, these
days, from doing any proper thinking. My only purpose was
to get thoroughly lost; to disappear into the hills and tarns
and miss my way home for as long as possible. If I could find
a string of swims and dips, each one surpassing the last in
aimlessness, so much the better. The great thing about an
aimless swim is that everything about it is concentrated in the
here and now; none of its essence or intensity can escape into
the past or future. The swimmer is content to be borne on his
way full of mysteries, doubts and uncertainties. He is a leaf on
the stream, free at last from his petty little purposes in life.

I took my Great Uncle Joe's copy of George Borrow's *Wild
Wales*, the account of a three-week walk across that country
in the summer of 1854. Borrow, who was a great swimmer as
well as walker, is in some ways insufferable. He never ceases
to pose on the page as he posed in life, and his prose is
generally heavier going than even the wildest of Wales.
Nonetheless, in his grandiloquent fascination with history
and language (he liked to call himself a 'word-master'), and in
his genuine curiosity about the lives of country people and

gypsies, he is hard to ignore, and wins you round in the end.

Borrow used to swim all over the Norfolk Broads, where he lived, all year round, and in the North Sea when he moved to Great Yarmouth. If he couldn't sleep, or was bored with the company at home, he would walk twenty-five miles to Norwich and, after a rest at his mother's house, tramp back. He was six foot three, with a mane of white hair and massive shoulders, and cut a striking figure in Great Yarmouth in his sombrero and long sheepskin coat, with his servant, Hayim Ben Attar, and his black Arab steed, Sidi Habismilk. In the summer of 1854, Borrow embarked on his Welsh walk carrying only a small leather satchel with 'a white linen shirt, a pair of worsted stockings, a razor and a prayer-book'. Great Uncle Joe had *Wild Wales* with him in Parkhurst prison on the Isle of Wight in 1892, where he was doing time at the age of twenty on the trumped-up charge that he was a dangerous anarchist. I have often imagined the young idealist reading the book in his prison cell, dreaming of the freedom of the open road and the hills.

The Rhinog Mountains stretch south along the coast for eighteen miles between Snowdonia and Barmouth Sands. It was to this trackless quarter that I drove from Stiffkey, arriving in the dark to camp by the sea on Shell Island, south of Harlech, where I had arranged to meet my cousin Adrian in the morning for the first day's walking and high altitude swimming.

We began by scrambling uphill from the Roman Steps, a haphazard stair of roughly flat stones that was once a trade route through the Rhinogs. We were aiming for the *llyns*, Welsh for tarns, higher up. Connoisseurs of these mountains like Adrian are used to the absence of paths, and after much toil we eventually hoisted ourselves level with the lofty Llyn Du. We looked across it to an almost sheer ascent of some 650 feet to the summit of Rhinog Fawr at 2,347 feet. A brisk wind coming up the mountainside off the sea ruffled the surface of the tarn, which must have been 350 yards long and half as wide. The immense shadow of the mountain rendered the water opaque and black. To judge by the almost vertical plunge of the mountain into the *llyn* on the far side, it must have been very deep. We were about 1,700 feet above the sea and feeling distinctly cool, even in our mountain gear. My companion began to shiver, and, lacking a wetsuit, decided to give this particular treat a miss.

This was a moment I had anticipated with relish. I slipped off a rock into the velvet deeps and swam suspended in what suddenly felt like giddy depth. It was icy. I swam straight out and across the middle of this chasm, gulping air and moving fast towards a sloping ramp of grey fissured rock at the far end of the ruffled tarn, entertaining the usual fantasies about what company I might have below. But it was still a beautiful swim, my feelings of awe intensified by the gothic mist. Adrian, who is Head of PE at a Gloucester comprehensive school, cut a reassuring figure across the water. The rock here is mostly Cambrian, a hundred million years old. The rock and the country are one and the same: Cambrian and Cambria. The two next oldest rocks, the Ordovician and the Silurian, are named after two tribes of ancient Britons who lived on the Welsh borderland.

Halfway across, I turned and swam on my back and confronted the dark presence of the mountain. I thought of the phrase 'deep as England' in Ted Hughes's poem 'Pike'. Wales may be yet deeper. I was a prehistoric creature in my glistening wetsuit, ready to be fossilised unless I kept moving. I scrambled on to the huge, grey, ramped rock at the far end, and slithered higher up it to enjoy the view for a few moments before the wind began to bite. I took a header back in off the rock, my highest dive yet. The imperative to keep moving kept my mind off the chilled water, and I soon acclimatised once I got into the rhythm of the breaststroke, urgent at first, until I began to relax. I doubt I would have had the nerve to attempt the swim had I been alone. It was far colder when I came out; this was no place to stand about with nothing on. Neither of us had any doubt that a warming assault on the summit of Rhinog Fawr should be our next move. The cloud had by now almost cleared, and views were opening up on all sides. Some chocolate, and we were off on a spiral route up the northern slopes of the mountain to reach the south-western ridge, and the summit. As we clambered up the last few feet of chaotic rock, the cloud was clearing, and there were views across the sea and up the coast to Anglesey, where the sun had come out, and along the other Rhinog mountains stretching south in line towards Barmouth Sands; Rhinog Fach, Y Llethr and Diffwys.

We now descended on a circular route to the next tarn, Gloyw Llyn, which winked at us from below. We followed a stream, at first a tentative rill amongst the rocks and tussocks, but soon growing into a fully-fledged torrent. Just as we were whingeing about the boggy going, and clambering round a series of minor waterfalls, we came upon a classic swimming hole. It was a verdant pear-shaped pool sheltered by a grassy bank to one side, with steep mossy rock rising out of it on the other, clothed in stunted gorse and tussocks. It felt warmer here, and we had both worked up a sweat. By now the sun was out, shining straight through the lens of water onto the golden peaty pebbles of the bottom. We stripped off and leapt in. It took our breath away. The pool was three or four feet deep with just enough room to swim, as in a treadmill, against the current. Every second was an eternity. Neither of us stayed in for longer than a minute but sprang out on the knife-edge between aching and glowing.

A buzzard circled overhead. It saw two figures bounding downhill over bog moss and cotton grass to the big tarn, Gloyw Llyn, now gilded by the sun. It watched them climb out on to an outcrop of rock, take off all the clothes they had only just put back on, and dive into the lake. As it soared higher into the sun, the bird observed the two pale, naked figures crossing and re-crossing the tarn, and diving far down off the rock several times into the deep, clear water. Then it drifted away across the mountain.

On the way down the mountainside we passed through an ancient grove of stunted oaks, the trees so encrusted with mosses and lichens they looked like old cheeses left in the fridge for too long. The second tarn had been more than twice the size of the first, and nearly as cold, and we still luxuriated in the after-effects of the soft, sweet-tasting water's rigour. It had provided the crowning swim of the day.

We returned to civilisation for dinner at the Victoria Inn at Llanbedr. It was the sort of place where Borrow might well have dined. To my sadness and his, Adrian had to return home that night. I was going to miss his wit as well as his pacemaking. 'Will there be anything else?' asked the waitress as she cleared our table. 'What would you suggest?' we enquired. 'Well, nothing really,' she said.

After supper I went back up the mountain and camped at the top end of a lake, Llyn Cwm Bychan, on a little sheep-mown peninsula where the river enters it. It had been in such flood a couple of weeks earlier that it would have submerged my tent to a depth of three feet. When it rains hard here, the water simply cascades off the mountains. It would be a perfect spot for an early-morning swim. I lay for a long while by the moonlit lake, imagining Borrow here, reflecting on the convivial pleasures of the day.

I always dream a lot when I am camping, in the sweet repose that comes with exercise and physical fatigue. 'The dreams are getting obsessive and I don't even know if I should own up to them,' I put in my notebook. 'By now I am dreaming almost continuously of rivers, seas, tides and ponds.' Tucked up on my peninsula with the sound of the river vibrating through the turf, I dream I am swimming in a still, black canal overhung by a cobbled wharf with a high roof, like a pagoda. At one end of the wharf there are wooden lock gates in deep water, and beyond the gates is something, I don't know what, that needs retrieving. I am with my dream friend from childhood and the other members of my own version of the Famous Five. We are definitely trespassing. One of us is going to have to creep on to the wharf and plunge down under the lock gates to reach the other side. I am the one who dives and I swim down and down under the looming gates in the green water, but I never know what is on the other side because that is the moment I wake up.

I woke to the beginnings of a fine day and bathed in the lake off my peninsula, swimming through lingering miasmal mists rising off the surface. Thoreau describes Walden Pond at such a moment: 'As the sun arose, I saw it throwing off its nightly clothing of mist, and here and there, by degrees, its soft ripples or its smooth reflecting surface was revealed, while the mists, like ghosts, were stealthily withdrawing in every direction into the woods, as at the breaking up of some nocturnal conventicle.' It is a marvellously unconscious evocation of the kind of scene Courbet loved to paint, of women undressing to bathe.

Searching the map, I had seen some promising upland streams, a waterfall and a tarn, so I hiked off uphill through the bracken. There is so much of it in the Rhinogs that the sheep all carry it around on their coats like camouflaged soldiers. I watched a ewe standing between two big rocks the shape of goats' cheeses. They were just far enough apart to allow the animal in, and I began to understand the relationship Henry Moore perceived between sheep and stones. He saw sheep as animate stones, the makers of their own landscape. By grazing the moors and mountains they keep the contours – the light and shade – clear, sharp and well-defined, like balding picture-restorers constantly at work on every detail. The black oblongs of their pupils set deep in eyes the colour and texture of frog skin are like the enormous slate coffin-baths you see in the farmyards here; seven foot slabs of slate hollowed into baths. Quite why the farmers made such things is a puzzle, when there are natural baths and pools in every stream inviting you to 'wash away the night', William Morris's phrase for the morning ablutions of his questing knights in *The Water of the Wondrous Isles*.

I climbed up a *cribin,* or *moel,* a rounded rocky outcrop commanding a view of the valley, and settled down in a warm sheep hollow. Every tree up here has a hollow the size and shape of a sheep, the roots exposed and polished by generations of them hunkering down. I sat perched on the first of a series of tumps rising in succession up a ridge, their rocks rounded by cushions of turf. I was level with the tops of hawthorns, rowans and ashes that grew on the slopes and grassy hillocks. There was birdsong everywhere; the rising notes of pipits, like the turning of a rusty wheel, the mew of the buzzard as it spun into view. Redstarts flew from tree to tree, taking the line a slack rope would take slung between them. Economy in flight is what makes it graceful. Look at the swift, which hardly seems to move its wings at all, or the planing buzzard, ascending a thermal. The redstart flaps its wings just enough to get from A to B and always lands on the upward beat, under full control. Birds always land rising, coming up to a branch or ledge, never down.

I removed my boots and stretched out to enjoy the sun. The hollow-sounding ground was still damp and my glasses, left lying on it, soon steamed up. With my face close to the turf I observed a faint mist rising from clumps of tiny flowers peopled with tiny insects: yellow tormentil, stonecrop, sage, thyme, sorrel, bell heather, foxglove, innumerable grasses, mosses, twayblade and heath bedstraw (now rumpled bedstraw) where I had been lying.

Wandering further on amongst these tumuli, I came upon the entrance of a cave, with a dozen steam genies twisting out of it where hot sun played on its wet, peaty floor, well manured by the sheep that must squeeze in and shelter there. I got my head and shoulders in, and waited for my eyes to grow accustomed to the dark, then used the reflected sunshine in my watch, a tiny sun dancing about the walls, to see how far it stretched into the hill. The cave had filled up with centuries of sheep-shit and ran for at least fifteen or twenty feet in a perfect five-foot arch of slate, with the rotten remains of wood protruding from the walls. I could have entered on all fours, but there was something unappealing about the idea of crawling in wet sheep-shit. Was it a slate mine, a lead mine, or a tomb? There was a stone circle not half a mile away.

I found two more cave entrances close by, both nearly blocked with loose earth, guarded by brambles, thistles and foxgloves. This was *Rogue Male* country, practically unmapped, and unfrequented. I made a mental note that I could go to ground here, as the nameless protagonist of the thriller goes to ground in Dorset, in the event of some future political or personal crisis, living on berries and mutton, and communing with the weasels. Here, too, was a roofless, circular, stone-walled chamber and three more tunnels running into the hill from higher up. They were much easier of access, five feet wide and four feet high, well lined with slates which now dripped on me as I crept in and explored. Practically

92

brushing my cheek, a wagtail flew off a nest of five pale speckled eggs hidden in a sage plant and a hart's-tongue fern near the entrance. I crept in some twenty feet until the shaft ran off to my right in utter darkness and I lost my nerve and retreated gingerly, suddenly fearful of the rock-fall that clearly hadn't ever happened in several hundred years.

There was no sign of these tunnels on the map, and I was content for them to remain a mystery. Indeed, it was infinitely preferable to me that they should not be on the map, and never should be. This was one of those magical places the people of northern Greece call *Agrafa*, 'the unwritten places'. They are the remote and secret places in the Pindos mountains, bordering Albania and Macedonia, that were deliberately left off the map by the inhabitants so as to avoid the imposition of taxes by the occupying Turks. Borrow would certainly have gone and knocked on the nearest farmer's door and demanded to know the full history of the earthworks. No doubt his curiosity was laudable, but it also often seems impertinent and condescending. He would ask total strangers what they thought of their landlord, whether their parents were still living, or about their religion. It says much for the civility of the Welsh country people that they always seemed to give him straight answers.

I had been following a tributary river of the lake uphill and now came to a meeting of the water. I took the left fork and followed a delightful little rushing brook about four feet wide that ran steeply over a series of waterfalls between two and ten feet high. It ran alongside a south-facing stone wall that acted as a sounding board for its song, a continuous chord composed of the deep notes made by the spouting of water into stone hollows and the descants of the shallower rapids. Thus serenaded, I cooled off in a pool below a waterfall, so shaped that I could lie facing the morning sun with the cascade on my shoulders. By angling myself further back, I could get the full, icy force of the water over the back of my head, a sensation more often associated with warm water and the hairdresser's chair, and utterly exhilarating. Behind the curtain of water I saw the secret green lushness of liverwort. The view over the whole bowl of mountains was magnificent, and I hadn't seen a soul all morning. Wedged in the rocks were some old split hazel fencing stakes or wattles, eroded almost to a wafer by the stream. Just the knots and sinews of the wood remained. I retrieved a half-melted chocolate bar I had left to solidify under the water and soon dried off in the warm sun.

My next swim was about a thousand feet up, below the mountain succinctly known as Clip, in the comparatively balmy waters of Llyn Eiddew-mawr overlooking the vast estuary sands of Porthmadog. The tarn must be half a mile long, and it was perfectly clear, with a brown peaty bottom shading into invisible depths. The sun had been shining on the water all day, and I swam across and back very comfortably, having warmed up on the ascent. By now it was tea-time, and I lay on the bank eating nuts, dates and biscuits, wondering if the tarn had ever contained the 'afanc'. This is a creature that reputedly once lived in the Welsh lakes. It was considered by Borrow to have been the crocodile, and by others to have been the beaver. Myth has it that Hu the Mighty, the inventor of husbandry and a leader of the ancient Cymru, drew out the afanc from the water with his team of four oxen and banished it. Certainly there would once have been beavers in Welsh lakes, and, at one time, crocodiles. Musing by just such a lake as this on his walk, Borrow felt sure that if its depths were searched, 'relics of the crocodile and the beaver might be found'. 'Happy were I,' he says, 'if for a brief space I could become a Cingalese, that I might swim out far into that pool, dive down into its deepest part and endeavour to discover any strange things which beneath its surface may lie.' I had swum out far, but I had not dived down. The afanc was possibly some kind of plesiosaur, a fifteen-foot creature resembling a crocodile, one of whose fossil skeletons was discovered in the summer of 1844 at Kettleness on the Yorkshire coast. It is now built into the wall of the Whitby Museum.

I hiked downhill along one of the enormous stone walls, some up to eight feet high, that thread across this rugged country. Their only logic seems to be aesthetic. Only the longer ones appear to do much, like mark a boundary, or keep sheep in or out. These walls are reputed to have been built by French prisoners of war from Waterloo, and enclose wide 'fields' on the hillsides and tops, perhaps sixty or a hundred acres at a time. The work must have been immense. Maintaining them is a life's work too. I couldn't help thinking of the hernia unit at the Harlech General Hospital. It must be a busy place on market day.

I could hear the sound of laughing water across nearly a mile of hillside, and could soon see it too, tumbling, white and sparkling, over a ramp of black rock thirty feet high, like a leaking castle. Feeling like a striptease artist by now, I hung my clothes over a bilberry and climbed up the falls to the top. Water was gushing and surging up through a moraine of massive boulders, then sliding down a forty-five degree slab of rock, black where it was wet, and purple where it was dry. Lying back against the sloping rock I let the water flood over me, then swam against the current in a substantial pool lower down. Water rushed about everywhere here, and amongst the remains of a settlement I found a spring inside a kind of stone temple covered in ferns. I went down to drink from it, and felt its atmosphere and power. The sense of a Delphic presence was so palpable, the Oracle might just have gone for lunch. The cottages had been tiny; no more than eight feet square. The walls of one were still standing, and its hearth, too. On the old track that led away downhill was the most luxuriant bed of wild thyme I have ever seen. None of the ruins were marked on the map at all, which only made discovering them the more thrilling.

I climbed into the river where it ran on through a miniature ravine full of the bright, rich pinks of heather, bracken, stonecrop, thyme, gorse and the little yellow tormentil. I followed it down through a ladder of waterfalls and pools, some of them deep enough to swim, interspersed with straight, high-speed runs between great slabs of rock. Here and there the stream would bend sharply to the left or right and the water would climb up the rock wall and spout into thin air like an eel standing on its tail. Then it merged with another stream, running down an almost parallel ravine, and I slid, scrambled, waded, swam, plunged and surfed through it all until I was delivered into a deep, circling pool. A little further on, a solitary sycamore stood sentinel over a sheep-nibbled lawn of buttercups and daisies by a waterfall and another pool, long and deep, between black slabs of rock, where I swam against the stream and hovered in the clear black water. Here I made my camp, hanging my towel to dry in the sycamore branches. I made delicious tea with the river water, devoured bread, goats' cheese and pennywort leaves, and fell into a deep sleep, lulled by the song of the waterfall, of Minnehaha, Laughing Water, the bride of Hiawatha, watched over by the dark shapes of menhirs on the hilltops.

I awoke to the croaking of a raven overhead somewhere, dreaming a nonsense of what E. M. Forster in *Howards End* called 'Borrow, Thoreau and sorrow', and squirmed half out of the sleeping bag like a caddis larva, watched by a curious, timid ewe and her lamb. There was a ruined roofless building by the bank of the waterfall pool and a rounded containing wall with a gate. I realised that this must have been a sheep wash. It would explain the presence of the solitary sycamore providing shade over the lawn where I was encamped, and a gnarled holly overhanging the river as a sign for the shepherds. It might also be the reason why this was the only place I had found daisies and buttercups in the Rhinogs. They belong in the lowland grazing meadows and would have been carried up here as seeds or roots by sheep.

I leapt straight into the pool like a self-dipping sheep. It was six feet deep, and I swam up to the waterfall and hung there again in the bracing stream like a seagull following a boat. Then I waded a little way downstream through the dis-ordered, foaming boulders to the next pool, in a gorge of gleaming, mossy rock crossed by a bridge of six-foot stone slabs slung across the water like the lintels of Stonehenge. It was the wildest natural jacuzzi. Currents jostled me from all directions and I climbed out stunned and galvanised. I made tea on the gas stove and breakfasted on more goats' cheese and bread. Although not quite up to the standards of George Borrow, who sometimes breakfasted on eggs, mutton chops, boiled and pickled salmon, fried trout and potted shrimps, it was made special by the place, with its buttercup lawn shaped into an inverted comma and enclosed by a stone wall that retains the ancient, sloping track running past at a higher level, and tapers from five feet to nothing in a way that a modern architect would completely approve. There were surely never any drawings for this, yet the proportions and sense of harmony with the natural architecture of the water, rocks and trees were very fine. Whoever built it had, as Alexander Pope put it, 'consulted the genius of the place'. It was highly distinctive, like a Greek stage, shaped by years of use and now all the more beautiful for being a ruin and so remote. I had not seen a human soul for thirty-six hours, just sheep and the powerful presence of the Rhinogs, whose peaks that morning were lost in clouds. I could have stayed there for days, walking to the next tarn on the map with an unpronounceable name, and unpronounceably freezing water.

9
THE LOST POOLS OF THE MALVERNS

Malvern Hills, 17 June
NEXT MORNING I drove out of Wales through the Black Mountains to the Malvern Hills in search of springs and open-air pools. I had read of the Malvern Festival, where, during the 1930s, the impresario and producer Barry Jackson used to première George Bernard Shaw's plays, ferrying in as many as sixty London drama critics at a time, by the trainload, and even planeload. Shaw would come for two or three weeks in August to walk in the hills, and swim daily in the spring-fed pools. Bathing was one of GBS's passions, and as a change from the cold Malvern water, he would often take the cast for drives round the hills or over to Droitwich Spa, where he would duck into the warm brine baths before driving back for the evening show at Malvern, with the salt still in his beard. The actors must have dreaded the drive home; Shaw was an appalling driver, with a dyslexic habit of treading on the accelerator of his Rolls-Royce when he meant to brake.

Nowhere else in Britain has anything like the profusion of natural springs Malvern enjoys, and in the nineteenth century the town was deliberately developed as a spa. It rises up the east side of the steep range of hills in terraces of fine Victorian villas, each set in its own spacious garden. To me, prospecting the maps for likely dips, it had all the signs of a swimmer's paradise. Malvern's springwater was famous from at least as early as 1620. Even then it was being bottled, long before Jacob Schweppes began selling the Holy Well water in 1850.

There are over sixty springs and wells around the steep green hills, but a great many of them turned out to have become derelict or disused since the 1940s or earlier. Inspired by tales of gondoliering and night-bathing in the pools, I tramped along the ridge path that leads to the summit of the Worcester Beacon, where you used to be able to have tea at the Beacon Café before it was burnt down by vandals a few years ago. During the festival, there had been donkey rides up these tracks. I had hoped to look down from above and spot the swimming pools glinting from below, but they were nowhere to be seen. Although one, at the Dingle, still survives as a sunken garden, none is any longer in use. High and dry on the Malvern Hills, I consoled myself with thoughts of Shaw in his tweed knickerbockers and his friend Elgar striding up here, and of the poet Langland, who wrote *Piers Plowman* as he gazed out over Worcestershire in around 1377. In the opening lines of the poem, Langland had impressed in my imagination a powerful notion that his Malvern foothills must be full of promising swimming holes:

> On a May morning on a Malvern hillside . . .
> As I lay and leaned and looked on the water
> I slumbered and slept, so sweetly it murmured.

All that I found in Malvern was an indoor 'leisure pool'. Forced to abandon all hope of bathing in the lost pools, I went instead in search of the miscellaneous spouts, pumps, fountains, wells and springs that abound here. The first surviving spring I found flowed into a stone trough from an iron pipe beside the road up on the beacon. This was the Chance's Pitch Spout, and I joined a queue of three or four other men with assorted plastic flagons waiting to fill them. As we talked, I was reminded what sociable places wells, pumps and springs have always been. Turning on the tap at home is a far less rewarding social experience. Sipped from cupped hands, the water tasted very pure, with none of the dreadful taste of iron or sulphur I associate with spas, and it was cold; it tumbles out of the hill at a steady forty-seven degrees all over Malvern.

My next spring was in a little fenced hollow in a field at the bottom of a slippery downhill scramble through a wood on the western slopes near the British Camp Hotel. Here I found myself face to face with a pair of foxes, who seemed quite as surprised as me. The dog fox scampered off, but the vixen and I just stood looking at each other for fully two minutes. I wasn't going to move before she did, even if we were there all morning. Then she turned and dragged herself away, towing her paralysed hindquarters after her. I stood for a long time by the living spring, too shocked to move, looking at the rank, parted grass where the dying fox had disappeared, wondering how long she could survive.

Sick or unhappy people used to come in their thousands to Malvern and its springs seeking a cure. Tennyson came, after a nervous breakdown, and said he was 'half cured, half destroyed' by the place. Florence Nightingale stayed in August 1897, and Charles Darwin arrived depressed and unable to write, but was so convinced by the effects of his treatment that he returned three more times. Visitors to the spa walked all round the Malvern Hills sampling water at the springs. It was famous for its healing powers, but low in minerals, so another form of water cure was also developed here. In 1842, two doctors, Wilson and Gully, introduced hydrotherapy to Malvern. Their methods were based on the work of the son of a peasant farmer in a remote corner of Austrian Silesia: Vincent Priessnitz.

Hydrotherapy goes back to classical times, but it was Priessnitz who had revived it and made it popular in the first half of the nineteenth century. He founded the first water cure establishment at the family farmhouse in Grafenberg, 600 feet up in the mountains, 160 miles north of Prague. Like Malvern, the village is surrounded by springs low in mineral salts, and offers strenuous hill walking as additional stimulation. Priessnitz had been run over by a cart when he was eighteen and suffered a great many broken bones. He was treated in a way that was locally traditional: strips of wet linen were wrapped about his broken body, and continually reapplied, soaked in cold springwater. Within a fortnight, so the story goes, Priessnitz was up and walking again, and he was back at work within a year.

Apart from the difficulty of the journey itself to Grafenberg, close to the Polish border, patients at Priessnitz's new establishment were subjected to spartan bedrooms whose windows were kept wide open to the winter night. You were woken at four o'clock in the morning and wrapped from neck to toe in wet linen. Thus mummified, you were left to sweat for an hour or so, then introduced to a thirty-foot cold bath, with water at forty-three to fifty degrees, for two or three minutes. By six o'clock, you were out walking in the forest, returning to a breakfast of brown bread and strawberries, followed by a rest. You were roused later for an uphill walk some way into the forest to the open-air douche. This was a natural mountain stream diverted into a pipe supported on a wooden gantry, spouting a waterfall from a height of twenty feet. You stood underneath, and the icy pummelling it gave you was a kind of cold-water massage. On the walk back, you would drink water at the springs. Priessnitz liked his patients to drink twenty or thirty glasses a day. The rest of the morning was your own to while away with a spot of wood-cutting in your bedroom, or snow-clearing. Then, shortly before lunch, you would spend a quarter of an hour sitting in a shallow, cold bath. Lunch was cabbage, gherkins and springwater, then a rest, followed by a four o'clock douche in the woods, a seven o'clock cold bath, supper of bread, butter and milk, and bed at half-past nine. On top of all this, there was a hefty bill to pay on your release, but Priessnitz claimed to be able to cure gout pains within a day. The sanatorium, known as 'the Water University', still exists at Grafenberg, with a statue representing Priessnitz and the spirit of cold water outside. In 1997, one of the patients attempted to blow it up.

The account of the Grafenberg daily regime comes from a Captain Richard Claridge, who stayed there in 1841, having spent two months in Florence unable to move with some kind of arthritic ailment. During his three-month stay, he drank 1,500 tumblers of springwater, walked 1,000 miles, and went away a new man. That year, more than 1,500 patients came to Grafenberg, and the year after Drs Wilson and Gully brought their own version of this treatment to Malvern, with equal success. Darwin was so impressed, he had his own cold water douche bath built at home, and immersed himself in cold water every day. George Bernard Shaw and Benjamin Britten also took daily cold baths throughout their lives.

The effects of cold water on the body have recently been re-examined by Dr Murray Epstein in clinical trials at the University of Miami School of Medicine as part of the NASA research programme, and by Dr Vijay Kakkar, Director of the Thrombosis Research Institute for the British Heart Foundation. The fact that some of us live in the Sahara and some in Siberia suggests that human beings have a great capacity for adapting to cold climates as well as hot. The temperature of your body is regulated in the brain by the hypothalamus. When you put your foot in cold water, the variation in temperature is transmitted via the cold sensors in your skin. There are more cold sensors in your feet than any-where else, which is probably why people instinctively tend to use them to test the water before bathing. Thus stimulated, the hypothalamus reacts by causing the constriction of certain blood vessels to divert the blood flow away from skin, fat and muscle to the internal organs to conserve heat. It also sends hormones to the pituitary gland, which in turn controls the activity of the thyroid gland, pancreas, kidneys, testes or ovaries. When you immerse yourself completely in cold water, your hypothalamus sends out signals all over your body to modify its metabolism in preparation for dealing with an emergency, which would, primitively speaking, be flight or fight.

In the clinical experiment on 'cold pre-adapted humans', volunteers began a twelve-week course of daily cold baths, graduating from five to twenty minutes at a time. In one trial, they acclimatised themselves by beginning in bathwater at, say, seventy-five degrees and reducing the temperature day by day to sixty degrees, which was considered adequately cold for the scientific observation. During the twelve weeks, cardio-graphs were taken, and blood pressure measured. Blood quality was also assessed. The findings were that in every case blood pressure and cholesterol decreased. People lost weight, reducing both fat and muscle, and the researchers were surprised to discover that whereas it had been thought that cold water must increase the predisposition of the blood to clot, the opposite was the case. The viscosity of the blood plasma was reduced, and there was an increase in other anticoagulants. Perhaps most interesting of all, there was an increase in the numbers of lymphocytes and white cells in the blood after leaving the water. This would increase the strength of the immune system. An increase in the production of thyroxine helped increase the oxygen capacity of the blood, and there was a beneficial increase in the thickness of heart muscle, together with a lowering of the pulse rate. Cold water, it was found, also dramatically stimulates the production of plasmin, a powerful enzyme which dissolves blood clots before they can build up to cause heart-attacks or strokes. As a further bonus, it was discovered to enhance the production of testosterone in men, and oestrogen and progesterone in women, improving fertility and stimulating the libido.

Such results may lend some credence to the claims made for cold bathing by certain English public schools, along the lines of 'mens sana, in corpore sano', although not the supposed bromide effect on the libido. It is ironic to consider that all those cold showers, at school or in the army, were actually heightening desire and increasing fertility amongst the nation's youth.

The fashion for hydrotherapy spread all across Europe, and by the 1850s the American *Water Cure Journal* had over 180,000 subscribers. In the same year as the two doctors arrived in Malvern, two more grand, elaborate hydrotherapy spas were built by entrepreneurs in Ilkley and Matlock. This was big business. Six years earlier, the St Andrews Brine Baths had been opened in a magnificent half-timbered barn of a building twelve miles from Malvern in Droitwich. A great many of the patients were referred by their doctors, and were actually suffering from depression (as in the cases of Darwin and Tennyson). After the Asylums Acts of 1828 and 1845, people could no longer enter asylums for voluntary psychiatric treatment without being certified, so they turned to the spas, and water cures.

In the old Malvern winter gardens, I found a disused drinking fountain with four bronze water sprites seated disconsolately around its dry marble basin. The council had demolished an elaborate Victorian memorial fountain to Dr Wilson, so it was a pretty good bet that the sprites had long since abandoned the town and its phantom pools, unwilling to be bottled by Schweppes. The following afternoon I decided to follow George Bernard Shaw's example and drive over to Droitwich for a warm salt dip.

Droitwich is next door to Bromsgrove and the well-to-do suburbs of Birmingham, and I passed the gothic spires of the splendid Impney Hotel, where Mr and Mrs Shaw once stayed, on the way in. The Brine Baths are in the centre of town in a new building next to the private hospital. The original St Andrew's Brine Baths next door, with their magnificent mock-Tudor entrance, have been turned into the Tourist Information Centre. The town has the prosperous air of an ex-spa; Georgian and mock-Tudor houses, and the half-timbered Worcestershire Brine Baths Hotel, suggest former glories. The main street was clearly once grander than it now is and probably had one of the original Sainsbury's grocery shops, with proper marble counters and tiled walls, butchers in ties with aprons and grey Brylcreemed hair, and no plastic pork-pie hats.

There is still something of that atmosphere when you go into the Brine Baths. Friendly, efficient women in crisp white aprons welcome you and there is an endless supply of generous white bath towels and gowns. Having slipped one on over my trunks, I entered the warm and slightly theatrical surroundings of the baths. Here I was met by Suzannah, one of the white-clad assistants, who offered me a table at the poolside and a cup of tea. Under the bright lights, it could have been a film set. Suzannah explained that to get the best from the brine bath I should stay in for at least forty minutes. Apart from the physiological benefits to the joints and spine through the total weightlessness you experience, immersion in the brine also lowers your blood pressure, and the effects last several days. You certainly do feel wonderful afterwards.

The brine bath is about forty feet by twenty, and raised

three feet off the floor, so you make a regal entrance up some steps, then along a bridge, then down into the pool. When I entered the amazingly dense water, I had to plant my feet into it really hard to stop them popping straight out again, like plastic ducks. They still keep it at the same temperature they always have since the spa began: ninety-two degrees fahrenheit. The pool is from three to six feet deep, and it is impossible to sink. Spending forty minutes in this was going to be no problem at all. When I floated on my back and stretched out my arms, I could lift my hands right up off the water. When I floated upright, my plimsoll line was across my chest, level with my armpits. I found I could propel myself around the pool with my head and shoulders clean out of the water, like Neptune. You can lean your head back in the buoyant salt and bob about like an astronaut, in an entirely weightless state. Your legs tend to pop above the surface, and your feet stick up absurdly. If you could walk on water, this would be the stuff to do it on.

The salt finds its way straight to even the tiniest abrasions, as I found out. I had a two-day-old bee sting on my thigh, and it began to itch deliciously. This was definitely bathing, not swimming. All my attempts at breaststroke ended in embarrassing capsizes. You tend to paddle yourself round the pool like a human lilo, eavesdropping on the small talk. There are jugs of fresh water and glasses at the poolside, in case you get salt-water in your eye or on your face. You have to be careful not to splash. Diving, I imagine, would be out of the question. You might break a bone.

In the early morning, before the doors open to the public at ten o'clock, patients from the private hospital next door use the baths to work with physiotherapists. Many will be recovering from operations on their backs or knees, and the hospital is popular with BUPA because of the accelerated rate of recovery from the use of the baths. Amazingly, the original NHS hospital had a hydrotherapy pool, but didn't use the brine, so its patients had to use rubber rings to keep themselves afloat instead. The salt-water does useful things to the crystals that form in arthritic joints, so there are a lot of regulars who come in twice a week, or even more, and experience genuine benefits. But at least as many people come here for the pure pleasure of it. I met a mother and daughter taking the afternoon off together, and you can quite happily spend all day in here if you like, reading the papers, drinking coffee, popping in and out of the sauna, shower or baths. All the other bathers were little groups of women in their sixties enjoying a good gossip and looking thoroughly at home.

The salt is entirely natural; indeed the original source of Droitwich's prosperity was from mining it, and much of the original investment in the spa came from John Corbett, the mine owner. The spa water is pumped up from a well halfway along the high street, and these days it is purified. But in the old pool, with its fine wooden beamed ceiling, teak-walled baths and corrugated iron walls, the water was its natural murky brown; 'the colour of the canal', according to Sylvia, the receptionist, who bathed in it before it closed in 1972. The water was kept at ninety-two degrees by steam from a coal boiler. Bathers were segregated, and allowed twenty minutes in the pool, then wrapped all over in hot towels like papooses and sat in a cubicle for twenty minutes.

German and Japanese tourists are puzzled when they visit our former spa towns, Bath, Leamington or Cheltenham. There are about 1,000 spas in Europe, and 320 in Germany alone, where 40 per cent of all hotel 'bed-nights' are sold in spas. In the nineteenth century there were some 200 spas in Britain, and even in 1946 there were 10. Now there are none, except for the limited medical use of Droitwich and Buxton. So it would be more truthful to say that on the following morning I woke up in plain Cheltenham, not Cheltenham Spa.

I began the day with about the nearest thing to a spa experience still available in the town, apart from a glass of San Pellegrino in a café; an early dip at the classic Sandford Lido, opened in 1935 when open-air swimming was at its height. Its fountain, and the white colonnaded symmetry of its pavilion, were reflected in the still blue water as I filed into the pool with several early-morning season ticket holders. I had the satisfying experience of being first in, diving into the perfect smoothness and swimming a whole length alone.

As I swam, I thought of a story my Norfolk friend Oliver Bernard told me. One warm afternoon in a school, he set a class to write the seventeen syllables of a haiku, and noticed one boy still chewing his pencil, unable to begin. He said he was 'no good at writing'. Oliver asked him what he liked, and he said 'swimming'. Then he wrote this:

> Water calm and clear
> I dive in, disturbing it.
> Bubbles rise and break.

The proceedings in the Cheltenham pool were regulated by the superintendent's white Jack Russell terrier whose single ginger spot gave him the air of a clown. However, he made it immediately clear that he was a deeply serious dog, and would take no nonsense from any of us swimmers. A plaque on the wall celebrated the pool's first sixty years, and named the guest of honour at the Diamond Anniversary celebrations in 1995 as Mr Raymond Green, who found his place in history by being the very first swimmer to buy an admission ticket here. There was also an interesting chart recording the number of swimmers each year. They had 76,816 swimmers in 1988, but 201,000 people bathed here in the hot summer of 1959.

Before the arrival of the spa boom, the entire population of Cheltenham in 1800 was hardly more than 3,000. By 1821 the town had a theatre, assembly rooms, a busy main street, and four times the population. It was in hot competition with Leamington, another drinking spa, which offered similar attractions and had grown from being a small village in the 1780s. Bath was the third largest town in England in 1810, with a population of nearly 40,000, and had three coffee houses to Cheltenham's two (one for ladies, one for gentlemen). The middle classes were becoming residents rather than visitors. 'Watering places', as William Cobbett called them, were run in a highly enterprising spirit by Improvement Commissions – and what he called 'silently laughing quacks'. Cheltenham was notably competitive. It engaged a Master of Ceremonies, who arranged and publicised the balls and a hyperactive social scene. There were clubs, subscription libraries, a social register, hotels, street lighting, schools like the Cheltenham Ladies' College, new churches and well-to-do doctors. The spa was continually unveiling new attractions like the 'Montpelier Pump Room', the 'Imperial Sulphurious Ladies' Marble Font', and, in 1818, the Cheltenham Races. Cobbett preferred to avoid spas on his rural rides. To him, they were the resorts of 'all that is knavish and all that is foolish and all that is base'. 'When I enter a place like this,' he said of Cheltenham, 'I always feel disposed to squeeze up my nose with my fingers.'

Still questing for the authentic naiads of the spa, I ventured over to Bath for the afternoon. During my map-swimming sessions in the University Library at Cambridge, I had originally intended beginning my journey in the Roman Baths themselves. To have begun in the national capital of bathing seemed logical at the time. Bath has been the Mecca of bathers since at least the first century. But when I telephoned to enquire about swimming in the ancient baths, I was told it was out of the question. The spring was apparently contaminated with a bacterium that enjoyed sulphur, and no one was allowed near the water. It seemed a fitting fate for the city Alexander Pope called 'a sulphurous pit', and Cobbett regarded as a 'wen'. As at Malvern, there was only an indoor leisure pool, and even that had been shut all through the previous summer because the council had privatised it, and the new swimming pool company had promptly gone bankrupt. Bathonians, faced with the sudden liquidisation of their public baths, had been forced to go to Bristol or Chippenham, unless they swam in the river pool at Claverton at the confluence of the Avon and the Frome, or even in the middle of the city beside the Pulteney Bridge. Members of the university, meanwhile, could use their new fifty-metre Olympic pool, but the pattern of dereliction followed by renewal of the city's bathing facilities seems to be historical, going back at least as far as the Romans, and, with the help of the National Lottery and the Millennium Commission, the city is poised to relaunch itself as a modern spa.

All through Bath's most recent heyday, in the seventeenth

and eighteenth centuries, people used to immerse themselves up to the neck for hours at a time in the Roman Baths, in the naturally warm, sulphurous springwater. They sat on stone cushions to adjust themselves for depth. Meticulous medical records were kept by the charitable hospital where they treated 'a great crop of paralytics that daily appear amongst tradesmen'. These were mostly lead workers and decorators suffering from the lead poisoning known as 'Painter's Palsy'. It began as abdominal pain and eventually led to paralysis. Drinking one-and-a-half pints of the vile-tasting spa water and immersing themselves for long periods, the patients experienced the natural diuretic effect of submersion on their kidneys, and excreted the lead about four times more efficiently as a result. The medical records classified patients on completion of their treatment under four columns: 'Improper' (meaning still poorly), 'Improved', 'Cured', or 'Dead'. Of 244 patients whose treatment was reviewed in 1778, nearly half were cured and 93 per cent improved. For most of those who migrated to Bath, however, the worldly pleasures of the place probably outweighed any benefits from the waters. On his visit around 1724, Daniel Defoe found it to be 'the resort of the sound rather than the sick; the bathing is made more a sport and diversion, than a physical prescription for health; and the town is taken up in raffling, gaming, visiting, and in a word, all sorts of gallantry and levity'.

Why were the spas eventually abandoned? The chief cause was the coming of the railways, which made the rival attractions of the seaside more accessible. Sea-bathing came into fashion in the nineteenth century, and was considered beneficial to health. Railways also brought the working classes into the spas. Some of the wealthier middle classes avoided the unwelcome intrusion by migrating to European spas like Marienbad and Baden-Baden instead. Brighton, once a spa town with its own horse racing, became a massively popular working-class resort. Encountering this succession of lost pools and dry watering holes felt like finding several pubs shut in a row. I decided to abandon the desert spas, and go looking for more full-blooded swimming.

10

TRIBAL SWIMMING

Worcestershire, 6 July

I WENT TO THE Vale of Evesham to meet a whole family tribe of river bathers who had written to me after reading a newspaper article I published on the joys of swimming. Their letter had enclosed a postcard of a mill on its own river island beside a weir and its pool, with a note on the back, 'This is where we swim.' There was an invitation to come and join them some time in the river.

Fladbury is a village a few miles upstream of Evesham on the River Avon. Not the Bath Avon, or the Hampshire Avon, but the Avon that runs through Stratford-upon-Avon. Shakespeare's Avon. I followed my directions to walk down an alley beside a house on the village green, found myself on the banks of the river just above a weir, and recognised the old three-storey red brick mill house across the water. A handbell dangled from a willow. I rang it, as instructed by my hosts, and waited. Two children appeared on the opposite bank and began to approach laboriously on a punt, propelled by hauling on a cable slung from bank to bank. I jumped aboard, was ferried back, and welcomed by Judith, my host.

I had entered a swimmer's dream. People lolled half-submerged along the top of the weir, reading or sunbathing, while others paddled themselves about the river in coracles, swam, dived, or just sat about in bathing costumes. It was a water rats' club straight from the pages of *The Wind in the Willows*. The mill sleeps twenty-eight, in an assortment of beds and bunks in more attics and bedrooms than I could

110

count. The children showed me up and down little flights of stairs, in and out of a warren of rooms, until I was dizzy.

Judith's letter had addressed the question of the right to swim in our rivers. The Environment Agency had written to her suggesting that it was irresponsible of the family to swim in the Avon, as they have very happily done for several generations. Judith was so upset by their patronising tone, and the implication that river swimming was strictly for crackpots, that she was considering starting some sort of swimmers' campaign.

The weather was perfect and the water tolerably warm, so, throwing caution to the winds, Judith and I set out upriver to discuss our mutual concern for the right to native swimming. We dived off an old stone landing-stage into sixteen-foot-deep clear green water above the weir and recklessly breaststroked a few hundred yards upstream as far as a bridge. Everyone likes to have a fixed point to swim to, even Channel swimmers. Walkers have their horizons and mountaintops, and swimmers count lengths, or go as far as the bridge, or the willow, or a certain boat at anchor, or the other side of the bay. We swam back with the gentle current, past back-garden landing-stages and several moored narrowboats.

Diving in again from the mill quayside, we felt the colder water below the warm layer on top and nosed upstream again alongside the boats.

Judith is part of an extended family of Quakers who have owned the mill for years and now share it, with their children and friends, booking themselves in a week or a weekend at a time to avoid overcrowding. Here was a strong family with a shared passion for the water, and certain characteristic ways of doing things. There is a tradition of coracle-building amongst them, and next door to the kitchen on the ground floor was the boathouse, with the little canvas-skinned craft hanging up like hats all round the walls, a larger curragh, an original wooden Rob Roy canoe, and a finely ribbed wood and canvas Canadian canoe. Each coracle was made to its maker's own special variation on the traditional design, with their name or initials carved into the wooden seat. Several of the children were out in the little craft, standing upright on the seats and deftly propelling themselves by stirring and twisting the paddle in the water ahead. The coracle, which weighs not much more than a rolled-up newspaper, spins about on the surface like the silver whirligig beetles that congregate on sheltered water in summer. One of the family sports is coracle polo. Another is a form of jousting in which you try to unbalance your opponent. I took a turn in one of these floating nutshells and soon found myself in the river.

Judith disappeared into the kitchen and found the Environment Agency's letter. I sat dangling my feet in the river, reading it:

> I feel it is my duty to draw your attention to the considerable risks associated with swimming in the River Avon.
>
> This river contains within its upper catchment a number of large industrial towns and cities including Rugby, Coventry, Warwick and Leamington. This inevitably means that the river receives a large volume of treated sewage effluent which, at times of low riverflow, can constitute as much as 80% of the total river flow. In spite of high treatment standards, this high proportion of sewage effluent poses a risk of bacterial contamination and many people who voluntarily or involuntarily swim in the River Avon suffer stomach upsets as a result.
>
> The most sinister risk of swimming in any river is the risk of contracting Leptospirosis which can lead to Weil's disease, a potential killer. The children's doctors should be made aware of this risk and any subsequent flu-like symptoms should be carefully monitored.
>
> Any river will have potentially dangerous currents both on and below the surface particularly in the vicinity of weirs and these cause the tragic and unnecessary deaths of many swimmers every year.
>
> I would strongly recommend that children are discouraged from swimming in the river but are taken to a local swimming pool instead. If this is not possible they should be constantly supervised by a trained adult and the risks should be made clear to the children, their parents, and the family doctors.

All the children I met at the mill appeared to be excellent swimmers and more than competent in boats. (They had certainly put me to shame in their coracles.) The smaller ones wore lifejackets as a matter of course and the bigger ones swam well and looked out for each other. The letter seemed a sad admission of the agency's failure to do the very job it was created to do.

As to the 'sinister risk' of Weil's disease, and the risk of drowning, a recent report entitled *Health Hazards Associated with the Recreational Use of Water*, published by the South West Regional Health Authority, concludes that the joy, pleasure and excitement that most of us get from water far outweigh the limited risks to our health. Weil's disease is the secret weapon of whatever dark forces are opposed to wild swimming. It has such a wonderfully sinister sound it would certainly have been invented by Steven Spielberg or Ray Bradbury if it didn't actually exist. It is caused by bacteria of the genus *Leptospira* carried in the urine of rats, cattle or dogs entering the human body through cuts and abrasions of the skin, or through the mucous surfaces of 'the mouth, nose and conjunctiva'. In response to public concern about the disease, Dr Robin Philip, an epidemiologist at the University of Bristol, has assessed the risks for 'recreational water-users' in Britain. He found that the risks of contracting Weil's disease, and of dying from it, were actually lower among this group (including swimmers) than for the total British population. He states:

> There are on average each year in the UK, some 2.5 cases of Weil's disease associated with bathing and water sports (i.e. one case among every two million annual recreational water users). As the case fatality rate in the UK is 10–15 per cent, the chance of dying from Weil's disease associated with bathing and water sports is about 1:20 million exposed persons (i.e. one case in the UK every four years).

Dr Philip analysed all the cases of the disease between 1982 and 1991, the majority of whom were not 'recreational water-users'. In fact, farmers and agricultural workers seemed to be the main occupational group at risk. He concluded: 'Despite the large numbers of people engaged in recreational water sports, the risks of contracting the disease, and of dying from it, seem to be lower among recreational water sports enthusiasts than for the general population.'

When the British Canoeing Union looked into the possible risks on behalf of the one million canoeists in this country, most of whom naturally get wet in rivers as a matter of routine, they found that the risk of a canoeist contracting the disease is about 1:200,000, and a canoeist heeding the preventive advice given to all river and lake users (see your doctor if you get any flu-like symptoms) would be a great deal less likely to contract Weil's disease than to die in a road accident in any one year (1:9,600). They put the chance of actually dying from Weil's disease for a canoeist at about 1:333,000.

We got back into the water, and splashed about near the weir. Judith showed me the work the Environment Agency had been doing to reinforce it. All sorts of little details were wrong, or unsympathetic to the place. An underwater toe-hold in the quayside, crucial for climbing out, had gone. It had been there for ever, and now Judith's mother missed it on her swims. An ugly iron ladder had been installed without consultation with the family. The top of the weir where they sit in the water was no longer as bum-friendly as the old flagstones had been. The family meant to have all this changed, right down to the toe-hold. I sat in the cool weir for a long while amongst the rippling minnows, teetering just above the white water the family sometimes shoots over in the curragh into the mill-pool below.

You can still dive out of the first-floor bedroom window into the river, and the iron handholds at the corner of the house by the weir were worn and polished smooth by generations of palms. There were photographs on the kitchen wall of the half-submerged family enjoying a floating picnic lunch in the river, complete with tablecloth. It is also a tradition with them once a year to set out the dining table on the weir and eat lunch in midstream. Judith and her family are serious amphibians who have swum in the Salt Lake in Utah amongst the salt-flies, and in the Snake River in Colorado.

Judith said that over the years they had noticed a difference in the way the water levels fluctuate. The river used to rise and fall slowly. During stormy weather the water would sink gently into the fields, draining gradually into the meandering streams and ditches, and eventually into the river. Judith often saw her grandmother cooking in wellingtons because the kitchen was flooded, and they would have to move up to the next floor while the river poured through the house. The mill was designed to accommodate inundation, with drains in the back walls. Now the river can often rise very sharply in the space of a few hours because there is so much tarmac and concrete everywhere, and such efficient field drainage. Streams have been straightened into concrete culverts; old flood meadows have been developed by supermarkets and even housing, so the water has nowhere to go except the river, and a flood can soon build up. In the most recent floods, the water level reached tabletop level in the kitchen, a boat smashed one of the windows, and the ferry was washed over the weir. There was mud everywhere downstairs, and all over the armchairs. Judith had resigned herself to 'two or three dusty years'.

Swimming is often enhanced by company, and sometimes by solitude. The same individual may swim for different reasons on different days. I certainly do. The joys of swimming are sometimes those of silence and solitude, sometimes of communion with nature, and sometimes the more friends who join you, the merrier. As with any mildly dangerous sport, there is safety in numbers when you swim in company, as when you climb or walk in the mountains. But there is also strength in numbers if your right to bathe in this or that particular mudhole is at all questioned.

Outdoor swimmers, especially in the wild, have always been outsiders with a shared vulnerability to the rigours of the elements and seasons, and to whoever seeks officiously to prevent them risking their necks, or disturbing the trout. Swimming without a roof over your head is now a mildly subversive activity, like having an allotment, insisting on your right to walk a footpath, or riding a bicycle. It certainly appeals to free spirits, which is why the talk is invariably so good in those little spontaneous bankside, beach or poolside parliaments that spring up wherever two or three swimmers are gathered, as though the water's fluency were contagious. That is why swimming clubs, lidos and unofficial bathing holes are such congenial places.

Next morning in cloudy Cirencester, Betty, the lady at the turnstile of the heated outdoor pool, took my £2 as I crossed the little river on an old iron footbridge. She told me they were thinking of closing at midday because of the weather. I hastened into the deliciously soft, warm water and set about swimming my mile: 56 lengths of the 30-yard pool. For a while I was alone. At about the half-mile point, the bottom of the pool suddenly lit up with the dappled reflections of wavelets like a David Hockney painting, and I felt the sun on my back. The management responded spontaneously by deciding to keep the pool open a little longer, especially as a trickle of swimmers, mostly women, had begun appearing. They ambled up and down together chatting.

The pool hasn't changed very much since it was built by a group of entrepreneurs in 1870. Steam power originally pumped the freezing water from a nearby well, but it was so cold it put people off swimming, so they switched instead to the 'warmer' water from the mill-stream. Heating and mixed bathing didn't arrive until 1931. Until then, the baths were filled every Sunday morning and emptied on Saturday evenings. At the beginning of the week, the water would be painfully cold. 'Fifty-eight degrees if you were lucky, fifty-five more likely,' according to one of the ex-grammar-school girls who were marched out every Tuesday to be traumatised in the icy pool for an eternal fifteen minutes. By the end of the week the water temperature might have crept up into the early sixties if the weather had been warm. There was no chlorination, so by Saturday, when the water was dirty and often covered in leaves and green slime, bathing was free, if you could stand it.

A group of passionate local swimmers, the Cirencester Open Air Swimming Pool Association, refused to see the original pool closed down by the council in 1973 when the inevitable indoor pool came along. Courageously, they took on the outdoor pool as an independent community enterprise, and have made it a success purely through their own hard work and enthusiasm.

To me, the marvellous thing about the pool is that it *hasn't* been modernised. It is a fine example of all the good reasons why it is often best *not* to spend money on things. The Cirencester swimmers have had the good sense to leave things alone. The result is an idyllic pool that has contrived to retain its old-fashioned charm. How much more delightful it is to change in a spartan breeze-block shed, hand-painted a jaunty bright blue by the swimmers themselves, and then to stuff your clothes into a vintage, battered wire basket which you trustingly take out on to the poolside with you. All I missed was the Brylcreem dispenser. This is really a miniature lido, with a lawn, a beautiful natural setting, and a bright Mediterranean-blue tuck shop serving Bovril, hot chocolate and something called 'Shark Bites'.

I discovered that to save water rates, the Pool Association had reverted to the use of water from the well, following the example of the original swimming-bath company, but also heating it. Hence the pleasant texture, 'soft as rose petals to the skin', to quote one of the pool's patrons, Winifred Waites, in her memoir of the pool. She describes jumping into 'that inviting blue water, soft as silk, with the blue sky above, the sun on my face, the birds singing, and the lap of the water as I swim'.

I lunched at Keith's Coffee House in Blackjack Lane, where all the talk was of the forthcoming Royal Show at Stoneleigh. 'Brilliant shops,' said the women at the next table, 'and lots of farmers.' On my way out of Keith's I lingered in the delicatessen department, full of cloth-covered jam-jars of rhubarb and ginger preserve, cream honey, raspberry honey and chutneys in hexagonal jars. I asked the assistant if these were all made on the premises. 'Oh dear no!' she said. 'I expect there's a factory somewhere which just makes them *look* home-made.'

Judith and the kamikaze swimmers at the mill had told me about a magnificent spring-fed flooded quarry on the outskirts of Bristol, where there had been a swimming club since the 1920s, and where there were diving boards. The wooded, hewn cliffsides of the quarry provided a sheltered suntrap, and there was a long waiting list to join the club. Fortunately, one of Judith's sisters was a member, and I wangled an invitation to swim there that very afternoon.

I was welcomed by the superintendent, changed in an enclosure where everyone just left their clothes trustingly on a peg or a wooden bench, and went in off the springboard for a long swim in the glassy, sweet-smelling springwater. It was medium cool, sixty-two degrees, and I shared the three hundred yards of lake with a dozen late-afternoon swimmers, all women. Some swam in conversational pairs, others alone, lost in thought, or just drifted about the huge surface as one might doodle on a piece of paper.

I had driven over through the Cotswolds and parked in a leafy suburban avenue in the north of Bristol, where I passed through the elegant ironwork gateway of the Henleaze Swimming Club straight into the 1920s. The lake shone like a river by banks of weeping willows and well-kept lawns dotted with little groups of sunbathers. It was long and deep, as though it flowed between the canyon walls of the old quarry. Gardeners and their sheds stood silhouetted along the clifftop. The club is only three miles from the city centre, and wildly popular. Membership is limited to 1,300, with a waiting list of about 800. You have to show you can swim at least 50 metres before you can join, and the lake still has a fine set of high diving boards. The 10-metre board at the top, from which Olympic divers used to give displays in the 1930s and '40s, is now reckoned too high by the ASA for the depth of water beneath it, so divers use the 7- and 5-metre boards and a 2-metre springboard. Everything is beautifully maintained.

I took advantage of the absence of congestion on the lake to practise my backstroke, always a problem style in the swimming pool because of the danger of collision with another swimmer, or worse, if you are preoccupied with some knotty philosophical question, concussion on the handrail at the other end. The coolness of the water was a sign of its depth, although the year before it had reached seventy-six degrees at the height of the season. They take regular samples, which are monitored by the public health people, and no one seemed to worry about sharing the lake with carp. This urban oasis was clearly dedicated principally to swimming and diving purely for pleasure, not competition, but from time to time there are friendly distance swims with other clubs. Diving boards are, sadly, becoming quite a rarity around pools, and with so little opportunity for self-education there must be some question about our future as a nation of divers. Mothers and children picnicked on the grass, and we were joined in the water by a septuagenarian regular of the club, clocking up one of her ninety-two swims of the season.

When the workmen struck springs in 1912 and the quarry flooded, it was bought by a local doctor. He was later approached by a group of enterprising Bristol swimmers who realised the new lake's potential and formed the Henleaze Swimming Club in 1919. The club was allowed to swim in the lake, and eventually bought it for £450 in 1933. Men changed behind a canvas screen; women in a marquee. Now there's a fine 1930s half-timbered women's pavilion and the men sunbathe and change in a sunny arbour with rows of the kind of cast-iron coat-pegs the bullies used to hit our heads against in the school cloakrooms.

Until recently, a member in his nineties used to swim in the lake most days. They also have two regulars aged eighty-four and eighty-two. One is thin and stringy and arrives after his three-mile run round the golf course in the morning; the other has legs like tree-trunks, arrives on his bike, and sits around smoking a pipe in the men's enclosure all day. As we changed, my hosts had described his swimming style arcanely as 'a gut-butting stroke'. By the sound of it, I think he may have been one of the last living exponents of the 'trudgeon' style of swimming, later to be superseded by the crawl. An English pioneer of speed swimming, Mr J. Trudgen, originally learned the stroke from the natives of South America, and caused a sensation here when he won an important race on 11 August 1873, swimming with something like an over-arm crawl action and breaststroke leg kicks. In a popular corruption of Trudgen's name, the style became known as the 'trudgeon', possibly by unconscious association with the dainty fish we used to haul out of the Grand Union Canal as boys, the gudgeon.

Over tea and rock-cakes on the clubhouse lawn afterwards, the Henleaze Club members were full of suggestions about interesting swimming holes I might sample up and down the country. Some of these sounded highly intriguing, like the two Devon waterholes known to their discoverer as Waterhole One and Waterhole Two: a pair of steep-sided disused quarry shafts he dives into to reach the black water eight or nine feet down. It is fathomless and icy cold as you go deeper, but when you climb out there's a warm, sunny knoll for sunbathing and drying off.

The beginnings of the Henleaze Swimming Club in 1919 leading up to its flowering in the year it bought the lake and quarry in 1933 coincided with a spectacular burgeoning of interest in swimming in Britain. In 1929 there were 276 swimming clubs in Britain, and the ASA issued a booklet on the construction of pools. By 1930, the Ministry of Labour was giving 41 per cent grants towards the cost of building swimming pools, and by 1931 there existed in England alone about 1,400 swimming clubs; a five-fold increase over two years. All over the country people were busy putting up diving boards and building or improvising their own baths. The swimmers at Bromborough in Cheshire were building their own pool, helped by the Price's Candle Company. The *Swimming Times* reported: 'They have a 50 yards straight away course and are aiming at one with a lap of 110 yards. The pool is the works reservoir, into which warm and perfectly clear water is constantly trickling. It is, therefore, slightly above *tea* temperature.'

A lucrative market in swimwear was also developing very nicely. Jantzen were advertising 'Kellermann Sea Togs', modelled on the pioneering one-piece costume worn by the Australian distance swimmer Annette Kellermann, who had done so much to make swimming popular with her spectacular public displays. Reports from new clubs flooded into the offices of the *Swimming Times*, under such *noms de plume* as 'Nauticus', 'Buoyant', 'Porpoise', and the joys of one new pool were described ecstatically as like swimming 'in the presence of St Natatious, the Bath Superintendent of Paradise'. Swimming cigarette-cards were issued by the Imperial Tobacco Company and the *Morning Post* carried regular articles on swimming and diving by W. J. Howcroft, Joyce Cooper, and Pete Desjardins, the Olympic high and springboard champion, and the only diver ever awarded maximum points by all judges.

On the lawn of the Henleaze Club, I was busy noting down more swimming holes from the generous collective memory of the members: 'You head for a little place called Bramford Speke by the Exe on the road out of Exeter beyond Crediton. Take a path off to the left by the bridge and the really great place to swim is across a couple of fields ...' Entering wholeheartedly into the spirit of my quest, they were soon poring with me over a map of the Severn hinterland around Nailsea, wondering about the swimming potential of Bathing Pond Wood near Wraxhall, or Watercress Farm at Long Ashton.

When I described my frustrating, non-swimming visit to Bath, several of the swimmers mentioned the Farleigh Hungerford Swimming Club eight miles away on the River Frome. During the hot summer of 1996, it had received a sudden influx of new members from Bath when the city's newly privatised pool went under. They put me in touch with Rob, the club secretary, and Phil, the farmer who owns their riverside field. They asked me over next morning for what they call in Farleigh Hungerford 'Real Swimming'.

I arrived in the mid-morning on an enchanting south-facing grassy hillside, swooping down to the riverside through a sheltered little water meadow almost within sight of the old castle at Farleigh. At the top of the rise was a wood-framed tin hut with 'MEN' on the door, hearts and arrows on the walls, and a pine floor worn smooth by generations of bare feet. It was a lot more commodious than the ladies' changing room, which was roofed by the sky. There were triple-tiered diving boards and, at the other end of the little concrete quay, a fine ash springboard, traditionally coconut-matted. I dived in off this and came up near the other side of the river in water that was deep and cold. There wasn't a soul about; everyone was at work, but I had been told to help myself to a swim anyway. Although I didn't realise it at the time, I have to own up to breaking rule six of the club, which stipulates that 'All members must wear bathing costumes or shorts (not slips), nor white.' Diving naked into a clear, black river pool off old-fashioned coconut-matted boards is not a pleasure that comes along every day.

The only sound was the roar of the weir just downstream, and the piping of an approaching kingfisher. Like a gas flame leaping into life, it suddenly burst over me. Later, as I lay sunbathing up by the hut, it came and flickered about the diving boards, fishing the pool. The river was fringed with old alders and willows, their gnarled roots exposed and polished by the toes of countless swimmers. Steel ladders led down the banks, which plunged vertically into deep water. I sat on the slippery stone steps of the weir and edged along them to the middle. Downstream the Frome was shallow, fast-running and very clear over a stony bottom dappled in sunlight. In wet mud by the diving quay, I saw the five-starred prints of an otter, so fresh that the mud still stood up where the claws had pricked it.

The place was refreshingly free of notices. A discreet message from the county council exhorted swimmers to cover up all cuts with plaster – always a wise precaution against infection – and not to drink the water. (They come and take a sample here once a month to make sure it is safe enough for swimming.) Five feet off the water, the springboard gave a reassuring clank each time I sprang off. Fish rose in the pool and I dived into the widening centre of each ripple.

The river swimming club at Farleigh Hungerford goes back some seventy years to 1930, when a group of local people were already swimming in the River Frome by the Greenhill brothers' farm. People would walk the three miles or so out there from Trowbridge for a swim and a drink at the Hungerford Arms – and perhaps a taste of the Greenhill brothers' cider. Others came to Farleigh to picnic at the castle or the watermill, or to visit the watercress beds there.

Originally, the core group of young swimmers bathed from the right bank of the river nearest the road. The four Greenhill brothers, keen swimmers themselves, had the farm on the other bank, and invited the bathers to use it, and to camp on their land.

By 1933 they had elected a president, George Kemp, and a secretary, George Applegate, and formed a committee. A swimming hole had become the Farleigh & District Swimming Club. They designed their own coat of arms, the club initials rampant around a castle, which they wore on their black one-piece costumes. A flag of the same design was run up the club flagpole whenever they swam. The original club was about thirty strong. George Applegate's dad, who was an engineer in Westbury, built the sturdy steel-framed diving board platform and a footbridge spanning the river. The club headquarters was the Hungerford Arms in Farleigh, and club rules were drawn up. Rule six was the one I had accidentally broken, against skin dipping, and rule seven said, 'Decency must be strictly observed.' Rule nine forbade members to use obscene language. A membership card for the 1936 season shows the annual subscription as 1s 6d (7½p, equivalent to about £5 today) and carries advertisements for Usher's Ales and B&B at the Hungerford Arms. Under the headline HAPPY DAYS, MINNOWS!, the local Trowbridge chemist (himself a keen swimmer) offered helmets, ear-plugs and water wings.

Bill Blick used to cycle over to Farleigh every morning for a swim all the year round, breaking the ice if necessary. There was a Christmas Day swim, with Arthur Wells's home-made wine to revive everybody, and there were days towards the end of the season when they would floodlight the river with the headlamps of cars and swim on into the night. Members included the local butcher and fishmonger, and Tom Clarke, a photographer from the *Wiltshire Times*. He recorded many of the idyllic scenes from those days, now in the club archive; groups of bathers cooling in the weir like Busby Berkeley's Babes, diving from the boards, or swimming in the pool. Half a dozen of the Farleigh swimmers – Les Prince, Roy Virgo, George Applegate, Les Wells, George Raymond, 'Timber'

Woodman and Frank Francis – would camp out in the Greenhills' apple orchard each year from Easter until September, swimming every morning at six-thirty before cycling to work at Trowbridge and helping with the hay-making.

The Farleigh swimmers set about building a wooden changing hut, the footbridge, toilets, wooden steps to the top of the weir, a wooden diving-stage (the steel one came later), and a primitive springboard improvised from a long plank nailed over a treestump: 'A bit dangerous when wet and slippery, but it served its purpose.' Later on came George Applegate's three-tier angle-iron frame with three extended springboards for diving into the deep pool. 'We made the foundation of cement and a lot of scrap iron including old cycle frames to bind it together. The diving-stage was the pride of our swimming club, and there were steps in and out of the river. A lifebelt was hung handy in case of emergency but most bathers were pretty safe with so many good swimmers around.' There were diving competitions, galas, swimming races with neighbouring clubs, and silver cups to be won. During the war, the Land Army women used to come from the local farms in hot weather to bathe. Not all the club swimmers returned in 1945. Their friends made a metal plaque in their memory and bolted it to the support of the springboard.

Eventually the farm was being run by just two of the Greenhill brothers. One of the early club members, Blanche Francis, remembered them. 'They were a couple of charmers, like the Marx Brothers. They let the boys roam all over their land, riding their motorcycles, camping and swimming.' When all but one of the brothers had died, in 1970, Castle Farm was sold, and the new owner took a less liberal view of the swimming. The club was faced with extinction when she eventually announced she would not continue their licence. But they were saved by the generosity of the farmer on the opposite bank. It cost them £1,000 and a lot of extra work to move everything across the river – diving boards, changing huts, toilets, steps, etc. – but they did it, and the club flag is flying again at Farleigh.

I ventured further up the river under a low canopy of alders, imagining the Marx Brothers farmers, the swimmers on their bicycles, and the camp in the orchard in those more welcoming, big-hearted days, before things became tight and private, fenced and tidy. Two moorhens taxied off before me like the Wright brothers, scampering ever faster across the surface until they just teetered into lift-off, trailing a gangling undercarriage of olive-green legs and spidery feet. The previous year, the Farleigh swimmers had been joined one hot Sunday by a bullock which leapt in beside them off an old diving board support. A crowd of 200 watched it swim downstream pursued by club members with a rope. It had eventually scrambled back ashore. Nothing like this ever happens in swimming pools.

One of the moorhens suddenly exploded like a car alarm and wouldn't stop its hiccupping, even when I climbed out and lay drying in the sun on the warm coconut matting, my head over the edge of the board gazing down into the water. Dandelion clocks filled the meadow, and the yellow smudge of ladies' bedstraw. A cabbage-white butterfly explored, alighting on a lost white sock, then a girl's bathing costume put out to dry on the hedge and left behind. It must have thought the badges were flowers, the way it pondered them as though slowly reading: 'Frome Girls' Swimming 25m', 'ASA Rainbow Award 50m'. The tin changing shed clicked as it expanded in the sunshine. A young pheasant cleared its throat and coughed haltingly in the hedgerow.

II

SALMON-RUNS

Dartmoor, 9 July

DARTMOOR LOOKED DAUNTING, especially on the enormous map, which had taken up the whole of my billiard-table desk in the Map Room in Cambridge. Even on paper, I kept losing my place, running my finger along rivers spawned amidst the thin brown contours of peat-bogs, hills and tors. By the time I actually crossed the moor in the car the following afternoon, I was in a suitably wild, dark mood after sweating in traffic for hours on the way down through Somerset. It was one of several moments when I began seriously to question the whole outlandish project. I had naively imagined bouncing along the lanes of England in some open-topped bus, bursting with friends, their towels and costumes hung out to dry like flags in the breeze, and me at the wheel like Cliff Richard in *Summer Holiday*. Instead, of course, they were all far too busy with their own lives, and my journey was proving a much more solitary, even fugitive affair.

A cold dip in the West Dart River by the stone saddle bridge at Hexworthy came along just in time. I threw myself into a deep pool just upstream, gasping at the shock, and swam down into the stony salmon-haunts below. Surfacing, my spirits began to revive. I was, after all, on my way to visit friends; a family of Dartmoor river-swimmers. The West Dart is spectacular just here, dropping fast over the moor, surging at giant granite slabs ten or twelve feet long. I climbed round into the rapids above the pool and shot down into the eddy in the shadow of the bridge, disturbing a dipper that flew a rock or two away. The water tasted cold and fresh. Watched by a group of Japanese tourists on the bridge, I wallowed, splashed and dived, washing away the journey, feeling a little like an inexpert otter in the zoo, then dried off on warm granite. Half an hour later, the salmon were leaping there.

On Thursday afternoon I went with my friends, under oath of secrecy, to a bathing place where the Dart is joined by an unusually cold moorland torrent. We will call it the Sherberton Stream. Almost from its source in two springs high up beneath the summit of a tor, the torrent rushes headlong downhill, shaded by dense woodland all the way. So the springwater emerges into the Dart as cool as it was underground. The Dart slid like a white glacier into a deep, black pool, through a steep valley of oak and holly woods.

My friend John and I, wearing masks, snorkels and flippers, dropped straight into deep water off some rocks and swam against the current up into the pool. What we saw there astonished us both. About ten feet down in the clear water, dappled with sunlight, lay dozens of salmon, many of them well over two feet long. They turned and nosed off languidly upstream at our approach, disappearing into the clear green bubbling river, or amongst the shadows of underwater rocks. We followed them upriver, then lost them. Coming back downstream in long, effortless strokes, we were ambushed from the left by the sudden shock of the chilly upland waters of the Sherberton Stream issuing into the pool. The unusually cold water, rich in oxygen, was the special attraction of this place for the salmon. John, who has swum here for over thirty years, had never seen this many fish in the pool. He is a geologist, now in his sixties, and during the 1960s and early '70s, he had his own flourishing Dartmoor tin mine. He still occasionally pans the river for tin or gold, more for pleasure than profit.

Dartmoor has always been rich in minerals. Ashburton and Buckfastleigh once had the biggest tin-mining industry in the world. They were the centre of a huge international trade that stretched all the way to Amsterdam, Byzantium and the Nile, and there is plenty of evidence of it in the river. John showed me the riffles where the mineral stones, sometimes gold or tin, collect in a natural pan. We waded about, looking for obstructions to the flow, like a quartz seam crossing the bed, and searched for tin and gold below them, panning the gravel with saucered hands. The metals are heavier than the rest of the river sediments and sink naturally into these hollows. We found tin nuggets, especially heavy and black, shaped like discarded chewing gum, but no gold. We scooped up haematite, too, named after the blood these dark nuggets of iron-ore resemble. Later on, in a field near the river at his home, John showed me the panning machine he had built in his workshop, a wonderfully Heath-Robinson affair with a rotating perforated steel drum that runs off a belt-drive from his tractor.

John and his family have developed their own river-swimming technique, and each year, before his daughters grew up, John used to take them for a long-distance swim down the river to Totnes. I tried out the novel style nervously the following morning in a fast stretch of the river that runs through fields near their house. John taught me how to swim the rapids, even sliding over the most unlikely shallows, by keeping my head down in the water and breathing through the snorkel. This automatically tilts the rest of your body higher in the water. You wear a wetsuit for protection from bruises, as well as cold, and you look ahead through your mask for fast-approaching rocks, keeping at least one arm outstretched to fend off as necessary. You propel yourself mostly with the flippers.

Seeing a boulder approaching you at high speed, with the irresistible force of the river behind you, is terrifying at first. But by surrendering your body to the current, it is surprising how easily and naturally you are swept down, like the translucent leaves you see dancing underwater in the sunlight. The current urges you along the best course, but you must keep steerage way as you would in a canoe, by swimming faster than the river. You realise why the otter's tail is called its rudder. Your mask seems to magnify things by framing them; and the sounds of the river, and your own breathing, are amplified underwater. You see churned gravel glittering like tinsel, old bricks with their maker's name nearly smoothed out, bright green pebbles, dark rusty haematite, a drowned plastic bag pinioned to a tangle of sticks, water shrimps, bands of bright shining quartz, passing fragments of flimsy waterweed, little bullheads dodging under stones, and now and again the shadow of a trout. I swept on through a series of long, narrow, natural pools, steep-sided granite tanks that barrelled the river into deafening violence, hurling me down their gullets over dark submerged forms glimpsed skidding away, on past the wrecks of jammed tree-roots into the sudden calm of a deep pool.

Making my way back along the bank in the wetsuit through a field of cattle, carrying my flippers, mask and snorkel, I met the farmer, who said he had fished the Dart for thirty years. He wore tweed, I wore rubber and stood dripping, but he seemed not to notice, or was polite enough not to say anything, and we chatted away by the bank about otters and salmon for some considerable time. Before the war, he said, a favourite evening pastime of the Buckfastleigh citizens was to gather beside their weir and watch the otters playing. He said it was a good year for salmon and otters; there were more of both than he had ever known. He saw otter pads and prints on the sand here night after night and, only a few days before, he had actually seen an otter bitch and a cub; a rare occurrence. The Dart used to be polluted by dieldrin from the sheep-dip chemicals washed out of the wool at a carpet factory in Ashburton. The drastic decline in otters which began in the 1950s and led to their virtual extinction over most of England and Wales is known to have been caused by this very chemical. To make matters worse, the detergent used to wash the wool began over-enriching the river with phosphate and froth, but at last the river seems to be recovering, and the otters with it.

With so much twenty-four-carat water everywhere, there's a tradition of wild swimming in all the towns and villages that fringe the moor. At Throwleigh and South Zeal, they have always bathed and learnt to swim in a remote natural pool in the valley of the Blackaton Brook, which runs between steep banks of gorse and heather from the Raybarrow Pool at the foot of Cawsand Hill. The tiny waterhole was already naturally dammed by boulders, but enterprising swimmers gradually enlarged it by building the rocks higher. I heard about it from Mrs Amy Harvey, then nearly ninety, who had lived on Dartmoor all her life, and swam in this bathing hole throughout her childhood during the 1920s. She had written me a moving letter full of vivid recollections of the place, which is still popular with the village children now.

At Peter Tavy they have their own village swimming hole in the Colley Brook: a secluded mill-pool to which the bathers have added stone steps and a life-belt. I also visited the charming village swimming pool at Chagford, fed by the River Teign, with an outdoor café. It is fringed with trees down one side and – the last thing you expect to see on the edge of Dartmoor – a vigorous hedge of bamboo. The pool is filled from the river by a fast-flowing mill-stream that flows alongside it. These days, the Health and Safety people make them put chlorine in the water, but Pam, who lives in the cottage opposite and is the keyholder, doesn't like to put too much in because it spoils the fresh taste and smell of the clear river water off the moor. Pam's eighty-seven-year-old father-in-law, who helped to dig and build the original pool in 1947, comes down every day in the season and makes tea.

Okehampton used to have a river-fed pool a hundred feet long which was owned by a syndicate of swimmers, but has since been filled in. People who grew up swimming here in the 'ice cold water' remember the strict pre-war caretaker, Mr Wallers. He would open the baths at seven o'clock on a Sunday morning so people could swim before going on to shiver in church or Sunday school. He then closed up for the rest of the day. This is what Dartmoor Puritanism is all about.

Rivers rise everywhere on the moor. In the peat beneath Great Kneeset, five rivers have their beginnings: the Taw, Tavy, Teign, Torridge and Dart. But of all the Dartmoor rivers, the Erme is the most secretive. It rises in the long shadow of Hartor Tor and flows south through Ivybridge into a farm landscape around Holbeton so hilly that everyone gets an aerial view of their neighbour. Fields, barns and hedgerows are tilted at all angles like the counterpane of an unmade bed.

I had been curious about the Erme ever since first hearing Mike Westbrook's *The Cortège*, a large-scale work for jazz instruments and voices in which one movement, 'Erme Estuary', is a response to the place where he and Kate Westbrook live. It ends with a long, other-worldly solo on the electric guitar. But the estuary was all too real, and none too warm, as I swam across it on the rising tide two days later, seeing it for the first time on a visit to my musical friends. I had crossed to the centre of the wide bay from Coastguard's Beach. A little group of surfers clustered waist deep, waiting for the big grey rollers that surged out of the open sea, breaking on a sandbar. I threw myself in with them and swam inland. I felt the incoming tide lock on to my legs and thrust me in towards the distant woods along the shore. Each time a frond of sea-lettuce lightly brushed me, or glued itself around my arms, I thought it was a jellyfish, and flinched. But I soon grew used to it; seaweed was all around me, sliding down each new wave to drape itself about me. I kept on swimming until I practically dissolved, jostled from behind by the swell. Then, as the tide rose higher, the sandy estuary beach came into focus. The woods reached right over the water, and began accelerating past me. I found I was moving at exhilarating speed, in big striding strokes, like a fell runner on the downhill lap. It was like dream swimming, going so effortlessly fast, and feeling locked in by the current, with no obvious means of escape. I was borne along faster and faster as the rising tide approached the funnel of the river's mouth until it shot me into a muddy, steep-sided mooring channel by some old stone limekilns on the beach. I had to strike out with all my strength to escape the flood and reach the eddy in the shallows. I swam back up to the limekilns and crawled out on to the beach like a turtle, but couldn't resist dropping back into the muscular current for a second ride down the channel.

Earlier, we had all picnicked on Mothecombe Beach together, to the west of the estuary, and Mike and I had swum in the bay. It was a Private Day at the beach, which meant that only bona fide local villagers from Holbeton were allowed access, and then only to one side, leaving the other free for the private enjoyment of the Mildmay-White family, who own it. The whole of the lovely Erme estuary might have been rechristened the Baring Straits, since all the surrounding land was originally purchased in the 1870s by the two cousins who controlled Barings Bank: Edward Baring and Alfred Mildmay-White. Mothecombe is a private beach, and the estate charges the public for access via a man in a small wooden ticket-office at the top of the cliff path. The wild beauty of the coastal estate was evidence of sensitive management.

Mike had come round by the cliff path to our rendezvous at the limekilns, and we stood gazing across the estuary. A dense unbroken canopy of English rainforest flowed down to the water everywhere. It was an almost tropical scene, with six or seven egrets decoratively arranged in an oak, or flying with their long legs outstretched. I had seen them the previous summer on the Arne peninsula in Dorset, where they have even begun to nest. They are now a regular feature of the south coast of England, no longer confined to Spain, Portugal and North Africa. As the tide advanced, we stood listening to the sucking of millions of tiny worms in their mudholes. On the far shore there stood a single boathouse, reflected in the mud, half-hidden in the woods.

As I changed on the beach, we witnessed a scene like a cameo from fifty years ago. A mother, grandmother and a little boy caught crabs in a net baited with chicken from under a rock the grandmother had known as a secret crabbing place from her own childhood. What I found so inspiring about this vignette was the element of continuity that it shared with Mrs Harvey's story of the Blackaton Brook bathing hole. Two generations later, the crabs were still under their rock, and the village children were still swimming in the wild pool.

On the way home, we passed a reed-bed alive with the free improvisation of a sedge warbler ensemble, performing solos like earthy, uninhibited saxophones. Westbrook clearly felt at home with them, quoting the birdbook description of their 'irresponsible song' with approval. We stood on a wooden bridge watching a procession of seaweed carried up by the tide. It created the curious illusion that we and the bridge were moving like a boat through the water, back out to sea.

12

THE RED RIVER

IT FELT UNTHINKABLE to be this close to Cornwall, with summer well under way, and not to return. After my taste of Cornish swimming in the Scillies and at Marazion in the spring, I was in the same position as the dreamer in Fauré's song 'Après le Rêve' ('After the Dream'), who awakes, and only desires to sink back into sleep in the hope of re-entering a delicious dream and continuing its bliss. My Scilly swims, and my memories of past summer bathing in Cornwall, were all so delightful that all I wanted to do was subside into the idyll of its sparkling seas again. And so I had crossed the Tamar Bridge and returned, heading this time for the luminous sandy bay, backed by tall dunes, that stretches along the north coast from St Ives to the lighthouse at Godrevy Point.

The mouth of the Red River at Godrevy is outlandish in a dozen ways. In its unassuming way, it embodies Cornish history. It is one of the few special places around our coast where you can swim in fresh water and look straight out to sea, and an ocean horizon. It was low tide, and I swam in the wide pool created by the rocks that form a dam before the river spills over them onto the beach. I floated twenty feet or so above sea level, with a panoramic view of Hayle Bay all the way to St Ives. I like to imagine Godrevy derives its name from some medieval hybrid of the French *rêve* and means 'God's Dream', but I know it's a hopeless conceit. It does suit the wild beauty of the place, though, on a glinting, sunny day.

The river's metallic gleam went deeper than metaphor. Where the Red River is concerned, 'The Cornish Heritage' means cadmium, copper, zinc, lead, as well as arsenic; all the toxic heavy-metal by-products of the deserted tin mines upstream. If you haven't ever taken a dip in dilute arsenic, or half a dozen other poisons, this is the place for you. Yet in this dazzling sunshine, the river could hardly have looked purer or more innocent of pollution. It burst out of its quiet, lazy post-industrial valley in the kind of blinding white-water rapids normally reserved for mountains. You felt there should be salmon leaping restlessly in the spume. It overflowed its rocky dam and leapt out to sea over the beach in a sweeping S, past rock pools freshly fed by the tide. On its journey across the wide strand, the Red River reinvents itself at every low tide, pencilling a delta like the winter twigs of a big tree in the fine slatey sand, streaking it into subtle shades of grey and yellow. It could have been the Nile, or the Rhône filtering through the Camargue to Saintes-Maries-de-la-Mer.

I climbed out of the pool and followed the river down the beach to the sea's edge, with the curious half-ticklish sensation of damp, corrugated sand in the arches of my feet. The sun was audibly frying the bright green Chinese-restaurant seaweed that fringed the rock pools, frosting them with salt, the grey stone acned with little moon craters gouged out by centuries of limpets. I swam out to sea, deafened by the waves as they broke over me, on into the rolling, buoyant water beyond for a short excursion, then back through the surf to the river.

In the days when tin mining was in full swing, the river really did run red, stained by the iron in the washings and tailings. The mines were drained by a system of 'adits', more or less horizontal tunnels which emptied into the river. Water from deeper down the mine, full of dissolved metals, was pumped up to their level, then flowed on to poison everything downstream. But now the river looks clear, and hurries down a bed that was artificially straightened by the miners with bundles of coppiced sticks to accelerate its flow and separate the surface deposits of the metal by 'tin streaming', the Cornish equivalent of gold panning. It is about ten feet wide and two or three feet deep. But then you notice something odd about it: there's no waterweed, nothing green at all. Even today, this is still one of the most polluted rivers in Britain, even though, since the closing of the mines, it is slowly recovering.

For years nothing lived in the valley but miners, from Camborne to Godrevy, but recently, to everyone's delight, a few brown trout have been discovered in the Red River in its higher reaches, as well as eels, sticklebacks and, in the peat pools of the valley, dragonflies. None of the snails, water shrimps, or other little creatures that usually live in rivers have appeared. That is because they normally live on the bottom in the silt or gravel, and it is still intensely contaminated. Looking at it, you would never guess the place is a kind of early Sellafield. All along the floor of the valley the tailings from the mines have been piled up in a moonscape which was completely bare of any vegetation all through the last century, but is now recovering.

The final collapse of the tin-mining industry recently led to equally dramatic red-river pollution on the south coast near Falmouth. In January 1992, Restronguet Creek, where the Carnon River flows into the lovely Carrick Roads, suddenly began to turn dark red. In the space of two months, over 10 million gallons of intensely contaminated water poured down into the sea via the hapless little creek.

You might imagine that the story would have led to some reddening of official faces too, but you would be wrong. It is a classic parable of how shaky the laws on pollution remain in Britain. When the price of tin and pyrites on the world market tumbled in the late 1980s, the South Crofty Mine Company decided to close down their big mine at Wheal Jane, north of Falmouth. Once its pumps were switched off late in 1990, groundwater in the mine began to rise into the shafts and workings, dissolving and flushing out the poisonous metals that eventually burst forth at the beginning of 1992. Besides copper, zinc, cadmium and arsenic, they included a good deal of iron, which is what turned Restronguet Creek rust-red as the toxic flood bled iron hydroxide into the sea down the Carnon River. Apart from the odd ragworm, there is no animal life to catch the eye of the naturalist here; no crabs, no lobsters, no cockles, and certainly no oysters.

As Wheal Jane headed for closure, everyone knew what could go wrong, but they couldn't agree what to do about it. The way the law stands, the owners of a mine are responsible for it as long as it's occupied, but the minute they abandon it they are absolved of all consequences. After a good deal of dithering, the Department of the Environment agreed to help fund a £14 million filtration scheme by the Environment Agency to try and improve matters. In other words, a private commercial company was allowed to leave a legacy of serious, lasting pollution for the rest of society to deal with at public expense. The polluter, meanwhile, walked off scot-free. The original principle proposed by Friends of the Earth, that the polluter should pay, seems to have sunk without trace, but the government has now introduced a law requiring written notice from the owner six months before a mine is planned to close. Since the mining industry in this country has all but closed down already, this might be construed as bravely closing the stable door after the horse has bolted.

The river at Godrevy may have been chemically red and dead, but it was also alive with the energy and imagination of what amounts to the National Theatre of Cornwall. Camped on a wide level place beside the banks on the way down to the sea was the Kneehigh Theatre Company; two or three vans, a cooking tent, a trestle dining-table, and a scattering of tents in the shelter of steep dunes that rose up thirty or forty feet behind them. Their stage was the river and the dunescape around it, and it was elaborately set for something that could have been *Day of the Triffids*, *Robinson Crusoe*, *The Tempest*, *The Adventures of Tintin*, or all of them rolled into one, which is exactly what the Kneehigh open-air show turned out to be.

Down along the river, members of the company in ragged-trousered wetsuits were scurrying about like the crew of a big sailing ship, adjusting rigging, arranging the wings of a giant puppet, building cairns, setting a driftwood bonfire by the shore, swimming in the same pool as me, for their show turned out to be the most aquatic production since the waterfall sequence in Busby Berkeley's 1933 film *Footlight Parade*. An upturned boat stood silhouetted against the sea on the pebble shoreline at the very mouth of the river. It was rigged with mast and flagpole, and curiously decorated with necklaces of big stones strung on lengths of flotsam rope, and the skeletons of fish delicately constructed from dozens of wire coathangers. Along the fringes of the dunes a string of tepees, improvised from torn scraps of washed-up black polythene and spars of timber, flapped in the breeze. Enormous triffids with yellow plastic-piping stalks and Coke-can stamens sprang out of the shale banks by the river bridge. All this junk, lovingly collected and re-worked by the sculptor David Kemp, cleverly evoked the dereliction behind the apparent idyll of the Red River.

A notice stuck on a pole in the sand announced the evening show: *Ghost Nets*. A chair and table were set up as the advance box-office at the head of the wooden steps down to the beach. Tonight's show was sold out. I puzzled about this. How could a show in the open air on a river bank and a beach be sold out? How many does a valley hold? Returning from my swim, I met Bill Mitchell, Kneehigh's joint artistic director, striding about the river bank in Doc Martens and a pair of bermudas rehearsing some of the actors in the water. He explained that they only sell 120 tickets a night because the audience has to move around following the action. Anything bigger would just slow things up too much. He called what Kneehigh Theatre do 'landscape theatre'. Film is probably its nearest equivalent. You have long shots with actors very tiny on the horizon, then cut to something very intimate, a close-up, with the audience clustered round two actors only feet away and speaking quietly. There the comparison ends, because anything less like watching TV or sitting comfortably in the cinema would be hard to imagine. With Kneehigh, you're on the move all the time. You're part of the show.

They had a few hours to while away before the show, and invited me to tea round the trestle table. They had all fallen in love with the place. There were glow-worms at night, and they told me how they would swim in the evenings between

137

the two winds, land and sea breeze, when the sea is like glass and the shore deserted. At dusk, they lit driftwood fires on the beach. Some days clouds of sea mist came right down to the sea and they lost all sense of direction, swimming blind in the still water. From their camp in the sand dunes, they watched people at play. The surfers came and went in their pick-up trucks and VWs, and parked up in odd corners in their camper vans. At six in the evening they noticed a distinct change of shifts on the beach. The holidaymakers went home for tea, and the Cornish came down to unwind after work.

The Kneehigh show was about a Cornwall that once boomed and is now bust, the 'ghost nets' belonging to the pilchard fishermen, who disappeared with their shoals of tea-time treats when the last pilchard swam out of St Ives Bay a few years after the war. There are still a few of the fishermen's 'huer' poles left standing on the Cornish coast. I saw a couple on the cliffs at St Agnes and one in St Ives, and they used to stand in the dunes all round St Ives Bay. They are 30 feet high with steps cut in them. A lookout would be up there all day, as high as they could climb, scanning the bay for the glint of a pilchard shoal. When pilchard were spotted the cry would go up: 'Hevver!' It would run through the villages and into the fields, and the people would drop everything they were doing and race down to the sea, load their nets, tear out to sea in rowing boats, and haul in pilchards by the cartload.

Everybody round St Ives had a boat, and probably farmed as well, because the Cornish have always had about three or four jobs, depending on the season and the trade. But this pilchard industry was a community effort. The nets were hauled in and the catch was shared out. Even the huer, who was probably the last to actually hit the water, got a fair share. Now the big Russian and Spanish factory ships suck pilchards out of the Atlantic far away, long before they could ever reach their long-forgotten Cornish bays.

The actors dived, swam and splashed in the river and the sea all through the show. In the pilchard-netting scene, the audience was led down to the wide, glowing beach at sunset. The players strode far out into the sea with their nets, several of them swimming on into the evening waves to encircle the imaginary shoal. Then they began singing and hauling the wet and heavy nets up the beach, and everyone found themselves wading in and helping. Then, as the big sun swooped low, the actors lit a fire at the centre of a circle of stones, having manoeuvred their audience into a perfectly-timed line of sight for a tableau of fire, dark sea, horizon, and the sun, balancing itself on the horizon, poised to drown.

Bill Mitchell said he and the cast had been determined to get wet as early as possible in the show. He remembered seeing a theatre company come down to Penzance and take over the magnificent Jubilee outdoor tidal pool. To everyone's astonishment they managed to do their entire show without a single one of them going into the water. All through the performance the audience had but a single thought: 'When are they going in the water?' People left shaking their heads in disbelief. So the Kneehigh approach was to go for total immersion very early on. By the end of the show they were diving in as mermaids, swimming underwater and popping up all over the place on cue to say a line, then ducking back under. They say the secret of acting is in the breathing, but this was something else. The National Trust, which owns the land here, made Kneehigh print a notice in their programme asking members of the audience not to drink from the river. You can't be too careful.

After the show, and a pub fish dinner, I spent a blissful night in the back of the sometimes-reliable Citroën CX Safari down a farm track in a Dutch barn alongside a combine harvester. This is the beauty of the Citroën shooting brake. You can stretch right out and sleep in it, curl up and read in it, spread out your dinner in it, and carry a small library. Some people have prim little curtains in the back windows, but I carry a big air-force-surplus silk parachute with me and spread it over the car when I'm in residence. It works like net curtains in the suburbs; I can see out but people, or just as likely cows, can't see in. It also diffuses the light beautifully, prolonging sleep by softening the intensity of sunrises. It's the kind of parachute they use for dropping food parcels in emergencies. It is big enough to stretch out by the guy-ropes into an airy Bedouin tent, its brown, orange, green and white silk disguising the presence of a motor car, if not exactly unobtrusive. It keeps mosquitoes and midges out and means you can leave all the windows and the back door open on sultry nights. Even if it gets drenched, it dries out quickly in the sun. Once, when I was encamped inside it in the chestnut woods near Souseyrac in France, I heard some early walkers marvelling, 'Mais alors, il est venu en parachute.'

Stimulated by Bill Mitchell's mention of the great tidal Jubilee Pool, I drove across to Penzance in the morning for an early swim. The place might not be everybody's idea of the perfect holiday resort, but it was at one time the capital of the Cornish Riviera. In some ways it resembles Calais or Dieppe; a perfectly good seaside town in its own right that is better known as a gateway. People pass straight through Penzance to the Scillies, or to the Land's End peninsula. What really propelled Penzance to fame in its own right was the Grand Opening in May 1935 of the Jubilee Bathing Pool, an enormous triangular open-air lido jutting out boldly from the seafront as if to emphasise its pre-eminent position as the southernmost pool in the British Isles. It opened in the same year as the magnificent Tinside Pool at Plymouth, another seafront lido which, to the sadness of that town's many swimmers, now lies neglected and semi-derelict.

With its dramatic ocean-liner decks, stainless-steel fittings, steps and tubular railings, the Jubilee Pool is highly theatrical. I felt I was going on stage as I made my way down to the imposing million gallons of sea-water that flood into this artificial rock pool at high tide. There is no such thing as a width or length of a triangle, no clear bearings for conventional pool-swimming. I wanted to get in some sea-swimming practice in preparation for my attempt to cross the Fowey estuary, and I found myself reacting like a goldfish in a bowl, setting off on a long-distance swim round the triangular perimeter.

About halfway round, I met Madeleine, a painter, who swims here every day, gently breaststroking fifty metres back and forth across the pool. Three of us had the place to ourselves, and the buoyant water made up in clarity what it lacked in warmth. We each had over 300,000 gallons of it to swim in, so we couldn't help falling into conversation; it was like running into another swimmer in the Atlantic. Now and again, as we swam and talked, a helicopter bound for the Scillies puttered past over the sea. Madeleine asserted confidently that swimming is better than sex, and that it is an invaluable inspiration to her painting. There was no arguing with that. Her comment was curiously in tune with the sensuous nature of these original lidos. Their emphasis was all on the sensual pleasures of water and sun, and many of them incorporated fountains as well as extensive sunbathing lawns or decks. The white-painted Jubilee Pool was designed as a suntrap as well as a pool. In this sense, it is a megalithic monument in the same sun-worshipping tradition as the Merry Maidens stone circle a few miles away on a hilltop near Lamorna.

Madeleine said the true Penzance swimmers go in the sea off the Battery Rocks over the swimming-pool wall. They're in all the year round at eight o'clock in the morning, and scorn the pool-bathers. According to Madeleine, who clearly returned the disapproval, they're always getting cramp and saving each other, and do an annual swim from Newlyn Harbour to the Jubilee Pool across Mount's Bay, which as recently as 1994 could boast a level of pollution 240 times over the recommended safe limit.

The Penzance pool was very nearly lost in 1990, when the local council proposed to turn it into a modern 'fun pool' in an indoor leisure centre. It was saved largely by the imagination and determination of John Clarke, the retired Assistant County Architect for Cornwall. He had the pool listed as a Grade Two building, then raised enough money in grants for its repair and improvement. The freshly painted blue and white pool was literally dazzling. It is pure 1930s in its exuberant, extravagant use of concrete and in the flowing lines of its romantic, impractical shape. At first sight I thought it more fascist than anything I had ever seen, with its serried ranks of open-fronted changing cubicles surrounding the water like rows of soldiers. The removal of the cubicle doors from their fish-finger-shaped openings (to avoid vandalism or worse) was an inspired stroke of minimalism, the piano-key contrast between light and shade creating the effect of sarcophagi. The whole thing is massively fortified, of course, against the huge seas that did once succeed in breaching its walls during the Ash Wednesday storm of 1962. Swimming round in unaccustomed triangles, it dawned on me why I felt so overawed by the place. It was actually an Egyptian temple to the water gods. Its grandeur belonged with the Valley of the Kings as much as the films of Leni Riefenstahl. If they ever played muzak here (and they wouldn't) it would have to be Wagner, or Verdi.

To my surprise, the architect of this modernist extravaganza was neither French, Italian nor Russian, but Captain Frank Latham, Penzance's Borough Engineer. The pool had opened at the height of Britain's interest in lidos and all they stood for: healthy urban living, sunshine and sunbathing, the new cult of the outdoor life. Many of these ideas had originated in the Weimar Republic of Germany, in the social ideas that produced the 'Volksparks', where outdoor swimming pools were not only part of the park, but very much its symbolic heart. As early as 1920, the Mayor of Berlin, Gustav Boss, had created the new people's parks with 'athletics fields, playgrounds and the free baths'. The new cult of the body in Germany found expression in Hans Suren's *Man and Sunlight*, published in 1925. It went into multiple editions. The London County Council had led the way in the lido boom, with its open-air pools in Victoria Park, Hackney, Brockwell Park and Tooting Bec, and George Lansbury, the leader of the Labour Party, had opened the Serpentine for mixed bathing in Hyde Park in 1929. In the same year as the turnstiles began clicking at Penzance, lidos also opened at Ilkley, Norwich, Peterborough, Saltdean and Aylesbury.

When the Jubilee Pool opened, the mayor led a procession from the Sailors' Institute and before cheering crowds Professor Hicks, the Cornish Veteran Champion, took the First Plunge, followed by a beauty parade of bathing belles, men's and women's hundred-yard races, an exhibition of trick and fancy diving by the Plymouth Divers, and a Grand Water

Polo Match between Penzance, the reigning Cornish champions, and Plymouth. The Penzance Silver Band played, and the *Cornishman* judged the new pool 'a work of art'.

Lidos were closed one by one in the 1960s and '70s, usually filled in or turned into car parks. Some, like the Tinside Pool at Plymouth, have simply been left to fall into disrepair. In 1991, the Thirties Society published a booklet, 'Farewell My Lido', which reported that budget-cutting on lidos in the eighties had meant that 'only a handful still survive, and . . . none is free from threat'. The lido movement was probably quite as strong in Britain as in Europe, yet we have almost written it out of our history. The collective primitivism it represented was a powerful force for good, not least in the nation's standards of health.

By the time the Jubilee Pool was opened in the 1930s, lidos and pools all over the country were so packed with enthusiastic swimmers that the first rumblings of the serious lane swimmers began to be heard: 'Couldn't we have a roped-off lane for fellows to be able to train without fighting through a morass of people fooling about?' wrote one correspondent to the *Swimming Times*. A dichotomy was beginning to emerge between those who simply swam for pleasure and those for whom swimming was a more serious business.

Every lido and pool had a club, and passions ran high in their rivalry. Nowhere were they more evident than in water-polo matches such as the annual fixture between Penzance and Plymouth. As early as 1926, the Olympic polo captain George Wilkinson wrote that 'the process of degeneracy has gone so low in some cases as to include deliberate "digging" in the ribs, "thumping" the arms, and despicable practices underwater.' By October 1929, *Der Swimmer*, reporting an international match in Germany, complained: 'The water polo games were fights. Our men had to put on no less than seven fresh costumes during the game.'

Long before football, swimming was acquiring its own brand of partisanship, even nationalism. You can sense the pitch of excitement popular competitive swimming had reached by the early 1930s in the tone of this letter to the

Swimming Times. It bears all the signs of the mental effects of too much cold water:

GO-GETTING HELL BUSTERS WANTED!

We want a leader in every club – a regular 'go-getting, hell-busting' leader. A man who will not take 'no' for an answer, who refuses to recognise the existence of the word 'impossible', a man who is not content with the 'any time will do' attitude which seems to be ingrained in so many people who are associated with swimming.

We can do it and we must DO IT NOW! I am not content to wait until I am an old man to see the West taking her proper place.

Ironically, it was to take Penzance another sixty years to find such a champion of swimming as this in John Clarke, just in time to save its Jubilee Pool from the bulldozers.

The public lidos represented a modernising trend towards a democratic concern for a freely available, healthy, convivial environment, putting pleasure and health firmly at the centre of civic life. The writer and social policy analyst Ken Worpole has pointed out the significance of the decline of the lidos: 'Their neglect in recent decades speaks volumes about our return to the private, the indoor and our retreat from collective provision.' Perhaps the restoration of the Jubilee Pool, the reopening of Brockwell Park Lido, the saving of Tooting Bec Lido in London, and the recent renaissance of R. W. H. Jones's streamlined, flowing Saltdean Lido near Brighton may point the way to healthier, happier, more sensual days.

I arrived a mile along the bay in Newlyn with the naive idea that I might actually go for a swim in the harbour, or off the beach. I was under the spell of a painting by Dame Laura Knight, one of the Newlyn School of painters, called simply *The Boys*. It is set in Newlyn harbour, with the sandy beach in the foreground, where a group of boys is dressing on an upturned boat after a bathe. Beyond them, dozens of other boys, most of them naked, are swimming in the turquoise waters of the harbour, and some are wading out to meet an incoming boat. Laura Knight had come to join the New Realist group of artists formed in Newlyn by Stanhope Forbes in 1899. Forbes and his friends had rebelled against what they saw as the sentimentality and romanticism of the Royal Academy, forming the New English Art Club in 1886. Their mission was to paint in the open air the real day-to-day lives of Newlyn and its ordinary working people. As Forbes said: 'Every corner was a picture; the people seemed to fall naturally into place and harmonise with their surroundings.' With Penzance railway station a mile or so away, the place became the focus of an artistic and social world; on the beach, in the harbour, and in and out of the converted fish-loft studios. It was at one of the parties given in Newlyn by Forbes and his wife, Elizabeth Armstrong, that Laura Knight and Alfred Munnings met, and became life-long friends, much attracted to one another.

The last of the fish was being sold in an open-sided shed, and men were sweeping crushed ice over the edge of the quay into the murky harbour twenty feet below. The prospect of a swim looked suddenly bleak. There were bright sounds everywhere. Hammers on metal, radios, welding, hosepipes, and the bass notes of big engines. Under the heavy stench of diesel the good ships *Avalon*, *Ocean Spray*, *Marina*, *Keriolet*, *Prevail*, *Girl Patricia*, *Try Again*, *Trewarveneth* and *Golden Harvest* lay at rest in the dark pine-green water. Men dangled in cradles, painting the *Rebecca Elaine*, or sat untying knotted nets, bare backs browning, while huge Mafia gulls with fish entrails dangling from their beaks flapped menacingly overhead, missing nothing. Bruisers of the bird world, the gulls circled and landed lightly in the rigging or shat casually on the decks. The boats were painted white with birdshit. Drums of cable, pallets piled high with chain, huge blocks of granite; everything was heavy-duty, and you had to keep your wits about you on the quayside, dodging forklifts, the odd flying rope-end, and the articulated lorries of 'W. Stevenson & Sons. Trawler Owners'. The black mud and garish green seaweed of the harbour, laced with scum and the rainbow marbling of slicked oil, were hard to recognise as the innocent setting for the Laura Knight painting.

I headed down the coast towards Land's End in search of turquoise water, and found it in the cove at Porthcurno. My first sight of the water's dappled beauty was from high above on the cliffs at the Minack open-air theatre. The higher you climb above the sea, the calmer and more beautiful it looks, the waves thinning to the faint pock-marking finish of Hammerite metal paint.

The white sands and clear green water looked inviting and a long way down. I descended innumerable steps cut in the cliff and found myself a perch on the crowded beach. The Bronzed Ones were out in force here, with a strong contingent from Birmingham, all encamped with windbreaks, voluminous towels and big picnic boxes. All family life was there. It was like being in a suburb and listening in to the conversations in every home, or watching a hundred Mike Leigh plays simultaneously. No one seemed the least inhibited about the people next to them. These were families, warts and all.

There were quite a lot of swimmers too, but mostly close in to the beach, which shelves sharply to deep water. It was perfectly clear and quite warm. I swam out of the main cove in a long arc to my left, round the rocks, past two more beaches that are only exposed at low tide. This was the clear, unpolluted Atlantic; the same sea that had been so unbearably cold forty miles west across open water in the Scillies in the spring. I struck out across the bay towards the Logan Rock, and eventually beached in warm shallows, on a just-submerged sandbar a hundred yards or so offshore. This further corner of Porthcurno is what is quaintly known as a 'nudist beach'. In France or Greece these days it would simply be a beach. Looking across to the cliffs I saw people taking enormous risks in their eagerness to scramble round the rocks to this place. Waves broke gently over the sandbar, and the moment I stood up I felt out of place in my black Speedos amongst the informally-dressed beautiful people who paddled elegantly, brownly, hand in hand in the sun. There was something subtly aggressive about their nakedness, and I was reminded of walking hatless once down a Prague street in winter, the fur-clad heads turning in my wake. Like the 'naturists' at Holkham, they wore their nudity like a uniform.

I had swum into a Bateman cartoon.

It was just then that I realised the tide was beginning to rise and I had left my togs rather too far down the beach for peace of mind. Setting off at a brisk breaststroke, I aimed for the distant spot of blue which was my shorts, then turned over for a stretch of backstroke, gazing up at the high cliffs and what the composer Imogen Holst once called 'the contrapuntal wheeling of the gulls'. I enjoyed the comparative solitude. It grew noisier as I approached the beach, and my shorts, rucksack and boots were but a few feet above the waterline with the surf licking hungrily towards them. I put on a finishing sprint to the rescue, then dried out and warmed myself, half-leaning, half-lying on one of the massive quartz-striated pale-grey granite slabs that surround the cove. I was joined by a painted lady butterfly, sunbathing on my blue cotton French Connection shorts.

I looked around me at the British at play. I have always been persuaded by the marine biologist Sir Alister Hardy's aquatic theory of human evolution, which he first suggested in an article in the *New Scientist* in 1960. His ideas were later developed by Elaine Morgan in her book *The Descent of Woman*. Unlike Desmond Morris (who was put off swimming by nearly drowning when he was seven) they believed we spent ten million years of the Pliocene era of world drought evolving into uprightness as semi-aquatic waders and swimmers in the sea shallows and on the beaches of Africa. We went through a sea change to become what we are, and our subsequent life on dry land is a relatively recent, short-lived affair.

Apart from the proboscis monkey of Borneo, we are the only primate that regularly takes to the water for the sheer joy of it. We are also singularly hairless like dolphins and, alone amongst the primates, have a layer of subcutaneous fat analagous to the whale's blubber, ideal for keeping warm in the water. Hardy's ideas were sparked off by the curious fact that the vestigial hairs on our bodies are arranged in a quite different pattern from those on other apes. Hardy spotted that if you were to put a swimming human into a water tunnel, the hydrodynamic lines would coincide precisely with the lines drawn by the pattern of body hairs. This is just what you would expect to find in a creature evolved for streamlined swimming whose babies take quite naturally to water. My young friend Stan took his first swim in the bath just after birth, and was already a leading light in the Hoxton Ducklings Swimming Club at the age of one. Herman Melville's experiences in the South Seas, recounted in *Typee: A Peep At Polynesian Life*, convinced him of our natural affinity for water:

One day in company with Kory-Kory, I had repaired to the stream for the purpose of bathing, when I observed a woman sitting upon a rock in the midst of the current, and watching with the liveliest interest the gambols of something, which at first I took to be an uncommonly large species of frog, that was sporting in the water near her. Attracted by the novelty of the sight, I waded towards the spot where she sat, and could hardly credit the evidence of my senses when I beheld a little infant, the period of whose birth could not be extended back many days, paddling about as if it had just risen to the surface, after being hatched into existence at the bottom. Occasionally the delighted parent reached out her hands towards it, when the little thing, uttering a faint cry, and striking out its tiny limbs, would sidle for the rock and the next moment be clasped to its mother's bosom. This was repeated again and again, the baby remaining in the stream about a minute at a time. Once or twice it made wry faces at swallowing a mouthful of water, and choked and spluttered as if on the point of strangling. At such times, however, the mother snatched it up and by a process scarcely to be mentioned obliged it to eject the fluid. For several weeks afterwards I observed this woman bringing her child down to the stream every day in the cool of the morning and evening and treating it to a bath. No wonder that the South Sea Islanders are an amphibious race when they are thus launched into water as soon as they see the light. I am convinced that it is as natural for a human being to swim as it is for a duck, and yet in civilized communities how many able-bodied individuals die like so many drowning kittens from the occurrence of the most trivial accidents.

As D. H. Lawrence says in his essay on *Typee*, 'we are most of us who use the English language, water-people, sea-derived.'

Beach anthropology only tends to confirm my enthusiasm for Hardy's hypothesis. I contemplated the webbing we (but no other apes) have between our thumb and forefinger, and the splashing humans, hairless apes squealing with pleasure in the sea, and wondered about the transformation that comes about in most of us – when we sit on the beach, or bathe, or swim – from *Homo sapiens* to what Norman O. Brown calls, in *Life Against Death*, *Homo ludens*; from neurosis to playfulness. Perhaps we are simply more at home in or around water than on dry land. Perhaps dry land is our problem.

People certainly work, or play, hard on the beach. They build the most elaborate sandcastles, construct dams and create lagoons, race the tide in elaborate water games, spend hours skimming pebbles on the sea, lug heavy equipment for miles down cliffs, through sand dunes, up cliffs again. They spend fortunes on elaborate, powered water toys, wait for days for the right wave to surf, make beach camps like nomads, sit in beach huts all day gazing out to sea, or simply take off their shoes and socks and paddle. The painter L. S. Lowry would sometimes experience such a compulsion to sit on the seafront at Sunderland that he would take a taxi there, 135 miles from his home in Cheshire. My own version of regressive heaven was to spend the rest of the afternoon very much like the swimming pigs I had met with Dudley on Kythnos, alternately toasting on my rock with Margaret Forster's biography of Daphne du Maurier and ambling down the beach to wallow in the pure turquoise water.

13

CROSSING THE FOWEY

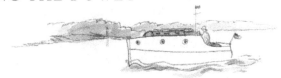

Cornwall, 18 July

IT WAS AFTER dark when I drove through the maze of
twisting lanes that leads to Polruan down the east bank of the
Fowey River. In places they are so narrow you brush the steep
banks on both sides. I spent the night in the Citroën at the top
of the cliffs by the coastguard's lookout cottage. I woke up
gazing out at a heavy sea mist from the open back of the car,
and lay dozing for a while under my parachute, listening to
the muffled engine of a boat coming round under the cliffs.

Polruan and Fowey face each other across a natural
harbour formed by the deep estuary of the river, sheltered by
the hills on which the two places stand. Conservative Fowey
calls Polruan a Socialist Republic, because they come under a
separate district council which has always been more radical.
Fowey has never quite recovered from the council houses
Polruan built all over the hilltop and skyline opposite.
There's a sense that they have still not resolved their enmity
in the Civil War, when Fowey was Parliamentarian and
Polruan Royalist.

Besides the pervasive presence of the ghost of Daphne du
Maurier, Fowey and its river have always held a special
importance for me because it was a favourite haunt of my
mother, and my Uncle Laddie, who spent most of their
childhood in Cornwall. My grandfather was public health
inspector in Truro, and the family had moved there from
Walsall. There were seven brothers and sisters altogether, and
they grew especially close because of the relative social

isolation of a Staffordshire family in a Cornish school. When they first arrived, the Cornish children thought they were from Warsaw and spoke to them in pidgin English. As outsiders, they continued to relate far more within their own family than outside it. Laddie, who was the oldest, eventually acquired a boat, a modest cabin cruiser in which the brothers and sisters led a Swallows and Amazons existence up and down the River Fal and on voyages to Fowey and Polruan. Here, too, was the summer cottage of a girlfriend, whom I would visit on absurd, marathon, all-night drives to and from London in my mid-twenties, in the best romantic traditions of du Maurier.

I knew it was not going to be easy to swim across the mouth of the Fowey River from the moment I arrived. The root of the problem is that ever since the days when du Maurier and her dashing chums lived here, it has been a place for showing off. The moment you go on, or in, the water, you're on stage. The town is stacked up the hill like a grandstand, and it bristles with binoculars and probably telescopes too. Everybody has a scenic window, the kind that would cost a fortune if you broke it, as a lookout point. Everyone is watching everyone else, giving running commentaries on the trim of their sails or the condition of their paintwork, or describing the course they would be taking if *they* were at the tiller. There are coastguards on patrol, pilots leading enormous cargo ships up and down the river to load up with china clay from St Austell, tugs, ferrymen, water taxis, and the Fowey Yacht Club, all keeping a weather eye on the cut of your jib.

I walked down the steep narrow streets into Polruan to catch the ferry across the river to Fowey, taking my place on the quayside behind an orderly queue of dogs. There always seem to be more of them than people on the ferry. In August, every dog in the land converges on Cornwall for its summer holiday and there is much throwing of sticks on every Cornish beach. On the way over I pondered the tidal currents of the harbour. In town, I looked up the tides, ate baked beans on toast in the Lifeboat Café, and tried to decide on my best course over the river.

After much debate with my friends in Polruan, I decided the ideal place for a crossing would be the harbour mouth, from the rocks below the ruined castle on the Polruan side to Readymoney Cove on the Fowey side, close to the open sea, a distance of about half a mile. If things went well, I said flamboyantly, I might swim both ways. The best moment was going to be half an hour or so before the top of the high tide, so that I would be able to take advantage of the slack water before the tide began to ebb again. At all events, you want to be out of the water by the time the tide turns because it is at the beginning of the ebb and flow that the tides run with greatest power.

That afternoon, I swam out into the harbour mouth on the high tide simply to get the feel of the water and currents. I hadn't intended it to be more than a short trial run, but was just settling nicely into the rhythm of the swim and deciding that I might as well keep going, when I was suddenly intercepted by the coastguard. A big grey powerboat, a-quiver with antennae, came sprinting across the water out of nowhere, and snowploughed to a halt like a skier a few yards off. 'Are you all right?' they called.

'Absolutely fine, thanks,' I said, trying to strike the same note as you would for 'Just putting the milk-bottles out'. 'Just taking a swim.'

They explained sternly that I shouldn't swim in the harbour without permission from the harbourmaster, and told me to turn round.

'But I'm halfway across already. I might as well keep going to the other side,' I suggested, feeling like a fish arguing with an angler.

They disagreed, and it was getting too chilly to tread water and engage in debate, and besides, they were bigger than me. So I headed back to Polruan, my spirits a little dashed, to the amusement of my friends on shore.

Over dinner that night at a cottage on the waterfront, we laid the plan of action. It was the weekend and there might be too many sailing boats to make a safe crossing. My only option, apart from giving up, was going to be to swim concealed from the coastguard by my friend Brian's boat, hoping, if caught, that they would forgive me if I took the sensible precaution of swimming with an escort.

Next day, we took the escort boat to the appointed spot with perfect timing. I went in off the rocks and began the swim. Brian and his children, Holly and Joe, chatted away as we went, and I eased into a steady breaststroke, keeping to the seaward side of the boat, out of sight of the harbourmaster's office. The necessary subterfuge added to the fun. If this were a Channel-swim report, I would add that I was swimming at 29 strokes per minute and had set off at 4.25 p.m. The Fowey River is 40 feet deep at high tide, and I began to feel the depth of the water beneath me. Roy, of the *Tregeagle*, one of the two tugs that lie at anchor just off Polruan, had told me that at a point opposite the ferry from Fowey to Bodinnick, further upstream, there is a 50-foot hole in the river bottom with a fresh-water spring in it. We were giving it a wide berth.

I tried to avoid swimming into floating seaweed, but each time it wrapped itself around an arm I would shake it off with an involuntary shudder. The fear of unknown things in the deep is never very far away. There was one nervous moment when an enormous rubber-hulled Galaxy SP24 racing power-boat with twin Mercury 75 engines appeared to head straight for us like a giant black condom, travelling fast with its nose in the air and a ten-year-old at the wheel. Otherwise, there was little traffic on the water, so we could maintain a reason-ably straight course, heading out towards St Catherine's Castle to the seaward side of Readymoney Cove to com-pensate for the tide, which was still rising and carrying me upstream. It was calm, but a sea breeze made it choppy enough to break off my sentences now and again with a salty slap in the face as we conversed. The children in the boat kept watch for jellyfish, but none appeared.

As I approached Readymoney Cove, my mind drifted back to my Fowey girlfriend. The little sandy bay held romantic associations, and memories of night-swims to the diving rafts moored offshore. Fowey figured in my childhood mythology as the place where Uncle Laddie often moored his boat on the trips from Falmouth, and loved to swim. He and my mother would set off exploring upriver, having brought the little craft over on one of their camping trips. On other expeditions, they would rove about the Fal and the creeks of the Carrick Roads, or go up the Helford River. The stories of their adventures, of driftwood fires and night swims, were the stuff of my bedtime stories.

I swam right into the cove and waded through the clear, sandy shallows on to the little beach. It may not have been quite up to the standard of Philip Rush's three-way Channel crossing in 1988 (in 28 hours, 21 minutes), or Dr Chris Stockdale's Channel swim, followed by a 203-mile cycle ride to Solihull from Dover and a full marathon round Birmingham, but it felt good all the same. It had been a straightforward crossing, so far unnoticed by the coastguards, and not wishing to cool off in the breeze I plunged back in for the return trip to Polruan, still shielded by the boat. A swim over any sort of distance is very like climbing a mountain. You look ahead from the shore and feel daunted. Your objective looks so tiny in the distance. Once in the sea, though, you begin to relax and lose yourself in the rhythm, feeling the texture of the water, opening up your lungs and breathing deeper, becoming aquatic. I was by now swimming confidently, although still conscious of the great depth of water beneath me, and the need to reach the other side before the tide turned. I now had the advantage of slack water, but once the tide begins to run, with a twenty-foot head of sea-water combined with the fresh-water stream of the river itself all wanting to escape to the open sea, there is a sudden unleashing of massive pent-up energy through the relatively narrow channel of the harbour.

We were a couple of hundred yards from the other shore, and just congratulating each other on giving the slip to the coastguards when they suddenly appeared from nowhere, bearing down on our little unofficial combo with a determined air. For a moment things looked tense and we saw a loudhailer being tuned up for maximum embarrassment. Their opening salvo came as something of a relief: 'Oh my God, not you again!'

'It's all right, we're on our way back now,' we said quickly, and apologised for any inconvenience we might inadvertently have caused. They were remarkably good-natured, giving us a slightly tongue-in-cheek telling-off, the nautical equivalent of letting you off with a caution. A few weekend high spirits were in order.

By now I was beginning to savour the notion of the hot bath Brian had mentioned might be available back at his place. My fingers and feet were feeling numb, and a triathlon swimmer had told me, one windy morning on a lake near Leicester, that water conducts heat away from the body twenty times faster than air. Thinking of warm towels, bath salts, and a hot tap opened to full throttle, I swam on with renewed vigour through the moorings off Polruan and clambered ashore on the rocks just below the cottage, where I fancied I could already see steam curling from the bathroom window.

In Polruan, swimming is taken seriously; the harbour has claimed the lives of too many inhabitants over the years, some of them young and high-spirited, returning late at night in a borrowed dinghy, having missed the last ferry after a night out in Fowey, or upset on one of the powerful waves that sometimes drive up the harbour in a storm. People are constantly crossing and recrossing the water in all weathers, so there is a natural reason to be a confident swimmer, and the village school has a long tradition of teaching every child not just to swim, but to swim strongly over a distance.

Every year at the end of June, the ten- and eleven-year-olds in years five and six swim across the harbour. Many of them swim both ways. The day is chosen by the teachers and the harbourmaster to take advantage of a morning high tide at about ten o'clock. At the appointed hour the children, well-greased with Vaseline, start from the Polruan quayside at the ferry landing-stage. The quay is packed with younger children from the school, parents, villagers and holidaymakers, all cheering like mad. Each child has their own attendant rowing boat for safety, and the harbour is cleared of traffic for the occasion. The older children from the school, who may have done the swim the previous year, are sent on by ferry to the other side to supply moral support. As each child touches the harbour wall on the Fowey side, a great cheer goes up. Some are ferried back, and some turn straight round and swim back to Polruan, where they are greeted by redoubled cheering, wrapped in towels and whisked home shivering for a hot bath before the traditional gathering for hot chocolate and cream buns at the Singing Kettle. The distance at this point is about 500 yards in open water which can get very chilly out in the deep channel in the middle. The young swimmers train at Liskeard pool, and in the harbour with their parents. By the time they come to do the harbour swim, most can swim a mile. It is hard to imagine a more nourishing educational experience; this is quite literally a rite of passage.

Next morning it was raining. Over breakfast in the Lifeboat Café, I was studying the map of the Land's End peninsula for signs of holy wells. This was to be a day of amateur anthropology. What better way to spend a rainy day than poking about wells? The more I travelled and swam, the clearer it was becoming that, as I had suspected all along, our relationship to water is a great deal more mystical than most of us admit. How much of the ancient folk-belief in the healing powers of water still existed? There are holy wells all over the country, but since the advent of mains water supplies in the 1920s and '30s, many of them have been forgotten. However, this end of Cornwall still seemed adequately supplied.

I went first to Madron, two miles out of Penzance, and found myself standing, dripping, by a holy well in a sallow thicket, tatty with lichens. Tits sang in the rain everywhere, or at least whistled. I had trudged a muddy path through undergrowth bowed down by the rain, then plunged down a dark corridor of gnarled blackthorn to emerge in a place where three streams converge, then apparently disappear into a small boggy pool the colour of vinaigrette. Christian mothers brought infants here to be baptised in the little stone baptistry a few yards along the path. A long-suffering sallow by the pool seemed to carry the world's woes on its slender limbs. It was festooned with all manner of tokens silently crying in the rain; a yearning choir of pilgrim voices. Finding so much stuff, so many things, hanging at eye-level in a wood, my first thought was of the gamekeeper's gibbet, another living relic of our former lively dialogue with the deities.

There were handkerchiefs, bits of coloured ribbon, a pack of cards, someone's tie, shoelaces, gloves, a skein of a woman's hair, long and brown, skanks of bladderwrack and kelp, a restaurant bill, strands of wool, an improvised mobile of drinking straws, a star of painted lolly sticks on a silk cord, threaded bottletops, a plait of bracken, hairbands, posies of wild flowers, a size-38 clothing label, even the business card of a Welsh 'Osteopath, Iridologist, Psychotherapist' with sixteen letters after his name and a Llangollen telephone number, 'By appointment'. Pencilled on another piece of card were the words 'To find the truth and recognise it, and most important to act upon it.' When Daphne du Maurier came here, she 'broke off a twig and turned it nine times against the sun', no doubt for good reasons. I made a secret wish that I would succeed in the most ambitious of the swims I had in mind: the crossing of the Gulf of Corryvreckan. This damp shrine could have been Lourdes, it could have been almost anywhere on the Ganges. The bits of clothing and relics left behind on the tree symbolised the 'old' person before their ritual cleansing in the water. The rain fell steadily on all these prayers, these dampened hopes, and they dripped. And three streams kept on disappearing into the well.

The odd thing about the place was that the streams were running *into* the well, instead of out of it, like most springs. I glanced at my watch to make sure it wasn't running backwards. I wondered how all this related, if at all, to the advertisements you see in the back of *Old Moore's Almanack* for 'Lucky Cornish Piskies'. Looking through a copy of this year's edition, which still looks as if it has been typeset on the original Gutenberg printing press, there are now two contenders for your faith, and money. Joan the Wad claims to be the 'queen of all the lucky Cornish piskies'. 'Each charm', we read, 'is guaranteed dipped in water from the lucky Saints Well, Polperro.' Various forms of good fortune are on offer: 'Lottery win, luck on the horses, bingo, health, job promotion, happiness.' You can carry Joan the Wad on your person in a variety of forms – charm, brooch, earring or ring – in solid silver or brass. The slick copyline runs: 'Good fortune will nod/If you carry upon you Joan the Wad!'

Joan the Wad's rival spirit is Lowender, 'The Genuine Lucky Cornish Piskey for your good fortune and happiness'. This hand-crafted charm is 'washed in the mysterious "Pool of Dozmary" on Bodmin Moor – home of the lucky Cornish piskey'. Lowender is a male piskey, and is available from 'Merman' in Bodmin. I thought I might find one or both of them hanging in a tree by one of the wells I visited, or even meet the real thing, but saw only a damp St Christopher.

I found another of these poor people's spas at St Uny, where the water springs into the holy well from under Bartinny Hill, the last high point before Land's End. There were stone steps down to the ferny, echoing well and a piece of cardboard with a written notice: DO NOT DRINK THIS WATER. IT IS NO LONGER SAFE TO DO SO. There was no explanation. Again there was the wise-looking gnarled tree, this time a hawthorn, and the fluttering votive offerings. A pigeon had woven some of them into its nest. I noticed twigs had been broken off the sacred tree as keepsakes, and there were seashells, pearls, necklaces and ancient watchstraps thick with algae. The well was only a few yards down a path from the Iron Age village of Carn Euny, where I was alone with its ghosts. Some of the buried houses are almost complete and I stood inside one of them looking out past the massive granite lintel across the Land's End peninsula to the church towers of Sennen and St Just. As I walked up Bartinney Hill the clouds lifted in time for a beautiful sunset over the clearly visible Scilly Isles forty miles to the west. Then a tide of mist began to roll up from Penzance as I waded downhill through thick heather.

Two miles away at Sancreed I walked up past Glebe Farm in the dusk to a third holy well. The path was overgrown and indistinct, but showed signs of occasional use. The still, clear well, eight steps down into an impressive granite-built grotto, was 'cleared and kept as befits a holy place' by a couple who are buried nearby. There are the remains of a small stone chapel, a Celtic cross, and a sacred hawthorn laden with tokens, many of them plaited from the orange day lilies that grow here in abundance. There were more offerings in stone crevices in the walls of the well: coloured sea shells, patterned stones, a horse tooth, the St Christopher, a garlic bulb. All these things were rich with meaning, but a powerful, silent mystery too. No doubt the placebo effect is the pre-eminent healing process at these traditional healing wells, but the mere process of taking control over your own health and doing something to help your condition must in itself be beneficial.

I had the same sense in these places that I often have inside a country church when I look in the visitors' book. Apparently lonely and deserted, each well was at the same time crowded with presences. In Cornwall, the religious connection with the sea and Poseidon, as well as the nymphs of the wells, goes back a long way. Graveyards are full of drowned sailors, and at Zennor, west of St Ives, there is a famous carving of a mermaid in the wooden end of a pew. Where English churches imitate the sacred groves of the forest, early Cornish churches, with their ribbed and curved roof timbers, imitate boats or even the skeletons of fish.

I know another such powerful and mysterious place as these holy wells. Two miles out of Newmarket on the old road towards Bury St Edmunds you come to the Moulton crossroads. In the verge you will see a mass of flowers, some fresh, some plastic, on a little grave. This is the tomb of Joseph, the Unknown Gypsy Boy, reputedly killed in a cart accident at the crossroads during the last century. There is a simple wooden cross bearing his name, and the colours of the graveside flowers on the eve of Derby Day are said to foretell those of the winner. I met a policeman there last year, whose patrol takes him past the grave several times each day or night. He confirmed the story I had heard from stable lads in the town that although there are always fresh flowers on the grave, nobody ever sees anyone putting them there.

I was left wondering about the nature of the wishes, prayers really, being offered up in these places. I suspected not many of them were simply hoping to win on the lottery. It was pain that I mostly sensed, and grief, but perhaps that was power of the elements, throwing down a month's rain in twenty-four hours. I had a kind of Stanley Spencer vision of all the troubled souls rising out of the water, beseeching the spring-gods for redemption. I hope not too many of them telephoned the enterprising Welsh Iridologist and Psychotherapist. These residual beliefs die hard. The new Castle Mall shopping centre in Norwich hardly looks like a great pagan shrine, yet the indoor fountain at its centre has to be cleared of coins every week. In Derbyshire, and all over the country, wells are still dressed with flowers in annual ceremonies that hark back to the Roman Fontinalia, the flower festival in honour of the nymphs that inhabit the springs. And of course, babies are baptised in the symbolic holy wells we call fonts in churches everywhere.

I drove in the dusk down to Ruan Lanihorne, a village near the River Fal, where I stayed with my friends Olivia and Gary in a rented cottage. Next morning it was raining again, but we were all determined to go up to the north coast near Padstow and investigate the natural rock pool at Treyarnon, in Constantine Bay. We were soon reminded it was holiday-time, driving behind a massed cortège of caravans and Dutch motor-homes, slowing to walking pace every hundred yards in the Cornish lanes to squeeze past each other. I've noticed the motor-homes always have bicycles hooked on the back, presumably decorative. Traffic calming was invented by the Cornish in about 1450. Wales or Wiltshire may be sleeping giants, but Cornwall is a sleeping policeman. In Cornwall, what looks like road-kill usually turns out to be somebody's swimming trunks, or a towel, spreadeagled and mangled by the tyres of a thousand mobile motor-homes.

At Treyarnon we parked next to a VW camper with a blown exhaust and a ragged blue tarpaulin over a roof-rack piled with surfboards. Painted across the back was the legend, 'One Hundred Per Cent Funky'. A thumping sledgehammer base threatened to dismantle its rusting frame. Through the steamed-up windows a group of surfing dudes could be dimly perceived in attitudes of extreme relaxation. The harder it rained, the more determined we were to go through with our plan, and our bedraggled little swimming party in bright blue and yellow Gore-tex clambered down the low, stepped, slate cliffs to the big tide-rinsed natural swimming pool.

A tall, solitary figure was changing into his trunks on a table-top rock below, covering his clothes with a mackintosh. Then he dived and swam with a beautiful black retriever. Gary and I went in too, and the retriever, called Moll, we discovered, swam over to greet us. She looked magnificent in the water and moved with instinctive grace, snout just clear of the surface, tail out as a rudder. The pool was forty feet across and up to six feet deep, full of mussels, sea anemones, limpets, starfish and barnacles. As Moll swam alongside us, it struck me that there is hardly an animal that hasn't the capacity to swim. Even cats will swim if they have to, and hedgehogs, hares, squirrels, moles, stoats and deer all take to the water from time to time. Recently I watched a cock pheasant swim across my moat when it accidentally ran across the lawn and on to a floating patch of duckweed it mistook for more grass. Giraffes are about the only mammals that can't swim, because their long necks upset their balance and they capsize.

At Newmarket, there are several elaborate open-air equine swimming pools, and all the trainers now regard swimming horses as an essential part of their routine. It tones up the animals and improves their fitness and breathing. It might, in fact, be much better for horses to swim their races than to run them. This is exactly what the Thais do with elephants. Elephant swimming races are major national events in Thailand, and the champion animals are heroes every bit as famous as Red Rum. One of the current champions is Hai Pok, a twenty-five-year-old elephant, who was recently cheered on to victory by crowds lining the banks of the Moon River, to the north-east of Bangkok. He beat the other elephants by swimming 260 yards over the river and back again in just over two minutes. He then narrowly outpaced two students in a one-way swim across the river.

In *The Descent of Woman*, Elaine Morgan argues that the elephant, like the whale, evolved as an aquatic creature. In water, weight was no hindrance, and size a positive advantage to the conservation of body heat. Elephants still instinctively use their trunks as snorkels when crossing over the beds of deep African rivers, and their baggy, almost hairless skin suggests that their layer of subcutaneous fat was once bulky enough to fill it out more smoothly, like that of their nearest mammal cousin, the sea cow. Elaine Morgan quotes the case of an elephant that went for a two-hundred-mile island-hopping jaunt in the Bay of Bengal. The journey took twelve years to complete, and some of the hops from island to island were across at least a mile of open ocean.

The writer and naturalist Robert Burton has suggested that the hallmark of a truly aquatic mammal is that it 'progresses not by paddling but by movements of the tail or sinuous movements of the body'. Whales, seals and sea cows obviously qualify, but Burton points out an interesting line to be drawn between otters and mink, noticeable when the species are compared swimming underwater. Mink swim with a dog-paddle, and are not in the same league for speed and agility as the otters, which swim by flexing the tail and lower half of the body up and down like a whale, rather than side to side like a seal. They also have their main sense organs – eyes, ears and nose – on top of their heads, like the hippopotamus, a sign of true aquatic adaptation. The only dog I could think of that shows any sign of true physical adaptation to swimming is the rare Portuguese Water Dog, which has webbed back feet. It very nearly became extinct, but is now being bred again. Moll was obviously enjoying her swim very much, and when she eventually came out and shook herself all over us, it was raining so hard we scarcely noticed, and we promptly dived back in.

The magical thing about tidal pools is that the water is naturally renewed by the moon twice a day and has a chance to warm above sea temperature in sunshine. The summer before, I had swum in another famous rock pool at Dancing Ledge, on the Dorset coast near Langton Matravers. Miles from anywhere at the bottom of the steep rolling downs, you climb through an old quarry and scramble down a bit of cliff on to a spectacular wide shelf of pocked grey-brown rock with a deep oblong pool cut neatly out of it. It was originally dynamited by Eric and Geoffrey Warner, the brothers who jointly founded Spyways, an extinct prep school in Langton Matravers where Derek Jarman began his education.

The Dancing Ledge is a dramatic petrified beach, with the waves sliding in across it, kicking spray high into the air as they slap and thump into the cliffs beside it, hollowing them out with great thuds you can feel through your feet, ricocheting in reversed surf that races back out to sea and collides head-on with the incoming waves in more fireworks of spray. The restless Dorset sea fondles and gropes at the rock-shelf like a lover's hand sliding up a stockinged thigh. The pool is a gash in the rock pavement ten feet wide and twenty-five feet long, and when the tide is up the snowy waves shampoo over the rocks and waterfall off its seaward rim. A thousand streamlets flow restlessly back into it each time the water recedes, and a dozen suns shine back at you off the cratered rock.

The little pool swirls and buffets the swimmer to a soundtrack of the muffled explosions of waves in the hidden caves under the cliffs. Its perpendicular walls are seaweedy, and getting out would be difficult if it weren't for the fact that at one end, the water comes right to the very lip, so the swimmer can flop out like a seal. When the tide is low, and the sea calm, Dancing Ledge can be a swimmer's idyll. You can lie on the warm grey rock amongst ammonites the size of car tyres, drying off in the sun, then tip yourself back into the rectangle of fresh sea-water. There are signs of a steel ladder or railing having once been fixed into the rock leading to the pool. Now there is nothing, and a refreshing absence of lifebelts or warning signs. The owners of this lovely stretch of coast must have decided that you would need your head examining if you didn't treat the sea here with the respect it deserves.

Paul, Damian and Andy, the Treyarnon lifeguards, sat in their wooden hut with their feet up on the counter looking out to sea. Business wasn't brisk today; there wasn't a surfer in sight, and the only swimmers were Olivia, Gary and me. We left Moll and her owner at the rock pool, and took to the waves in what was now a full-blown thunderstorm, having consulted the three in the well-fugged hut, who clearly thought we were mad. 'There's a current that swings clockwise into the cove on the right and out to sea on the left, so keep right and you're fine.' Though they have to rescue more surfers than swimmers (people who paddle blithely out to sea on their boards without any respect for its tiderips or the tendency of the wind to blow the board along), they had been called out a few nights back to rescue a whole flotilla of tipsy midnight swimmers who had gone too far out into the treacherous current that drags round the point of the cove and were being carried along out to sea. The lifeguards and several volunteers formed a human chain to the east of the point down-current from the troubled swimmers. Holding hands, they stretched out to form a living boom that would catch them as they swept round the point. The strategy succeeded and everyone had returned to the beach in safety.

The lifeguards blamed the molly-coddling of indoor swimming and warm-water 'fun pools' for preventing young swimmers from learning a proper respect for the sea. There is a growing tendency to go out and surf or swim with no thought of self-reliance, only a bland assumption that the lifeguards are there to rescue you should anything go wrong, as though the ocean were a giant fun pool.

I awoke in the cottage at Ruan Lanihorne next morning with the first signs of a cold, but it was my friends' last full day in Cornwall, and the night before we had planned an adventure I was determined not to miss.

Ever since I stayed one summer in a house across the Helford River at Calamansack, I had imagined swimming Frenchman's Creek, the mysterious wooded inlet where Daphne du Maurier set her famous novel. I had sailed across there with my son in a dinghy one midsummer evening on a rising tide. We ventured respectfully into the shadows of the silent creek. It felt mysterious all right, full of the dinosaur skeletons of half-submerged oaks dripping with seaweed and the bow-waves of the mullet shoals that come up here to spawn. We had nosed softly up between the dark trees that crowded to the water's edge as far as we dared, sensing the ghosts of the place.

This was where Daphne du Maurier spent her wedding night on 19 July 1932, moored up with her dashing Guardsofficer husband on his twenty-foot motor cruiser *Ygdrasil*. Tommy 'Boy' Browning was the youngest major in the British Army. He had been awarded the DSO at the age of nineteen, was an Olympic high hurdler, and had bobsleighed for England. He and a friend had appeared late the previous summer in Fowey on *Ygdrasil*. He had read du Maurier's first novel, *The Loving Spirit*, and had gone down to Fowey to 'meet the girl who has written it'. He succeeded, and at seven-thirty on that July morning was on his way by boat up Pont Creek beside Polruan to the remote church at Lanteglos, where Daphne, who had also gone by boat, was there to marry him at eight-fifteen. With typical disregard for convention, Daphne had arranged the wedding early so that she and Tommy could catch the morning tide in *Ygdrasil*. There was a hurried, bleary-eyed wedding breakfast at the du Maurier house by the Fowey River at Ferryside, and the couple changed into their old boating clothes and set off for the open sea, the Helford River, and Frenchman's Creek.

At Fowey, I had bathed in the quiet cove below Menabilly, the house secluded in the wooded hillside to the west of Fowey where Daphne du Maurier and her family lived for twenty-five years. I had walked through the Menabilly woods over Alldays Field to the cove where she used to swim, and waded in over the smooth pebbles between rock pools full of delicate green sea-lettuce and sea-anemones. Venturing alone into the entrance of the deserted cove, I had circled it several times, looking back at the woods that hid the house. I share du Maurier's predilection for quiet, sequestered places, and a swim in Frenchman's Creek seemed a natural sequel to the Menabilly cove and the Fowey River.

There can be few more inspiring sights than the oak-wood that crowds the water's edge and spills over the Helford River, stretching out branches far over the narrow strip of beach that disappears under a spring tide when the river is brim-full. The oaks are ancient and mossy. They have grown undisturbed for centuries, and when you walk along the beach at low tide you have to duck them as they gesture towards the water. They are like the limbs of the wayside trees

Thomas Hardy describes in *The Woodlanders*, 'stretching in level repose over the road, as though reclining on the insubstantial air'. There's a crab under every stone you overturn, and rogue oysters on the mud. Green wood, blue river; that is all there is.

When we arrived in Helford village, we tried and failed to find a boat to hire as an escort for a river swim. We had planned to cross the Helford Passage to Calamansack and start from the far shore, but, since this was now impossible, we debated which way to swim the creek: up or down. The tide decided things by turning, so we hurried a mile along a woodland path to the muddy head of the creek and in I went without further delay. There wasn't a soul about, but there was so much mud that my companions wisely elected to stay on shore.

I could have been swimming down the Limpopo. The tide was just beginning to ebb, the water oozing from the mudbanks. The first hundred yards of this bayou were deep, silky mud the consistency of yoghurt, then a wallow of thin brown soup under a roof of outstretched oak boughs. Every sound I made echoed round the silent woods. The creek was dark and much impeded by the serpentine hulks of fallen trees and floating festoons of tangled seaweed. I lay full length on my belly rowing myself along with my hands like a walrus. As there began to be a puddle's depth, I proceeded like one of the mud-hoppers that live in the mangrove swamps of West African rivers. Feeling deeply primeval, like some fast-track missing link in our evolution from the lugworm, I eventually squirmed into the relative luxury of deeper water and lengthened into a loping breaststroke, passing under the arch of a fallen tree. As I left it behind, I thought how much I had enjoyed my communion with the slime and I realised that I had also just re-enacted the evolution of swimming. The experience was so unexpectedly delightful, and the mud so curiously warm and friendly-feeling, that I even began to wonder if perhaps I had stumbled upon, or wallowed into, a whole new form of therapy; something along the lines of the primal scream. Mud, I decided, is one of those things in life that is only congenial once you're in it.

I was soon in much deeper water, entering the green pool where, in the du Maurier novel, Dona, the heroine, first discovers the Frenchman's ship lying at anchor in its hiding-place. In du Maurier's own phrase, I felt 'a trespasser in time', and her remembered evocation of the place long after the ship had slipped away to the open sea at dawn rang true: 'No rakish masts pointing at the sky, no rattle of chain through the hawse hole, no rich tobacco smell upon the air, no echo of voices coming across the water in a lilting foreign tongue.' A heron checked me with a quick glance as food, then took off in slow motion, a misty wraith rising out of the water and evaporating over the low treetops. I swam on down the middle of the deepening channel of the creek, and petulant little waves began to slap me in the face. I tasted brackish brown water, but consoled myself with the knowledge that the Helford is one of the least polluted rivers in the whole of Britain. Recently, though, some problems have arisen from the new fashion for growing bulbs in some of the fields by the shore and fertilising them with nitrates. The chemicals dribble into the river and do not agree with the famous Helford oysters in their beds. Nor would they please the mullet and bass that run up the river, or the sea trout that pass upstream through the narrow bridge at Gweek.

I swam about a mile down the creek out into its mouth, imagining Uncle Laddie's navy-blue motorboat chugging softly through these waters on the high tide to explore the creek, and silently humming bits of James Taylor's 'Mud Slide Slim and the Blue Horizon'. Straight ahead, across the Helford Passage, I could see the house at Calamansack where I had stayed. An east wind was driving straight up the open channel from the sea. Miniature waves beat gruffly at the sandy beach, and I landed by one of the massive, spreading oaks. My friends were waiting generously with my pullover and a welcome towel. As we walked back to Helford village for hot chocolate and cream tea I felt elated, as I usually do after a long swim, but my voice was beginning to crack up. I thought little of it until I woke up in the night with a raging fever and a sore throat.

We had to leave the rented cottage in the morning, so I

dragged myself over to Fowey, took the ferry to Polruan, and holed up alone in the cottage by the water for a whole lost weekend of fever, hallucinating and dreaming of the Corryvreckan whirlpool, which was already making me nervous. I dreamt of its untold depths and steely cold, making a maelstrom of my bed, half drowning under the billowing duvet, only vaguely aware of the sun outside and the flapping sails of the boats sailing placidly in and out of Fowey harbour.

14

THE BLANDFORD BOMBER

Dorset, 31 July

I HAD LOST THE rest of a long weekend altogether in Cornwall, in a welter of feverish dreams, mostly filled with anxiety about the troublesome task with which I had somehow saddled myself. The idea of swimming another stroke seemed entirely out of the question and I was no longer even sure which day it was. Visions like the sea paintings of Hokusai gripped me as I rose and dipped giddily in and out of consciousness. I was at the mercy of great tidal waves, or swept, gasping, down gigantic white-water versions of the Thames or Humber. The alarming thought occurred to me that I might actually be *turning into* Ned Merrill. In 'The Swimmer', Merrill sets off on his triathlon of swimming, jogging and drinking his way through the private pools of Long Island in apparently good condition, but then things begin to go subtly wrong, and he eventually finds himself wading through a thunderstorm, half-crazy, and on the verge of hypothermia. Sentences from the story floated into my mind and haunted me: 'He had swum too long, he had been immersed too long, and his nose and his throat were sore from the water.' Was this Weil's disease, come to catch up with me after my dismissive comments amongst the coracle swimmers on the River Avon?

I have a vague recollection that it was Monday when I dragged myself up to friends in Dorset for a rest cure in a hammock in a hilltop orchard. The weather, with its usual sense of irony, was magnificent. The doctor said it wasn't

Weil's, just flu or a throat infection ('Probably picked it up in the sea,' he said cheerfully), and after two days aloft in the hammock, and many cups of tea, I was ready for the beach and the cold-water cure of the Dorset coast.

Some of the best sea-bathing in the whole of England is to be had in Dorset, from the glamorous sands of Bournemouth all the way to the crumbling cliffs of Lyme Regis. Given the right weather, it is an ideal place to indulge yourself in some serial swimming. It was in Dorset that I had first tried out my idea of an amphibious ramble, when I had swum consecutively, the previous year, off Studland Bay, Dancing Ledge, Kimmeridge Bay, Lulworth Cove, Stair Hole, Durdle Dor, Ringstead Bay and Chesil Beach in the space of a few days. At seaweedy Kimmeridge I mingled with mullet too lazy to move, and lay so long on the hot rocks, the fossilised relics of a 140-million-year-old tropical seabed, that ammonites imprinted themselves all over me. I hadn't quite reached Burton Bradstock, two miles from Bridport, which is where we now descended from the hilltop.

On our way to the beach, we chanced upon Peter and Barbara, some friends of my hosts. They were a handsome, bronzed couple from Portland Bill who confirmed to us that they practically lived on the beach. We encamped together under the hot cliffs on the pebble ridge of high tide. When I suggested a swim, Peter began earnestly rummaging in our pile of clothes for change, and ended up having to borrow ten pence from his wife. 'An offering to Aphrodite,' he explained as he tossed in the coin. He normally invested as much as a pound, he said, in propitiation of the sea gods, and traced the origins of the habit back to his time in the navy. It was plainly important to him, and I said I thought Neptune must think me something of a cheapskate, only ever having poured the odd dribble of wine to him over the side of a sailing boat. I took to the water with trepidation and was pleasantly surprised at its kindly embrace. The beach shelves steeply here and the water is soon deep and dark. We swam out and looked back from the sea to the little resort, all yellow and blue like the classic seaside posters on post-war railway platforms. The bright orange cliffs are layered like Battenberg cake and there's no telling, even by the geologists, how many years separate each layer. They are full of fossils waiting to be discovered by the hammering of the next winter storm. Some lie about in the rocks below the cliffs, wherever there has been a tumbling down of debris. On the beach, the pebbles are tiny, rounded and flat, very comfortable for bare feet. They were hot that day, too. Two swans flew overhead across the lazy sea with whistling wings, heading towards the great swannery at Abbotsbury behind Chesil Bank.

Peter returned to the others and I looked back at the beach café, where people sat out in the sun, eating real Battenberg and gazing out to sea. Burton Bradstock is clearly a place where locals like to come, planning a day around its simple attractions: the beach, the bathing, a spot of fossil hunting, the shelter of the cliffs, the exceptionally good café, the odd frisbee, a magazine, or perhaps a book. There was definitely a higher-than-average proportion of readers on this beach and it was unusually quiet, like a library, or a club. There were several serious swimmers, too, and the heads bobbing in the sea here and there were reassuring company.

I swam along on my back, gazing up at the jackdaws and swallows that trafficked above the cliffs, feeling, or fancying I felt, a great deal better than I had on dry land. Perhaps it was just the body's bravado. Skirting the edge of the sea and daydreaming like this, I was also skirting the boundaries of unconsciousness: the line between dreaming and drowning. At the same time, part of me felt I could continue with ease, all the way to Portland Bill, twenty miles away along the massive pebble embankment of Chesil Beach. It curves away to the south from Burton Bradstock, and its stones are so precisely graded by the sea, from fine at this end to huge and smooth at Portland, that they say a fisherman lost in fog and coming ashore anywhere between Lyme Regis and Portland Bill can tell exactly where he is from the size of the pebbles on the beach. I had swum off Chesil Beach itself the previous year, far out of my depth even a yard or two out, and felt the strength of the longshore tidal currents. John Bayley, in his memoir of Iris Murdoch, relates her narrow escape from drowning on one of their Chesil swimming expeditions with the Dorset artist and designer Reynolds Stone. Emerging from the sea up the steep shingle, the two men were so engrossed in conversation that they did not notice their companion very nearly sucked into the undertow, dragged under by a wave, and only saved by the impact of another. It is not until much later that night in bed that Iris mentions the incident, more as a curiosity than a matter of life and death.

Safely back with our little group on the beach, I sat about with them on the rocks telling swimming stories. Barbara's concerned a radio ham who lived on Portland Bill next to the coastguard cottages there and swam in the sea off Chesil Bank every day of his life, until he was struck by lightning during a sudden thunderstorm on one of his dips and died. Peter's narrative was equally gloomy and concerned an incident at Gilbert Scott's St Pancras Hotel in the 1920s. In high spirits after a jolly evening, one of the guests climbed into the big water-tank in the roof and went swimming. He drowned, and wasn't discovered until four or five days later, when the hotel water began to taste odd and a plumber was sent to investigate.

Another of the swimmers' tales was about Jeffrey Bernard and the actor John Le Mesurier. They were old drinking companions, and would invent ever more absurd private games to amuse themselves secretly in company. A long-running favourite was to see which of them could casually insert the most outrageous clichés into a conversation undetected by anyone else. They had entered a pub in a small Devon seaside resort, and remarked to the landlord how inviting the sea looked that day. 'Ah yes,' he said, 'but it can be treacherous. Only last week, a young boy went swimming out there and drowned.' Everyone in the pub fell into a respectful silence, and, after a pause, Le Mesurier said, 'Well, it just goes to show, you can't be too careful,' at which Bernard snorted loudly into his glass, burst into fits of uncontrollable laughter, and the pair were obliged to leave, never to return.

Looking at the towels drying on the balconies of the Cliffs Hotel, up winding steps cut in the sandy cliff, I was reminded of *Monsieur Hulot's Holiday* and the beach hotel in which the film is set. You can saunter out from the hotel in the morning straight on to the beach and bathe before breakfast, just like Hulot. The hotel where Jacques Tati shot the film is still there at St Marc near St Nazare in Britanny. A Tati afficionado I know went and stayed there recently. Apart from a little modernisation inside, nothing had changed. The place has stayed true to the film, and therefore timeless. In fact, Tati had a false entrance to the hotel constructed on the beach, making it look closer to the sands than it really is. Everything else was authentic. The dining room remains the same, except that it has one or two discreet photographs of the director and his crew on its walls. The tall, questing figure of Hulot is never still, and always inclining forward towards *je ne sais quoi*. Like a bicyclist, he must always keep on the move. This leaning man with a spring in his step somehow defies gravity. His lightness of being stands for a gallant, Quixotic, other-worldly idealism. As a man out of his time, he would have been quite at home on this beach.

Burton Bradstock is one of two seaside places within easy reach of Bridport, a traditional stronghold of sea-swimming. Of the two, West Bay, which the older inhabitants still call Bridport Harbour, is much the closer, a few hundred yards from the main part of the town, and it is where the Bridport people used to learn to swim. There was no pool, so they swam in the harbour mouth from a wooden platform with a ladder. Bridport Swimming Club had its own water fenced off by buoys and, in spite of the swell that often surged through the narrow harbour entrance, novices were harnessed with a canvas strap around the waist and climbed down the ladder into what one Bridport swimmer remembers as the 'black, icy depths'. When they reached the water the rope was pulled taut and the instructor walked along the planks above like a dog-walker. As your confidence grew, the rope was paid out and slackened, and you literally swam for your life.

The Bridport Swimming Club was pioneered by one George Elliot, the proprietor of Elliot's Stores in the town, and his friends Andrew Spiller and Colonel Roper, reputedly a one-armed swimmer. Spiller swam a great deal from the beaches and in Bridport Harbour from around 1908, in the local sea-swimming races. Their friend and contemporary swimmer,

George Wadham, was returning to England from abroad in 1918, and entering the Mersey during the blackout, when his ship collided with another. Although a strong swimmer, Wadham somehow drowned, and his body was washed up three weeks later on the Welsh coast. It was picked up by a boat whose captain actually knew Wadham, who had been wearing only his underpants and a wide money-belt containing eight guineas when his ship went down. Much to his mother's annoyance, he had a tattoo on his arm: 'George Wadham, Bridport'. He had five children, all first-rate swimmers except his daughter Gladys, who hated the sea because it drowned her father.

Gladys Wadham's daughter, Elizabeth Gale, still lives and farms in Bridport and spent her schooldays swimming in West Bay, often cycling the four miles each way from her home in Burton Bradstock to the swimming club three times a day. Her Uncle George, Wadham's eldest son, was also a famous Bridport swimmer, polo player, and a mainstay of the club. He survived two wartime shipwrecks, always took cold baths, and swam in the sea off West Bay well into his seventies. He would swim far out to sea alone as often as the weather allowed, and once swam up to a fisherman's boat a mile out to ask the time.

SECOND DAY, June 8th, 1808, we again met at *King's Mill Bridge*, where we got into a Boat, and sailed down the River to an island, a few yards below the Bridge, which we claimed a right to by Landing a Boy of the name of Jervis, and it may from henceforth be called *Jervis' Island*. From thence we sailed down the Stream to the first bed of Rushes, and having cut some Rushes therefrom proclaimed the Right of Manor down the River as far as our yesterday's Perambulation, as far as the meadow called *Lewisham Mead*. We then turned back, up the River to *Lydlinch Water*, commonly called the *Leaden Water*, which we sailed up to a Rush Bed . . . From thence round *Ham Meadow* to the Watering Place, opposite to a meadow called *Hayward's Meadow*, where John White swam across the River, with Levi Warren on his back, and landing in the said Meadow proclaimed Two Acres thereof as belonging to the Parish of Marnhull . . . John White swam across the Meadow and landed in *Brownes Meadow* on the opposite side of the River proclaiming One Acre.

from 'An account of the Perambulation of Marnhull,
upstream of Sturminster Newton on the River Stour'
by John Hussey, Lord of the Manor,
June 1808

It is striking how much water there was in the Dorset Stour two hundred years ago, and in June, too. Now it has been banked up to prevent the seasonal flooding of the water meadows that once made the valley so rich and varied through the year. As a consequence, the river winds almost invisibly through Dorset, hidden from view for much of its journey, or fenced from public access. The account of the 'Perambulation of Marnhull', which could have come from Richard Jefferies's *Bevis*, or Arthur Ransome's *Swallows and Amazons*, is a vivid evocation of the English obsession with the finer points of ownership that still separates us from contact with most of our native rivers. Like a good many of them, the Stour is in a critical condition, however beautiful it may still seem. There comes a point when so much water is abstracted from a river that it almost ceases to flow. Water is drained from it for the public supply at twenty-one different places. Industry and agriculture also take river water. Agricultural fertiliser drains into the sluggish, depleted river and favours the growth of too many algae and weeds. It is a different river from the one Hardy knew when he lived by its banks at Sturminster Newton and wrote *The Return of the Native*.

Next morning I went down to the Stour by the deserted boathouses of the Bryanston School Rowing Club. Coming round the corner of some tin-roofed sheds, I came upon a grass snake sunbathing on a bank-side lawn. She spotted me straight away and poured herself away through the grass, with her little head held up high, a flickering tongue, and the flash of white collar. It was good to see the snake; they are excellent swimmers and becoming all too rare, but I was more interested that morning in entomology. I had come to the river out of curiosity about the Blandford Bomber, an almost mythological insect that has terrorised the swimmers, and ordinary terrestrial citizens of the Stour valley, for years.

I went in off a concrete slipway and swam downstream between banks of trees in water that was still and soupy, but smelled clean enough. The bow-wave I made stretched in a wide arrowhead from bank to bank. No sign of the Bomber. I drifted gently down from the boathouses and along the Bryanston playing fields as far as the old school bathing place above the weir, now reduced to a concrete platform where diving boards once stood. Old boys who were at the school in its days of river swimming remember that their naked bathes here would invariably be accompanied by giggling from amongst the trees on the opposite bank from Blandford girls who would congregate to watch. Sometimes, too, there would be a yelp, if one of the swimmers was attacked by the Bomber.

The Blandford Bomber is a sub-species of a kind of blackfly, *Simulium posticatum*, that emerges from the river in enormous numbers in summer. Naturally, half-naked river swimmers are at special risk. The Bomber's bite can cause severe swelling and pain commonly lasting a couple of weeks, and one victim I spoke to described standing in his vegetable garden like St Sebastian in shorts, blood streaming down his legs from a low-level Bomber raid. In some years, there have been well over a thousand reported victims.

The most interesting thing about the diminutive insect is the rich and imaginative mythology which has developed around it. To local folk it has always been an alien creature, an illegal immigrant with wings, from Africa or South America. One popular version had the fly brought in accidentally with a consignment of butterflies from a South American entomo-logical expedition by the biology teacher at Bryanston school. Others firmly believed that the insect came in as eggs in African mud caked on the boots of soldiers returning from the Congo to the Blandford camp. At one stage alarming rumours that the Blandford Fly might spread river blindness, as similar blackfly species actually do in Africa, began to circulate the town. None of this had any foundation in truth, but those who felt the town was in danger of expanding too fast when the Prince of Wales proposed developing nearby Poundbury were only too happy to fan the flames. One resident actually suggested adding the words HOME OF THE BLANDFORD BOMBER underneath all the town signs on the way in. All these myths tell you far more about English xenophobia than about the Bomber, which is in fact one of our forty native blackfly species, and has been here for millions of years. It needs a specialised habitat, which the Stour happens to provide.

The secret weapon system of the Blandford Bomber is the anti-coagulant in its saliva which helps the pregnant female fly, desperate for protein, to suck your blood. Besides giving you a mild dose of haemophilia, it often causes an allergic reaction. Most victims are bitten on the legs, and the curious fact is that there have always been a lot of boys in shorts trotting about in the Stour valley. Besides Bryanston, there are three other independent boarding schools within bombing range of the river. Well-fed, and possibly even blue-blooded, successive generations of pupils have been attractive targets for the Bomber. Direct hits on boys anxious to get off lessons or games, feet up with the *Beano* in the sanatorium, must have been well-documented by matrons and teachers.

Bryanston schoolboys were segregated on their stretch of private river, which was kept free of weed for the benefit of the young oarsmen, and they were allowed to bathe in it. Most public schools seem to have colonised their own swimming holes, well-mapped in the arcane mythology of the upper classes and arranged into the characteristic hierarchies. Winchester had Gunner's Hole, the Milkhole and Dalmatia. Harrow had its own pond, where Byron swam, and Etonians bathed near the college on the Thames. Thomas Hughes gives a good idea of the importance of river-swimming in the Avon to the school life of Rugby in *Tom Brown's Schooldays*:

> This mile of river is rented, or used to be rented, for bathing purposes by the Trustees of the School, for the boys. The footpath to Brownsover crosses the river by 'The Planks', a curious old single plank bridge running for fifty or sixty yards into the flat meadows on each side of the river – for in the winter there are frequent floods. Above the Planks were the bathing-places for the smaller boys; Sleath's, the first bathing-

place, where all new boys had to begin, until they had proved to the bathing men (three steady individuals, who were paid to attend daily through the summer to prevent accidents) that they could swim pretty decently, when they were allowed to go on to Anstey's, about one-hundred-and-fifty yards below. Here there was a hole about six feet deep and twelve feet across, over which the puffing urchins struggled to the opposite side and thought no small beer of themselves for having been out of their depths. Below the Planks came larger and deeper holes, the first of which was Wratislaw's and the last Swift's, a famous hole, ten or twelve feet deep in parts, and thirty yards across, from which there was a fine swimming reach right down to the Mill. Swift's was reserved for the sixth and fifth forms, and had a spring board and two sets of steps: the others had one set of steps each, and were used indifferently by all the lower boys, though each house addicted itself more to one hole than to another. The School house at this time affected Wratislaw's hole, and Tom and East, who had learnt to swim like fishes, were to be found there as regular as the clock through the summer, always twice, and often three times a day.

The Blandford town children all learnt to swim in a different stretch of the Stour before the river-fed open-air baths were built in a 'brick tank' by the town bridge in 1924. They would plunge into the river off the railway viaduct, now demolished, to collect enamel plates from the murky bottom and, when the baths were opened, the tradition was upheld with an annual plate-diving championship. What would an anthropologist coming to Blandford from, say, the Amazon Basin make of such rituals? To the viaduct-divers, getting bitten by the Bomber must have seemed a comparatively minor risk.

Swimming back upstream, I could hardly detect any current at all, nor any sign of the elusive blackfly.

15

A SMALL WORLD

Suffolk, 2 August

ALTHOUGH MUCH RECOVERED from my Frenchman's Creek swamp fever, I still felt the need for the comfort of my moat, and drove east next day from Dorset to Suffolk to take stock of my wanderings in Wales and the West Country before striking north. When I arrived home in the night, I met a hedgehog outside my back door, floodlit when I turned on the light. He was foraging amongst the dried rose petals of a Buff Beauty. The little aesthete appeared to be eating them, crunching them loudly like crisps. He was in a world of his own, apparently oblivious of me, except that if I moved my foot or made a sound he would freeze. We continued our game of Grandmother's Footsteps for some minutes before he trotted off at surprising speed, the shiny coat of spines rippling like silk above his trousers of speckled fur.

The moat had warmed up into the almost-seventies, and I swam the sixty lengths of a mile. It doesn't look any bigger than the local twenty-five-yard swimming pool, but it is five yards longer, and about twenty degrees cooler. When the water is colder, I often swim just two, four, or six lengths: always an even number because I can only climb in and out at one end. Each length takes seventeen breaststrokes, so a mile is about 1,020 strokes. I wondered idly, as I shuttled back and forth, how many strokes I had so far put in on my peregrinations, and how many more there might be to go, and felt thankful that I was not being sponsored, and not in competition with anybody, even myself. I am just an ordinary man-in-the-pool swimmer of no more than average ability, quite happy as long as I am afloat somewhere interesting and preferably beautiful.

In *Recollections of the Lakes and the Lake Poets*, De Quincey describes the close connection between Wordsworth's inspiration and his long daily walks, and reckons up the poet's total mileage in his lifetime: 'I calculate, upon good data, that with these identical legs Wordsworth must have traversed a distance of 175,000 or 180,000 English miles.' My swimming was never going to be in that league. Nor, I feared, would I ever equal the estimated 127,575 arm strokes and 214,326 leg beats put in by Philip Rush on his 1988 three-way Channel swim. The important thing, I told myself, was that a mile in my moat felt every bit as good as a Channel swim to me, and that was all that counted.

The wild, biologically purified water of the moat is quite different from the abstract tap water, which is much more like electricity or gas: something you turn on or off, something you control, and pay for. As Colin Ward argues in his book *Reflected in Water*, to have turned water into a commodity is unnatural, because water is a gift, like air and sunlight. It wasn't until the 1920s that mains water began to arrive in many places in Britain, and people began the adjustment from the familiar taste of their own living, local water to the lifeless ubiquity that comes from a tap. Water used to be an absolute; now there are two kinds, the living and the lifeless.

All artificial, semi-natural systems need maintenance and generate work. The moat is no exception. Once the birds have flown from their nesting, the hedge along the south bank needs trimming to let in as much sunlight as possible. Wearing my goggles, I could see pondweed reaching towards the sunlight like Gaudí's cathedral spires. Newts swam straight up from the clear green depths to gulp air, then down again, like pearl divers. The immediate task was to take out the excessive waterweed. Left alone, it would simply rot down in the moat, silting it up, and eventually deoxygenating it. It would also prevent me swimming.

I used the weed-crome I have improvised out of an iron-headed garden rake heavy enough to sink when I cast it in across the moat on the end of a length of cord. I hauled in the dark bundles of weed, and pitchforked them on to the bank. In every skein of brilliant green weed something shone or wriggled, or there was the metallic glint of a water beetle. The job took me far longer than it should, because I always sort through each soggy bundle I have trawled for signs of life, rescue it, put it back in the water, and watch it swim off; young newts, a water-boatman, caddis larvae in their stick houses, or a handful of the countless water snails of different kinds that continuously filter the water. Sometimes I put them temporarily in the aquarium to observe. The water-boatman rows his vivid turquoise body just like a penguin when it swims, and the great water beetles are streamlined with the same torpedo shape. I leave each pile of weed beside the bank for a week or so to drain, and the water voles move in underneath, creating a labyrinth of runs under the cool roof of weed.

It is always hard to know how much weed to take out and how much to leave in, because all sorts of creatures, including newts and dragonflies, lay their eggs on it. I cleared the centre and left weed along the margins, which were still full of life; a single sweep of my net brought up five great crested newts, one common newt, two great water beetles, two big water snails and a mass of little ramshorn snails, like tiny ammonites. Around the banks, the subtle crimson flowers of figwort were just coming out, and when I swam, I saw one of the water voles sidling along under cover of the reed-clumps, disappearing into the bank. From water level, I observed the mating dragonflies joined in flight like refuelling aircraft, and the random progress of the dandelion clocks that drifted on the thermals over the moat. No doubt the air is cooler over the surface, as it is in the shade of the great willow at one end, where the moat-water flows up to the sky as sap, through a waterfall of rustling silver leaves.

As I had swum my mile, I kept meeting a solitary whirligig beetle making its way from one end to the other in a series of loops and circles, like calligraphy. Like the pond skaters, it wasn't swimming at all, but walking on water, on a raft of its own meniscus. Its apparently random progress set me wondering where it was going and why. But it might just as well have wondered the same thing about me. The encounter made me think about the individuality of insects, which we are used to imagine as automatons, all programmed to behave exactly alike. The year before, *Microcosmos*, a French feature film about the real lives of the insects in an ordinary field in southern France, had impressed me with its evocation of the little everyday aspects of an insect's life – preening its antennae, or making a bed in a campanula flower. Such scenes gently reminded us of our own ways; of our kinship with creatures we often think of as in a world apart.

The two directors, Marie Perennou and Claude Nuridsanay, had soon found insect individuality manifesting itself in the differing acting abilities and temperaments of their little thespians, and it had proved necessary to hold casting sessions. In one scene, a ladybird was to climb a blade of grass and take off from its tip. Out of twenty ladybirds, the directors found just three natural actors they could rely upon to play the scene as scripted. And out of several dung beetles auditioned, they found only one who would roll his dung-ball obligingly before the camera. The others had obstinately refused to demonstrate their *savoir-faire*. Amongst amphibians, I have certainly noticed marked individuation in the garden toads that often stray into the kitchen, possibly because there is an Aga in there. When I pick them up to carry them back to the vegetable garden, where they are supposed to be on pest control duty, some go quietly without a murmur, but with others there is an unseemly struggle as they try to escape, and they perfume my hands with the slightly noxious imitation venom that is supposed to make you drop them in disgust.

Swimming the last few lengths, I thought what a moated people we are, suspicious of Europe, and not at all sure about the Channel Tunnel. No wonder moats were such a popular idea in the sixteenth century, when the French, Spanish or Dutch might invade at any moment. Every Little Englander could have his own personal English Channel. I realised then that I was indeed swimming the Channel; that I was no different from Wemmick in *Great Expectations* in the little moated cottage home he invites Pip to visit:

I highly commended it. I think it was the smallest house I ever saw; with the queerest gothic windows (by far the greater part of them sham), and a gothic door, almost too small to get in at.

'That's a real flagstaff, you see,' said Wemmick, 'and on Sundays I run up a real flag. Then look here. After I have crossed this bridge, I hoist it up – so – and cut off the communication.'

The bridge was a plank, and it crossed a chasm about four feet wide and two deep. But it was very pleasant to see the pride with which he hoisted it up and made it fast; smiling as he did so, with a relish and not merely mechanically.

16

EXTINCTIONS

Suffolk, 4 August

NEXT DAY I met an otter in the Waveney. I swam round a bend in my favourite river in Suffolk and there it was, sunning itself on a floating log near the reed-bed. I would have valued a moment face to face, but it was too quick for that. It slipped into the water on the instant, the big paddle tail following through with such stealth that it left hardly a ripple. But I saw its white bib and the unmistakable bulk of the animal, and I knew I had intruded into its territory; knew also that it was underwater somewhere close, sensing my movements. It hadn't paused to puzzle over my unconventional mode of approach. It just went. It didn't miss a beat. We can scarcely be said to have communed, yet I can replay every frame of the brief encounter in slow motion, right down to the just-vacated wet log rolling back into balance, oscillating slightly, and my own emotions, a mixture of elation at a rare moment's audience with the most reclusive animal on the river (Ted Hughes called it 'a king in hiding') and shame at having interrupted its private reverie.

That otters came within a whisker of extinction in England and Wales during the late fifties and early sixties is well known. It happened suddenly and insidiously. But there are hopeful signs that they are now gradually returning to many of their traditional rivers. It has taken thirty years for the powerful poisons that killed them, organochloride pesticides like aldrin, dieldrin and DDT, to flush out of our rivers, and for people to realise that otters will only thrive in waters that are left wild and untutored, as well as unpolluted, with plenty of wet woodland, untidy wood stacks, nettles, story-book gnarled trees full of hollows, and as few humans as possible.

I was swimming ten miles from the moat, where the Waveney defines the border between Norfolk and Suffolk. It is a secret river, by turns lazy and agile, dashing over shallow beds of golden gravel, then suddenly quiet, dignified and deep. It winds through water meadows, damp woods and marshes in a wide basin that was once tidal from Yarmouth to Diss, close to its source in the great watershed of Redgrave Fen, where its twin, the Little Ouse, also rises and flows off in the opposite direction, into the Fens. With its secret pools and occasional sandy beaches, the Waveney is full of swimming holes, diving stages improvised from wooden pallets, dangling ropes, and upturned canoes pulled up on the bank. Every two or three miles you come to a weir and a white-washed watermill.

I swam on beyond the otter pool, under some sort of spell. It struck me that the animal's particular magic does not stem so much from its rarity as its invisibility. It is through their puckish, Dionysian habit of veiling themselves from view that otters come to embody the river spirits themselves. Henry Williamson knew this when he wrote his great mythic poem of Tarka the Otter. In the best traditions of spirits, the otter reveals itself through signs. You hunt for their tracks on sandbars, or for their spraint, the aromatic dung they leave behind to mark their territory, like clues in an Easter-egg hunt, under bridges or on the lowest boughs of willow or alder.

That otters were once plentiful in the Waveney was clear enough until recently if you went to the Harleston Magpie, which used to be a principal meeting place for the Eastern Counties Otter Hounds. Before the pub was altered, there were still otter masks and pads on the walls there, and up the road at the De la Pole Arms in Wingfield they have even installed entire animals, mummified in glass cases. One of my Suffolk friends inherited a red and blue tweed hunting coat that would have been worn by a member of the Eastern Counties Otter Hounds. It must have been hot work, hurrying on foot up and down the river bank, and from pub to pub along the valley, in tweed suits. A student of rural customs, he also once saw an otter pad mounted on a wooden shield with the enigmatic inscription: 'Shanghai Otter Hounds, Wortwell Mill, 1912'. Quite by chance, he stumbled on the explanation in a bookshop the following year, looking through the memoirs of an officer of the Shanghai Police, Maurice Springfield, who, it seemed, had been the Master of the Shanghai Otter Hounds, and bought some of the dogs in Suffolk around 1912 to take back with him to China. He must have been allowed to hunt them with the East Anglian contingent, perhaps by way of a road test, running down the unfortunate otter at Wortwell Mill.

In the autumn of the year before, I had crossed Suffolk to Westleton Village Hall one Saturday morning to attend a training session in animal tracking organised by the Suffolk Wildlife Trust so that we could take part in a survey of the Suffolk rivers for otters, mink and water voles. About forty of us sat in the hall studying slides of their footprints, and learning more about their ways. Small plastic tubs containing otter and mink shit were solemnly passed round. It was a bit like a wine tasting. You waved the poos under your nose, sniffed, then passed on the sample to your neighbour. Our tutor described otter spraint as 'fragrant', with something of the quality of jasmine tea, but perhaps an added nuance of fish oil and new-mown hay. A sample of jasmine tea was also circulated. You need a good nose to be a successful otter detective. We took it on trust from our tutor that otter spraint is also 'tarry and tacky'. Mink, on the other hand, have, or do, 'scats'. Scats look quite like spraint, but smell like burnt rubber or rotten fish. I felt the aesthetics of the matter posed some threat to our scientific objectivity.

That afternoon, we had all gone down to the Eel's Foot at Eastbridge, within sight of the Sizewell B nuclear power station, and walked along the bank of the Minsmere river in a crocodile looking for real live otter spraint. The Minsmere otters, no doubt observing all this from the safety of some hollow tree, would have witnessed the unusual spectacle of forty humans queuing to lie full-length on the bank and sniff small dollops of poo, making appreciative sounds. Someone spotted a bubble and all forty of us froze, bright-eyed and bushy-tailed, but it was just a bubble. I find I have since rather gone off jasmine tea.

I had met my Waveney otter downstream of Mendham Mill, near where I began my swim, diving in from a lush meadow where giant puffballs grow in late summer, once in such profusion that I mistook them at first sight for a flock of sheep, or the naked bottoms of swimmers. The breaststroke had again served me well by being so silent. I swam on downstream, over festive streamers of waving ribbon weed, brushed by the floppy leaves of yellow waterlilies, through endless meandering bends, past swans that hissed, but swam away, and turned off into the still, secret world of one of the drainage channels that run in straight lines across the flood meadows. It was five feet wide, full of moorhens and humming with insect life. Damselflies of all hues and patterns courted each other madly right in front of my nose, quite unconcerned. They even flew about *in flagrante*, performing the extraordinary feat of flying and copulating at the same time; a kind of insect Mile High Club. Huge dragonflies, some blue, some brown, hawked up and down the water right over me, or perched undisturbed on lilies. As I pushed through between the reeds, rows of bubbles rose ahead of me as eels sank deeper into the mud, or where a moorhen had dived and was swimming off underwater. Eels are the favourite food of otters, and the most nutritious of all fresh-water fish. This was just the sort of haunt that would have appealed to the animal I miss most on this river: the coypu. It set me thinking about the different attitudes we adopt towards animals. Like the otter, it was a good swimmer, had luxuriant fur, and was recently driven to extinction on this river by the activities of humans. In its special way, it has also created its own myth; indeed the legend is all that is left of it, for since it became extinct in Britain, no one, apparently, would even dream of reinstating it.

The last coypu on the Waveney was martyred like Hereward the Wake in some reedy outpost of the marshes in 1989. There used to be plenty of them pottering about incautiously along the river. I saw my last one in July 1986, preening itself on the banks of a stream at Thornham Magna in the headwaters near Eye. I also met several on canoe trips down the Waveney. Like mink, these harmless vegans originally escaped from fur farms. They are a native of South America, and probably suffered from some of the same animal racism now directed at the mink. They lived in the rivers and marshes and had all the usual rodent propensities for breeding and occasionally bingeing on carrots or sugar beet. Another of their favourite activities was to burrow teasingly into the banks of rivers and flood defences, thus whipping up even more paranoia amongst the farmers about the danger of inundating large parts of East Anglia.

The animals were good swimmers and had webbed feet. The females produced quins twice a year, and had their nipples high up on their bellies above the plimsoll line, so they could suckle their offspring as they swam alongside, keeping themselves well hidden in the marsh. Coypu could grow to over a yard long, and twelve stone in weight, so they never really had any natural predators in East Anglia. Being very big as well as very fecund and very greedy, they were too much for the Ministry of Agriculture, who, like Pat Garrett before them, hired a posse of men to hunt down every last coypu in the marshes. Cage traps the size of garden sheds began to appear up and down the Waveney, baited with carrots and sugar beet. Men in peaked caps and white vans buzzed up and down the valley. The operation dragged on for years, until someone at the Ministry twigged that it wasn't only the coypu who were adept at self-preservation. The very last thing the good ol' Norfolk and Suffolk boys at Coypu Control wanted was to see the last of the coypu exterminated. Rumour has it that they were eventually persuaded to finish off the job by the mention of generous coypu-sized redundancy packages.

The *Waveney Clarion*, community newspaper, voice of the people of the Waveney valley, was quick to recognise the rich symbolism of Coypu Control. If an animal chose to immigrate to the Marshes, why shouldn't it be welcome, whatever country it hailed from? True to its liberal traditions, the newspaper came out in full support of the colourful blend of fun-loving, gourmandising, hard-drinking Latin-American culture and general laid-back rodent mischief-making embodied in the fat-bottomed coypu and its struggle against the dastardly, jackbooted, but gullible Coypu Control. And so Mick Sparksman's Coypu Comix cartoon strip was born.

The *Clarion* was one of the most successful community newspapers of the 1970s, and circulated amongst the growing colony of romantic, liberal-minded people who lived, or had settled, in the general vicinity of the Waveney and shared the Whole Earth Catalogue ideals of the Woodstock era. Many had come from London, like me, and were working hard at the country life. Coypu was the star of the paper. Dressed in plaid trousers and a knotted scarf, he was a hippie Rupert Bear, getting up to all the tricks the Chums had hardly dared to dream about. Yet he was an innocent too. With his friends Reg Rabbit, Ramblin' Dog and Shiftless Mouse, he was forever having near squeaks with the Coypu Control officers. He had a weakness for Adnams ale, carrots, sugar beet, freshwater mussels and jugs of home-made sugar beet wine. He was always 'starving' and always escaping by hopping into disguise, as a duck, a rabbit, a scarecrow, even a snowman. He once hitched a lift to London in a Lowestoft bloater lorry, feasting and sipping Adnams all the way. In the Coypu v. Rabbit Annual Cricket Match, the rabbits got all the runs and the coypus were sixteen all out. Coypu was an active member of the bungling Coypu Liberation Army and helped organise their annual Reggae and Cider Bonfire Party. He also staged a successful raindance during one of the East Anglian droughts. His favourite hymn, whistled at times of crisis, was 'All Things Bright and Beautiful'.

I returned through the meadows, swimming upriver against the gentle current to Mendham Mill, where the painter Alfred Munnings spent his boyhood. Munnings's brother, Frederick, eventually took over as miller from their father. His nephew Robert Moss gave me a lively account of his swimming education on holidays there as a child during the First World War.

The young Robert and his cousins learnt to swim in three

stages. First, in March, they were driven forty miles in the open back of the mill's lorry to their Great-Aunt Ellen's house at Mundesley, on the north coast of Norfolk. Here, they were taken to the shore clad in striped bathing costumes and totally immersed in the sea. It was believed that wetting their heads protected them from chills. The old lady came in with them in the icy March winds, and the rule was, 'No bathe, no lunch', whatever the weather. Even during a year's sojourn with the navy in the High Arctic at 80 degrees north, Robert Moss was never so cold again.

Swimming lessons were resumed at Mendham Mill, where a huge weeping willow stood by the boathouse, and the river was shallow enough for the children's mothers to stand where the willow branches dipped in the water, but too deep for the children, who supported themselves by holding on to the tips of the willow twigs, gaining confidence from the sensation of actually swimming. Their mothers caught hold of their feet and taught their little legs the breaststroke.

They were then ready for Stage Three, in the confluence of the main river with the mill's by-pass streams. Here they learned to use the traditional technique of the village children. It depended on a bundle of reeds about five feet long and eighteen inches thick, bent into a gentle V-shape and tucked under the armpits to act as primitive water-wings. There was an ample harvest of buoyant reeds in the overflow channel between the floodgates. They feature in Alfred Munnings's painting in the Royal Academy of a young man and woman rowing their boat into the bank of reeds in that very channel. The bundle was tied with hempen yarn, usually scrounged from the man who mended sacks at the mill. It required skill to make it. It had to be tied not too tight and not too loose, so that each time it was used a few of the reeds would escape. The theory was that by the time the bundle had finally disintegrated, the aspiring swimmer would no longer need its support. It worked, too.

That evening, I went to Bungay in search of 'Bungay Beach', one of the town's swimming holes, across the marshy wastes of Outney Common, where the river kinks into a two-mile oxbow. The path led over a slender single-span footbridge of cast iron and concrete that is only sixteen inches wide; just wide enough to walk. The town reeve had it built in 1922, and its economy of design is breathtaking. It has a single handrail on one side only, and spans twenty-five feet. It is like a bridge on a willow pattern plate, and it can only be there for swimmers. The path now ran through a densely wooded island to its upstream end, where rhythmic thwackings I couldn't quite place echoed round eight giant horse chestnuts that supported several dangling ropes with wooden handles over a deep, green pool surrounded by polished roots. Two boys were drying their costumes by flogging them against the trees. Swimming up to the tangle of tree roots in deep water, I experienced one of those sudden intimations of dread, known to all wild swimmers, about what could be lurking beneath the surface. This was a perfect pike pool; what if a big pike was hiding up in one of the holes in the bank beneath the roots? I swam quickly for the open water in mid-stream.

Some weeks before, I had discussed such fears, rational or otherwise, with Stephen Rees, a plumber who swims in the Cherwell, a few miles to the north of Oxford. One afternoon in the late August of 1996, Mr Rees was swimming in one of the Cherwell mill-pools between Somerton and Upper Heyford. He swam across to the far side of the pool where a lasher, a fast-flowing channel of white water, flowed in. He was about to swim up it, but waited for his companion, catching hold of a willow branch with his left arm. Almost immediately he felt 'a bash' in his right arm, which was trailing in the fast water. He told me he thought for a moment he had hit it on a sunken branch. Then he looked down and recognised the head of a pike holding on to his forearm and saw the flash of its body as it spun away. 'It was about ten to fifteen pounds, say about two-foot-six long. All I saw was the head and a flash as it disappeared. Then the water began to turn red. I wasn't exactly tanned, so I suppose the pike saw what it thought was a white fish in fast water. I had one large rip in my arm and a lot of puncture holes. I got out straight away and had to drive back home with my shirt wrapped round the wound, feeling pretty shaky.'

Mr Rees ended up in the hospital, having eight stitches in his arm and a tetanus jab. The experience hasn't put him off river-swimming, and he has even been back to the same pool for several dips since. He also returned with rod and line to exact revenge, but only managed to catch a 4-pound specimen. Mr Rees happens to be the water bailiff for the local fishing club, so perhaps it was just that the pike recognised him. He knows there are some big pike in the Cherwell; a friend of his father caught a 34-pound fish near the millpool a few years ago. Mr Rees considers the chances of being bitten by a pike while swimming to be infinitely small. His theory is that his assailant had been trapped in the pool for some time, unable to swim back up the fast-flowing lasher, and was hungry, having eaten all the available fish. In the blur of the white water, and desperate for a bite to eat, it bit.

I heard a similar tale from the Shetland swimmer Paul Guinea. As he got out of one of the lochs there recently, an eel wrapped itself around his leg and came into the boat with him. The notion that Stephen Rees might have been the victim of Fish Rage is not to be discounted. I read in *The Times* in October 1996 of an angler in Konakovo in Russia, who landed a ten pounder and tried to kiss it. The fish sank its teeth into his nose and doctors had to prise it off, even after it had been decapitated. A friend of mine once saw a fish van in Dresden with this succinct Teutonic witticism painted on its side: SHARKS EAT PEOPLE. THEY ARE FISH. FIGHT BACK – EAT MORE FISH!

I escaped from Bungay Beach quite untroubled by anything but my own dream-pike which, once conjured into the place, could not be banished. It was a delightful place to swim, and seemed popular. I passed another young party as I departed over the swimmers' bridge. Looking down, I noticed a pair of abandoned swimming trunks floating off downstream.

The following afternoon, I swam the length of Benacre Broad at Covehithe a few miles up the coast the other side of Southwold. It is a silty fresh-water lagoon separated from the sea by a low spit of sand and shingle beach, and its days are numbered. The bleached skeleton of a single tree stood defiantly in the middle of the sands. As I swam back in water like cooled tea towards the spit, and the sea beyond, rooks cawed in the dark woods behind me, and a curlew called from the reed-beds. Long Covert, the old bluebell wood beside the broad, is blindly marching into the sea. In spring, bluebells and pink campions grow right up to the pebble strand, which is strewn with the decaying roots and stumps of oaks and syca-mores. Meanwhile, the sea was pickling the trees at the edge of the wood to extinction. First it shrivelled their leaves, then it blasted them until the trunks were white and bare. I stepped thirty paces over the beach and swam out into the North Sea.

I had come down the path along the disintegrating cliffs from the magnificent ruined church at Covehithe. Each year, the path moves further inland across the fields because great hunks of England keep falling away in the winter storms. The previous year Roger Middleditch, the beleaguered farmer, had planted carrots. By the time he came to harvest them, they were sticking out of the cliff-top and littering the beach like fish. A year later, his rows of lemming barley grew right up to the cliff and toppled over it. During the winter, Mr Middleditch had lost about twelve metres to the sea. Two years before, he had lost twenty. Since the mid-1970s, when the erosion mysteriously began to accelerate, the waves have taken forty-seven acres of the farm. It was originally nearly 300 acres; now it is 240. Less than four acres of a twenty-one acre field that led the other way to the sea from the farm in the 1970s now remain. His philosophical words came back to me as I drove away down the lanes towards Dunwich: 'In less than twenty-five years the sea will have reached the church and our farm. The church will go, the farmhouse and buildings will go, Benacre Broad will disappear.'

Richard Mabey, who has often walked the East Anglian beaches, has a sense of the way this shifting coastline may work on the mind: 'I sometimes wondered if the closeness of these unstable edges of the land was part of the secret of Norfolk's appeal to us, a reflection of a half-conscious desire to be as contingent as spindrift ourselves, to stay loose, cast off, be washed up somewhere unexpected.'

That evening, I visited Suffolk's own lost city of Atlantis, and swam at nightfall over the drowned churches of Dunwich. Pilgrims have been coming here for years to gaze at what no longer is, or to look out to sea in rough weather and listen for the fabled submarine ringing of the bells of fifty sunken churches; perhaps even to pen a line or two like: 'Where frowns the ruin o'er the silent dead.' The tide was almost up, and I swam off the steep bank of shingle by the fishermen's huts. The clattering pebbles, dragged by the swell like castanets, were amplified by the night, and by the cool evening water. The moon was strung on the horizontal vapour trail of a jet plane like a musical note printed on a page.

There never were anything like fifty churches, although a Southwold historian, Thomas Gardner, had said so in 1754 and the exaggeration stuck, along with the underwater pealing of church bells, supposedly swung by the same rampaging sea that had demolished the medieval city and port on the night of 14 January 1328. Hundreds of homes, barns and warehouses in six parishes were eventually inundated. By 1573, only two churches were left standing, and most of what remained except for All Saints' church was destroyed in the great storm of 1740. But one of the church towers still stood perfectly upright on the beach at low tide, until it collapsed in about 1900. So thorough has been the sea's erasure that almost the only historical evidence left is in documentary records. The tempest didn't just take churches, shops and houses, it took hills, a whole hunting forest, and the major harbour on which the city's prosperity was founded. It washed them all away like a sandcastle and blocked the entrance to the harbour with a gigantic shingle bank, closing it forever. The contrast between the clamour of a medieval sea-port city at the peak of prosperity and the empty, silent horizon of today is enough to set the least reflective of souls thinking about the impermanence of things. All that is left of Dunwich now (apart from the car park) is a café, a pub, two fishermen's huts, a row of houses, and a nineteenth-century church. The one medieval building still standing is the ruined twelfth-century chapel of the St James leper hospital, once well outside the city walls. There is something of the myth of Philoctetes about its survival: the outsiders have endured in the end.

The uncomfortable pebble beach shelves steeply, and I was glad to subside into the sea, swimming immediately in deep water, black and treacly after the lightness of the Waveney the day before. Far out past the breakers, shifting like a porpoise in the swell, I had the illusion that the shadowy cliffs were visibly receding. The underlying boulder clay of Suffolk erodes easily, and the layer of shingle that lies on top of it is forever being washed away and moved about by storms and tides to create an undersea topography that changes so much, they have to keep redrawing the navigation charts. I was the only bather in the cool night sea, and everything was very distant. To the north, the lighthouse at Southwold; towards the horizon, a cargo ship and a fishing boat, and to the south at Sizewell, the brash twinkling of the nuclear power station. Moving through the night, suspended in the waves over the extinct city, was like swimming over the submerged Iron-age fields of the Scilly Isles.

17
THE WASH

Norfolk, 11 August

AT FIVE O'CLOCK in the morning I set out for the north, via
the Norfolk Breckland, the northern fens, and the Wash. The
sun was still rising when I swam at Santon Downham, a
hamlet of squat single-storey foresters' cottages in yellow-grey
Cambridge brick encrusted with lichens. The place was
dwarfed by the tree canopy that surrounded it in a sudden
clearing in Thetford Forest, down avenues of lime, Scots fir
and oak. Everything seemed little; the post office, the pretty
white criss-cross iron bridge, and the Little Ouse. I bathed
from a bay of sand so fine and clean it could have been the
seaside. I have known it as a swimming hole most of my life,
since coming here as a miserable little army cadet on a school
field camp when I was about fourteen. It was high summer
and the rough, woollen, khaki uniforms were prickling us all
crazy in the heat. So were the thick socks and heavy boots.
Someone must have taken pity on us because we were piled
into the back of a truck and bumped along endless sandy
tracks until we reached this mirage of a river, stripped off, and
felt its welcome embrace like all our mothers soothing and
kissing us cool. I felt then, as now, the caress of long tresses of
viridian water crowfoot swaying and trembling in the current.
The water was crystalline and sparkling, with the sun's
brightness reflected back off the fine, chalky, gravelly bed and
fish skidding in and out of the weed sheafs. The river here is
thigh deep and its silky waters suspend you almost stationary
as you swim upstream, like the countless minnows that

nibbled shyly at my feet as I sat in the shallows, glad of the early-morning solitude.

The Little Ouse is a wadi running through the Breckland desert. It comes as a surprise to find a river of such beauty in this arid, sandy place, like coming over a barren ridge and seeing the lush palm groves of the Draa Valley south of Marrakesh. In the neolithic days when the whole area was a populous centre of industrial flint-mining, the river must have been a busy place.

I left my clothes near the bridge and walked barefoot on the warm sand along the river bank upstream for a mile and drifted back down, swimming gently with the current, pushing between the sensual weed, past more sandy bathing bays and sun-hollows in the miniature reedy dunes along the banks. The river was covered in a fine orange dusting of poplar pollen only visible at surface level, and rainbows played in the spray curtains of water-jets hosing a potato field with pumped river water. Dark chubb dodged under the banks amongst the roots of crack willows, and every river stone I turned over had a whole caddis-larva housing estate hidden beneath it.

The Little Ouse is the reflection of the Waveney, rising out of the peat pools of Redgrave Fen to flow in the opposite direction and join the Great Ouse in the Fens at Brandon Creek. I dawdled and splashed back to the bridge between banks full of the lush rankness of willowherb, reed and loosestrife, reaching it just as the post van crossed, and the first bathing party of children arrived.

Driving on through Santon Warren past Grime's Graves towards Ickburgh, I turned off and parked, and set off on foot down a woodland ride and across a meadow. I heard the brimming river before I saw it, pouring and dancing more like mountain water beside a grassy path that bordered a marshy wood. This was the Wissey, a river so secret that even its name sounds like a whisper; a river of intoxicating beauty that appears somehow to have avoided the late twentieth century altogether and to know nothing of drought or over-abstraction, let alone pollution. It was full of fish and wild flowers, and, for all I knew, crayfish and naiads, wonderfully remote from any sort of civilisation. The banks were thick with purple water-mint, forget-me-not, hawkbit, and clouds of yellow brimstones and cabbage whites browsing on the purple loosestrife along the banks. The water was polished, deep green and gold, shining from its velvet bed of crowfoot and fine gravel; it seemed quite out of time, flowing as sweetly as the river in Millais' painting of the drowned Ophelia, decked in wild flowers. (He actually painted it near Ewell in Surrey.)

The Wissey rises in a moated fish pond at a farm in Shipdham near East Dereham in Norfolk and quite soon runs through the never-never land of an army training ground, forbidden to most of us for over fifty years, left undisturbed for months on end, and, crucially, unfarmed. Thus insulated from modern agricultural pollution, the Wissey is one of the purest lowland streams in East Anglia.

Feeling like a philanderer of rivers, with the water of the Little Ouse still in my hair, I went in respectfully through some reeds and began breaststroking tentatively downstream, in water that kept changing tempo, through chalky shallows and deeper pools under the intermittent shade of alders. At times it was so shallow I hauled myself along through nine-inch riffles, cushioned on lush beds of water buttercup. Then I would round a curve and be tilted and rushed downhill almost as I had been on Dartmoor, emerging into waist-deep water full of the fleeting shadows of trout or chubb.

The Wissey probably derives its name from an Old English word, 'wise', meaning simply 'river' and an early East Anglian tribe, the Wissa, may originally have been the People of the Wissey. But how did Wisbech, further west in the Fens, come to derive its name from a river that goes nowhere near it? It is interesting evidence of the dramatic extent to which rivers have changed course over the ages in the Fens. The Wissey, which once ran all the way west to Wisbech, has been intercepted on its way by the Ouse at Denver, and thus finds its way to the Wash at King's Lynn. Many of these changes have been caused by successive drainings of the Fens, beginning with the Romans. Fenland rivers build up silt in their beds and rise up above the surrounding land. Eventually, one may burst its banks somewhere and set off across country on a new course. The rich, silted beds of the extinct rivers and dykes are called roddons, and the twisting roads that cross the Fens follow the earlier meanderings of the rivers. Lines of old willows are also signs of ancient watercourses. At Cottenham, north of Cambridge, you can walk in the course of the old Carr Dyke, and the black, silt roddon of the prehistoric River Cam is clearly visible at Welney.

A series of wooden breakwaters set diagonally into the Wissey caught my eye as I swept along in a green tunnel. They were like paddles dug in to steer a canoe, and created similar eddies in the stream. These were croyes, constructed by the Environment Agency to deflect the current and enliven the river. They would have the same effect as rocks in the course of a Cumbrian river. By forcing the current through a narrowed gap they cause turbulence, which will gradually gouge out a pool downstream, flushing away the sandy bottom to reveal gravel. Different kinds of creatures live on gravel, so this enriches the diversity of the river's life. When the river is in flood, eddy pools develop as havens for fish and other creatures to hole up; shelter from the storm. In relatively straight rivers you can offset alternate croyes and help recreate the lost meanders. It seems odd that the same people who ironed out the meanders in the first place are now busy spending more of our money putting them back in.

There wasn't a soul about, and the insect hum of a really hot day was already building up. A kingfisher streaked right over me in a searing afterburn of blue. You always hear them first, piping a shrill little whistle as they fly, as if to clear the airspace, like Mr Toad at the wheel. Iridescent, black-barred demoiselle courting couples flew in and out of the rushes or rested on them in clinches. These graceful insects are aptly christened *Agrion splendens*. Blue was the fashionable colour in this river. Delicate blue damselflies and big blue aeschna dragonflies hung in the air just above the surface, taking no notice of me at all. I felt like Gulliver, moving through the Lilliputian fleet. Stones concealed caddis larvae like pearly kings and queens, and lively water shrimps scuttled for cover.

At Didlington bridge, a mile downriver, I found myself in a

natural swimming hole complete with the regulation rope dangling from a branch. The river was deep and free of weed and I swam in a shaded bower formed by a curious miniature grove of stunted oaks planted close together and never thinned. The ornamental cast-iron bridge was wreathed in wild hops, but the Breckland around Didlington felt abandoned; I had hardly seen a living soul all morning, except hundreds of miserable-looking white ducks standing about in a distant stubble field in the shade of green awnings like disconsolate wedding guests. At the Water Board's Gauging Station by Didlington weir, swimmers were put firmly in their place by an attractive red proclamation from the Environment Agency:

WARNING

IT IS AN OFFENCE: TO JUMP INTO THE RIVER FROM A BRIDGE, LOCK OR ANY OTHER STRUCTURE. TO SWIM WITHIN 36M OF ANY LOCK SLUICE, WEIR OR WATER INTAKE OR IN ANY LOCK PEN.

MAXIMUM FINE £50. WE CARE ABOUT YOUR SAFETY.

After a picnic lunch by the little river, I drove on to Hilgay, to the south of King's Lynn, where I swam by mistake in what turned out to be the poetical-sounding Cut-off Channel, one of the main arteries of the fenland system of drains. It runs west in a big arc from Mildenhall to Denver Sluice. I realised afterwards that I had misread the map, and was under the impression I was swimming the lower reaches of the self-same Wissey, when in fact it runs parallel through the same village half a mile away. Such is the confusion of interlacing water courses in the Fens. I crossed the somnolent water by Snore Hall, an ancient pile snoozing through the centuries, half sunk in the peat, that could have been a model for Toad Hall. The channel was forty yards wide, deep, and stretched away for ever in both directions. A pair of anglers watched me as I swam over, rescuing a roach en route. It had jumped and landed on a patch of tangled, floating weed. The puzzling experience contrasted wildly with my bathe in the upper Wissey. It was like swimming in warm minestrone. Much of the surface was choked with floating islands of half-rotten weed, and I staggered out gratefully through black water into a silty reed-bed, wondering what on earth had become of the pristine river of half an hour ago. I felt profoundly disillusioned, and it wasn't until later that I realised my mistake.

Just downstream from Denver Sluice, a gigantic arrangement of lock gates that controls the main outlet of the Fen river system, I swam the Great Ouse, which runs out to the sea at King's Lynn. The river here is a hundred yards wide, and I crossed its deep, thick, brown waters glancing nervously at an armada of swans bearing down on me from the massive green, steel hulk of Denver Sluice. I felt the depth and power of the river under me, and imagined it must feel something like this to swim the Ganges. The water was grained with silt, like an old photograph. Along the far bank was a gypsy scrapyard full of dead lorries and cranes and two piebald ponies trotting about amongst alarming quantities of ragwort. (It is very poisonous to animals, but the food plant of the beautiful crimson-winged Burnet moth.)

I swam towards the chimneys of a coypu's dream: the biggest sugar beet factory in Europe. On the verge near the roundabout leading to the giant factory I had passed a miniature encampment of chrome caravan, lorry, dog kennel and a small cabin cruiser up on chocks. I had entered gypsy country here, and it continued all the way to Wisbech. Horses are still grazed by gypsies along the river banks, but their numbers have declined since the days when fenland farmers like Coley Ambrose at Stuntney kept and bred over 200 working horses. The gypsies used to go beet-hoeing, and pea-, onion- or potato-picking all over the Fens. There was fruit-picking too, alongside the village women. I had met a woman in Wilburton a few weeks earlier who described how they followed the seasons' rhythms in their freelancing: 'We would start beet singling, then gooseberries, then plums, then apples, then potato-picking, then more apples, then we would be packing them in the sheds.' The days were often full of fen mists: 'We once went potato-picking and it was so foggy we thought we were alone, but when it cleared, the field was full of people.'

With one eye on the living swans, I almost swam into a dead one on a last journey to the sea, and when I hoisted myself to the bank, I couldn't avoid coming out like the Green Man, covered in duckweed. It was hard to accept, rowing myself through this turbid cocktail of dilute fenland, that the Great Ouse at this point included the sparkling Little Ouse and Wissey, the limpid Granta, the sacred Lark, and the sweet springwater of the Wicken Lode, all converging into the Great Ouse to run down to the Wash at King's Lynn. The Great Ouse. It sounded and felt like the origins of life itself, where we all began, where we all end, the Alpha and Omega of the Fens, the gateway of all the eels in thirteen counties, a port of call both ways on the Sargasso run. The swim and its setting were so bizarre that only the duckweed on my towel reminded me, days later, that it wasn't all a dream.

I drove on west, pressing deeper into the Fens, past houses tossed this way and that on sinking raft foundations, through Salters Lode and Nordelph to Well Creek, where I bathed in the Middle Level Drain in the evening sunshine. Well Creek is a narrow canal that follows the course of the original River Wissey, and forms a navigation link with the Old River Nene, the Twenty Foot River, and the Old Bedford River. It crosses over the Middle Level Drain at this point in an aqueduct, which I swam through for the perfectly good reason that I had never swum an aqueduct before, or at two different levels in the same place. There were some big sluice gates here controlling the Middle Level Drain, and water gushed into the canal, pumped up from the drain below.

A gang of boys was busy clocking up hundreds of pounds in Environment Agency fines, climbing up the sluice gates and leaping twenty feet into the Middle Level Drain. The canal narrowed to not much more than boat width where it passed through the aqueduct, and the boys further amused themselves by leaping aboard each narrowboat that chugged through, swaggering its full length in their swimming trunks, then leaping off the other side, to the dismay of its crew and much shouting on both sides. This, they explained to me, was traditional; a fenland pirate game since time immemorial.

At first disposed to regard me with suspicion, even hostility, as an oldie trespassing on their territory, the Well Creek Gang perceptibly mellowed when I executed quite a respectable, if furtive, dive into the Middle Level Drain then swam along it for a quarter-mile, past a charming waterside cottage with an old wooden landing-stage, orchard and vegetable garden. The scent of several thousand cultivated roses drifted across the water from the surrounding fields. The river was about thirty yards wide, surprisingly clear and warm, and as I swam due west up the middle, deep gold in the sun. It was the most beautiful drain I had ever seen.

All this was really a rehearsal for the grand swim I had in mind for later, by way of crowning the day, in the Wash itself. Returning to the aqueduct and sluice, I swam under them both to the far side with less than six inches' headroom above the surface. I blame Enid Blyton for such laddish behaviour; the Famous Five were always swimming in and out of smugglers' caves or in forbidden canals, usually at night, signalling to one another with torches. Everyone in Enid Blyton books always carried a torch, and the batteries never went flat. The improbable adventures were amongst my earliest stories, so I have only to see a sluice, or an aqueduct, and I am six years old again. There were no fines for the Famous Five; only a stern 'Now then children, what *is* the meaning of this?'

In the dusty sunset glow, I motored over towards the Wash to swim at last in the wake of King John, whose treasure has been lost in the quicksands since 1216. From the map, I had chosen Gedney Drove End as the most likely-looking starting point, on the grounds that it sounded remote and romantic. It was certainly remote. I parked outside the pub, then walked through a cornfield on a lonely footpath, almost obliterated by the plough, so that it constantly threatened to edge me off into the dyke. (De Quincey says this is what Wordsworth did to all his walking companions. He would start off on your left and edge you inexorably over to the right until you were nearly in the ditch, at which point you would move round to his left, and he would veer off the other way.)

I eventually reached the sea wall, a thirty-foot grassy bank with steep wooden steps and a rickety handrail. There were notices about the dangers of the tides and creeks, and another depicting a swimmer with an ominous red line through him. He looked remarkably like me. In spite of all this there was a stark beauty about the minimal landscape in the failing light. The creeks and marshes stretched away to oblivion and a watchtower for the RAF shooting range here was silhouetted against the sky. There was nothing but the last gurgling trickles of the departing tide.

Out on the horizon were three or four hulks, small *Belgranos* for the planes to strafe and bomb on weekdays. The watchtower door was heavily padlocked, yet someone had been unable to resist the opportunity to put up a notice: NO UNAUTHORISED PERSON BEYOND THIS POINT. There was a picture of an unauthorised person with a diagonal line through him. I fancied he, too, looked uncannily like me, and realised that the same compulsive urge that makes a great graffiti artist is also at work amongst the bureaucrats. I ventured gingerly out on to the marsh, a desert of cracked mud and little meandering creeks that suddenly came to life with dozens of crabs, running for their lives into the craters whilst gesturing at me defiantly, not to say rudely, with their front claws.

I had tiptoed past yet another sign: DANGER. UNEXPLODED BOMBS AND MISSILES. IT IS ILLEGAL AND HIGHLY DANGEROUS TO EXCAVATE ANY OBJECTS FOUND ON THE MARSH. THEY MAY EXPLODE AND KILL YOU. Now that was more like it. No piddling £50 fines for would-be paddlers, samphire-gatherers, or King John's treasure-hunters in the Wash. Just death. I glanced guiltily at the loudspeakers on the watchtower, half expecting a ticking-off. Peering into the middle distance I made out more targets planted in the mud like unauthorised persons stuck fast in their wellingtons.

I had been naive in imagining I might swim in the Wash. Even if it hadn't had the plug pulled out of it, I would probably have appeared on someone's radar screen and been strafed. I retired to the New Inn at Gedney Drove End, noted for its collection of several hundred china pigs, where I got my head in the trough, then zig-zagged back down the footpath, after the manner of Wordsworth, to camp for the night, an unauthorised person, on the lonely rim of the unswimmable Wash.

204

18

NATANDO VIRTUS

Derbyshire, 12 August

AS I ROLLED up my dewy tent in the early mist, it struck me that camping by the Wash had been just the right response to the place; the only kind of roots anyone should put down in such an uncertain mixture of land and sea, where the coastline was forever being redrawn. I love East Anglia's wide horizons, but if I stay too long I can feel becalmed; there's enough Celt in me to need the turbulence of the hills too, and the dashing upland rivers and streams.

I drove out of Lincolnshire across country, past Sherwood Forest and Nottingham (now re-christened 'Robin Hood Country' on the signposts), to the southern extremities of the English highlands in the Peak District of Derbyshire, where the rivers Derwent, Wye and Dove flow down to join the Trent in the Humber at Hull. Things changed dramatically at Matlock, yet another once-successful spa, as I wound up into the Peaks along the steep-sided valley of the Derwent, and then the Wye. I was unable to resist a detour at Ashford-in-the-Water to walk up to Water-cum-Jolly for a dip in this lively, wooded trout river. I still don't know for certain that the place-name wasn't a fiction on the part of the map-makers; that my swim in the big, deep, brimming mill-pool, walled by a limestone cliff, with a forty-foot wide cataract thundering into the mill-race beneath a shuddering wooden bridge, wasn't a mirage of the long-distance swimmer engendered by the rigours of the long road, and that enticing, almost pidgin English name. 'Water-cum-Jolly' seemed to embody in three words the very essence of the joys of swimming.

I arrived at Hathersage in time for a pre-lunch dip in the village swimming pool, an open-air, heated, miniature lido set high on a hillside with spectacular views of the Peaks on all sides, almost within sight of Kinder Scout, Jacob's Ladder and Mam Tor, but only twenty minutes' drive from Sheffield. The free-thinking traditions of the village stretch all the way back to Little John, first of the green activists, who is buried in the churchyard.

I had never seen a pool with a bandstand before; an imposing, octagonally-roofed, regency-looking structure shared with the bowling green just uphill. Inside, the pool was set in lawns, with the smell of just-scrubbed wooden benches in the changing sheds, copper beeches and sweet chestnuts, and a grandstand along one side. From the outside, the place looked more like a half-timbered barn, with hipped, tiled roofs and weather-boarded walls. There were tennis courts beside it, and a busy restaurant and café open to everyone. Everything was delightfully, and deliberately, unmodernised. The pool clearly occupies a central place in the social life of the village.

I immediately felt welcome, and all my frustrations at the Wash dissolved in the blue water, which was heated to a positively effusive 84 degrees fahrenheit. The pool was full of healthy-looking Hathersagians, all steaming back and forth, and fearfully good swimmers. No wonder that on hot days people queue round the streets of Hathersage eager for a dip, and the pool has been known to have to close its doors after the first hour of business.

I felt I had swum straight into the pages of Iris Murdoch's novel *The Philosopher's Pupil*, set in an English spa-town called Ennistone, where life centres around the swimming pools and baths, all naturally heated by the spa water, bubbling from hot springs. The motto over the doors of the Ennistone Baths is *Natando Virtus*, and the townspeople all swim there seven days a week, morning, noon and night, introducing their children to the infants' pool at the age of six weeks. As a focus of life in the town, the baths fulfil a similar role to the agora in Athens. 'Serious swimming', says the narrator, 'was a matter of pride in our town.' In the Hathersage pool café, swimmers were reading the papers and tucking into hearty, Little John-style lunches in the convivial north-of-Watford atmosphere that is such a welcome surprise to the alienated southerner: 'Afternoon, Mr Johnson. Have you got that quid you owe me?'

'Can we talk terms?'

The pool was originally given to the people of Hathersage by George Lawrence, a successful Methodist manufacturer of razor blades in Sheffield, and is still managed by the parish council. It used to be fed by a spring in the hillside, and heated by a coal boiler. When it grew muddy, the villagers would spend two weeks emptying it, and another two refilling it. The helpers all got free swimming. For years, it was closed on Sundays, according to Mr Lawrence's decree, but the village has elected to relax such puritanism, risking the charge of the visiting evangelist who came to Iris Murdoch's Ennistone and cried out, 'You have dethroned Christ and worship water instead.'

From the sparkling surface of the pool, I imagined the orchestral *thés dansants* that might have been held around the bandstand on such afternoons as this. It set me thinking about the close relationship between music and swimming. Rhythm is one of the principal pleasures of swimming, as well as its essence. I often have a tune in my head in the pool, provided it isn't being drowned out by muzak (chlorinated music), one of the best reasons I know for going native in a river or the sea. On the other hand, it might be interesting to think about using waterproof transducers to create an underwater sound system and perform live music from the poolside through the medium of water itself. Like whalesong, which can carry for 400 miles under the sea, music heard underwater is magically clear and wonderful.

Feeling distinctly jolly after my swim, I settled down on a bench in the grandstand with a mug of hot chocolate and the newspaper, next to a maths teacher relaxing in a bathing costume with a red biro and a stack of fourth-form equations. She told me the bandstand was always used during gala week, when the bunting was out, and brass bands would play. It is out of use at the moment because its guardrail doesn't conform to European Community standards.

I discovered another village pool three days later, in the Yorkshire Dales at Ingleton, built by the village miners in 1933. All the labour was voluntary, and the open-air pool was originally filled by a pipe running down from the River Doe beside it, and emptied on Sundays by opening a sluice at one end. Everyone would come down and help ritually scrub it out, and it would be filled again on Monday, gradually warming up over the week. One way of taking the chill off the pool, they reckoned, was the immersion heater effect of a body of swimmers at 98.4 degrees fahrenheit. (The collective noun for cold-water swimmers would be, perhaps, a shiver.) It was deep enough to dive into from the changing-room roof, and nobody ever suffered any ill effects from the unchlorinated river water. The pool may have been cold, but it was always free, and there were midnight swims after the Saturday night dances. In 1974, the Ingletonians tiled their pool, installed a boiler, and began charging incredibly modest admission fees. It was a delicious 82 degrees fahrenheit when I went in, and of course, heating the pool had rendered it even more magnetic as the self-supporting social centre of the village.

19

An Encounter with Naiads

Yorkshire Dales, 13 August

THERE IS A long tradition of wild swimming in Yorkshire. Sweating out a shift in the heat and dust underground, coal miners must have cast their thoughts longingly, in summer, towards the abundant cooling rivers and becks of the limestone country of the Dales. In no other industry was communal, ritual bathing such a deeply essential part of life; there were always showers or baths at the head of the pit. Getting into water is still second nature in this part of the world. Hill walking and cycling have always been popular in the north, and the Dales are full of tempting swimming holes to cool one's weary frame. The springs and underground streams burst everywhere from the labyrinthine limestone. Every village has its favourite places, some of them secret and difficult to reach, and often actually called this or that 'hole', like Foss Hole and Chemist Hole, in the superb River Doe above Ingleton.

The Yorkshire Dales have been shaped and carved by rivers. The Swale, Ure, Nidd, Wharfe, Ribble, Aire, Skirfare and Tees all rise in these hills, with the Lune running south to Lancaster out of Cumbria, and the Eden running north to Carlisle. With such abundance of water, few places are richer in wild flowers than limestone country, and Richard Mabey, an aficionado of the Dales, had intrigued me with a chance remark that set me off on a quest for a particularly remote and enchanting swimming hole above Littondale. His caution that I would probably have to abseil down to it only increased my curiosity. He described a clear tufa pool hidden in a cleft somewhere up a beck, guarded by a limestone canyon on the walk between Arncliffe and Malham. This was too interesting not to pursue, and in any case I couldn't get the place-names he mentioned out of my head: Cowside Beck and Yew Cogar Scar.

At the Falcon Hotel on the village green in Arncliffe, I was awoken early by the screaming of swifts, and a swallow singing in the eves over my open sash-window. It reminded me of home. The little hotel is a haunt of trout anglers on the River Skirfare, a tributary of the Wharfe, and nothing much seemed to have changed since 1950. It was just the sort of place I could imagine T. H. White holing up in for the weekend.

I set out across country towards Malham, climbing up along the top of the steep-sided gorge that contained the beck. The tiny figure of a cyclist laboured up the road on the other side towards Settle – 'a cruel road', they called it in the pub. Everything here carried the signs of use: the path, the sheep-holes worn brown into the hillside, the polished pine handholds of the stile ladders. Massive stone walls plunged almost vertically down the steep sides of the dale to the beck in perfectly straight lines, and the limestone strata showed through the grass like flock in a threadbare sofa.

The sun had come out, and glinted in the Cowside Beck, clearly audible three or four hundred feet below. About two miles further on up the high ridge path I came to a declivity diving towards the increasingly distant bottom of the gorge. There was no path, and the descent was so precipitous that it was impossible to see more than a few yards ahead at a time, but I decided to take the plunge, more or less literally, towards the beck. It was hard to know, even with the help of the map, whether I was heading down towards Yew Cogar Scar, the spectacular cliffs that walled parts of the gorge. They live up to their name with a perpendicular forest of gnarled yews that somehow clings to the rock face. The escarpment I hoped I was going down was Cowside. The descent was so dizzy it was hardly even grazed, so there were tussocks full of ankle-sized potholes. A stiff breeze funnelled up the gorge threatening to shake off the gaudy yellow-and-black-striped humbug snails that clung to harebells and yellow bedstraw. I felt for them, hanging on for dear life too, and creeping blindly down. The really amazing thing was that there were trees. Bent old rowan, ash and hawthorn grew from the most daring rocky outcrops, probably the only places where a sapling would have escaped being grazed. Fortunately, I had brought a climbing rope which I looped round a trunk wherever I could, and so slithered my way in stages to the bottom.

By now I was feeling the thrill of the chase, glancing eagerly about in search of hidden pools. I had landed in the canyon bottom just upstream from the cliffs of yew. The first thing I saw was a black rabbit disappearing into a stone wall, then another. Was there a whole colony of them marooned in here? Looking up at the imposing rocks, I could have been in California. I had no idea how I was going to climb out again. I followed the beck upstream, rounding each bend and contour with the warm glow of anticipated pleasure.

At length I came upon a small spinney of ash by the banks, and the promising sound of a waterfall. And there, just below, was the elusive tufa pool and the sparkle of animated water chasing its tail around in it. It was very nearly circular, and rimmed with moss. At one side, natural steps led into its perfectly clear depths, which ran to eight or ten feet by the fall. I stripped and dived in. It was so cold, I might have flung myself into a bed of nettles. Then came the heady rush of the endorphins, or 'endolphins' as a friend once called them, the natural opiates with which the body anaesthetises itself against the cold, and the adrenaline. As the *Oxford Textbook of Medicine* cautiously says, the mood changes they induce 'are difficult to validate scientifically, although feelings of well-being seem to occur'. For swimmers, my friend's inspired malapropism goes straight to the point: you come up feeling like a dolphin. The Cowside Beck dashed towards me like a wind under the trees, and spouted smoothly between two rocks to hurtle into the pool, which I now explored, feeling beneath the bubbling surface with hands and feet, diving under, and swimming against the current to hover in the middle. Immediately uphill, a tributary stream cascaded down a series of waterfalls and saucered pools over mounds of tufa accumulated through the centuries. If it weren't so natural and ancient, it would be easy to mistake tufa for the kind of artificial rocks you see at the Chelsea Flower Show. It is really petrified water that has built up, like the fur in a kettle, from the lime that is carried in the streams. It is voluptuous and spongy and loves to dress itself in fine mosses and algae.

I flopped out on to a rock, up the grassy side, and clambered, dripping, to bathe in a second pool some thirty yards upstream. The boisterous water took my breath away all over again and I returned to the circular pool, where I swam down once more to the bottom under the waterfall and surfaced inside it, coming out with head, hands and feet frozen, feeling wonderful. I thawed them in the gentle, dished, tufa pool, like a warm bath after the frigid beck, its water slipping over the sunlit stone.

I wondered how many walkers must have slid into these tempting waters, remote and hidden though they are. Sunlight reflected back off the rounded white rocks on the bottom, and soft cushions of fine, tight grass and thyme were scattered languidly around the margin, as though for some nocturnal gathering of the nymphs. J. B. Priestley, when he was travelling about these parts in 1933, met a woman who lived in one of the remote Dales farmhouses, 'a solid West Riding country-woman and not one of your fanciful arts-and-crafts misses', who swore that she saw faeries dancing on the hillside. There are still some places left in England that have unquestioned magic about them. This pool had me enchanted; I could have stayed there quite happily all day and night with the attendant naiads. But a man must take care never to kiss a water sprite. As the English folk-song 'George Collins' relates, it will lead to certain death, and that of any woman he subsequently kisses. The old pagan deities may have fled much of our land, but they have not yet forsaken all their haunts.

Made ravenous by the cold water, I demolished a prosaic sandwich lunch reclining on a cushion of thyme, with my head resting on a clump of moss the size and texture of a British Railways antimacassar, then decided to climb up alongside the tributary gill, through a scree of scattered rock, past the occasional modest waterfall, towards some caves at the top of Cowside. Sleepy dor-beetles crept about in the grass, and Yorkshire rabbits darted out everywhere, more agile than their lazy Suffolk cousins, bouncing between the rocks like bagatelle balls. The head of the steep cleft was a mass of springs spouting extravagantly over a giant sponge of tufa, decked out in mosses, ferns, liverworts and algae. I sat in the cave and ate another cheese sandwich, spiced with sorrel leaves I had gathered on the way up, grateful for the generous hint that sent me to this wild and beautiful spa.

In the morning, I drove over to Malham and walked out of the village in bright sunshine towards the headwater of the River Aire above the spectacular Gordale Scar waterfall. Some of the grazing meadows here contained great pastel blue pools of meadow crane's-bill, and it lined the roadside verges, with here and there a patch of the striking magenta bloody crane's-bill. The warm weather, and the previous day's rain, had brought on an abundance of grasshopper song and swelled the streams. Ascending the mass of tufa beside the waterfall, I reached the edge of the limestone pavements that stretch away above it to the north, and to the source of the Gordale Beck at the remote Middle House Farm near Malham Tarn. By the time it reaches Malham, the beck has gathered enough water to be worth calling a river, the Aire, that will flow on through Skipton and Leeds and into the brown expanse of the Humber at Goole, above Hull.

The path levelled out along a ridge, and I dropped down the stepped rock walls to the beck, half-hidden in a steep cleft as it approaches the waterfall. Here there were pools, dished from the yielding limestone and built up like coil pots out of tufa. It was sheltered, sunny, and warmed by great natural solar panels of white rock. I took advantage of the utter solitude for a delicious limestone plunge. I chose my bath with care, and soon settled on the right one, upholstered in moss and deep enough for an icy wallow in the hot sun. Rolling out, I contrived to lie reading on the rustic poolside with my toes in the exquisite coolness.

It wasn't long before I was joined by a leech, exploring my pool with great thoroughness and the most elegant swimming. It is hard to say how big it was because it kept changing shape, looping and stretching out its black stocking of a body as women do when they're trying tights for quality in Marks & Spencer. It varied between an inch-and-a-half and three-and-a-half inches, and it was the most graceful aquatic creature I have ever seen. Like pigs, leeches suffer in our language from the abuse of their name. There was a self-contained air about it as it inspected the rim of the pool, as well there might be, since leeches are hermaphrodites, like their relatives the earthworms. It seemed in no hurry; the leech family are an easy-going lot who put off breeding until they are six or seven, and can live to the age of fifteen. Of our eleven native species, only four actually suck blood. The rest prey on molluscs and small aquatic creatures and swallow them whole. A single meal will apparently keep a leech going for six months, a fact that causes Theodore H. Savory to recommend them as pets in *The World of Small Animals*. I was lucky enough to be taught zoology by Savory, who kept leeches in his laboratory at school, a magic land full of books, belljars and butterfly nets, peopled by Latin-labelled living spiders (his first love) peering at us bi-peds from mahogany-framed glass pens. I had felt instantly at home in his class-room, recognising the comforting aroma of my suburban bedroom, crammed as it was with semi-derelict vivariums full of my scaled and creeping familiars: lizards, newts, slow-worms, stick insects, tree frogs and white mice.

My leech could well have been a medicinal leech, although it hadn't shown much interest in my toes, or my arm when I put it into the water, and I imagine we must have been in there bathing together. Medicinal leeches seem to have become rare by 1802, when Wordsworth wrote 'Resolution and Independence', in which he meets an ancient leech-gatherer by a pond who tells him:

Once I could meet with them on every side;
But they have dwindled long by slow decay;
Yet still I persevere, and find them where I may.

However, they now seem to be relatively abundant in places. And they can still save lives: there is even a successful leech-farming business in Wales supplying hospitals all over the world. There are fish leeches, too, and the duck leech, which feeds inside the noses of birds. In order to spread to new habitats, a leech with wanderlust needs animals to come to its pond or stream and drink. Once attached, it can be carried to the next watering-hole by the unwitting host. Here in Gordale, leeches could well be carried by sheep.

An emperor dragonfly soared out over the waterfalls into the infinite blue air of the ravine beyond, and my leech continued its graceful undulating swim round the pool, then disappeared into a miniature cave in the tufa. There were tadpoles in there too, quite undeveloped, water shrimps and caddis larvae, and a drowned black beetle. Having tasted, and bathed in, the sweetness of the innocent Gordale Beck, it seemed extraordinary that its journey through a hundred miles of our land would turn it so quickly into the polluted tide of Humber. W. H. Auden's line: 'A culture is no better than its woods' holds true for rivers too.

20

SWIMMING WITH ANGELS

North Yorkshire, 16 August
SATURDAY DAWNED MAGNIFICENTLY blue, and the banks of the Wharfe at Bolton Abbey presented an almost biblical scene. On a bend in the river below the abbey ruins, there is a wide sandy beach and I fully expected to see John the Baptist rise up amongst the bathers and bless them all for having the sense and self-reliance to go swimming in the wild. It was still only eleven o'clock, and half Harrogate, Bradford and Leeds were already in the river. The scene was a hybrid of an L. S. Lowry beach picture, and Stanley Spencer's *Christ Preaching in the Thames at Cookham*. The thermometer was rising steadily towards the eighties, and Yorkshire was at play.

No one was making any money out of all this enjoyment on the river – least of all the Duke of Devonshire, to whom the land belongs – unless you count the busy restaurant and café on the banks. By bathing here for years, the Yorkshire people have established a kind of right, which, very sensibly, the Duke appears to recognise. I began swimming at once, from a point upriver where the water is forced into an exhilarating dash between massive rocks, then eases into a saunter through some of the deeper pools. Swimming and wading by turns as the capricious river bed allowed, I arrived at length at the populous beach below the abbey, dried off in the sun, and walked back for an ice cream at the café. It was like an inland Blackpool; men in deckchairs listening to the cricket, little football games everywhere, lilos and rubber boats. Here was a linear natural lido of spectacular beauty; proof that river-bathing and people in large numbers need do no damage to a river.

On the road past Skipton, on the way north-west towards Ribblesdale, Settle and Ingleton, I found myself at one of the most northerly points on the English canal-system: Gargrave on the Leeds and Liverpool Canal. It was two o'clock, and by now really warm, and I had been thinking about a swim in a canal for some time. Somehow, though, I had kept putting it off. I had heard rumours of a beach on the Venetian system of canals in Birmingham, somewhere near Spaghetti Junction, but no one seemed to know exactly where it was. I had contemplated the oily waters of the Caledonian Basin on the Grand Union Canal from the deck of a narrowboat, and I had even got as far as dipping a toe in the Monmouthshire and Brecon Canal near Talybont-on-Usk. Something was inhibiting me, I didn't know what, but I was going to have to cure myself. After all, according to John Betjeman in 'A Shropshire Lad', the ghost of Captain Webb, the original Channel swimmer, swam in the canal in his native Dawley, near Ironbridge:

> When Captain Webb the Dawley man,
> Captain Webb from Dawley,
> Came swimming along in the old canal
> That carried the bricks to Lawley.

I was never going to find a canal in better weather conditions than this, so I stopped the car, crossed a field to a lock, and went up the towpath to a quiet spot, wondering about old bicycles, prams and supermarket trolleys on the canal bed. I didn't dive. I went into the chocolate water feet-first off the stone parapet, expecting deep water. To my amazement, it was only knee-deep at the edge, shelving to a mud bottom I hardly dared touch, four feet six inches down in the middle. I reflected that barges are shallow-draught boats and don't need any greater depth, except in locks. The thought of the locks scared me. The idea of being sucked under the ponderous wooden gates was not appealing. But the immediate danger, I knew, was more from swallowing than being swallowed.

It was a good wide canal, with fine elevated views across the countryside north of Skipton. When the first narrowboat passed there was plenty of room for both of us, and the only danger came from the wash, which threatened a taste of the dubious-looking water, or a mouthful of gudgeon. I kept my mouth firmly shut and swam a token mile of the hundreds that thread this country, to just short of the next lock, and the Anchor Inn. The water was comfortably warm, and, slightly to my disappointment, there were no supermarket trolleys or prams. Not even a bicycle frame. I passed the Gargrave cricket match on my way, and could have continued swimming in the same direction all the way to Burnley, Blackburn, Manchester, Liverpool, Stoke-on-Trent, Birmingham and London. Or back the other way to Leeds and Sheffield. Instead, I climbed out (not always such an easy thing in a canal) and began to stroll back in my trunks.

It was by now such a hot day that I attracted little attention amongst the walkers on the towpath or the bargees. I was glad to have swum in a canal, and to sense the years of working traffic in the worn towpath flagstones and the churned water. I have friends who claim to have swum in the Kingsland and the Paddington Basins on the Grand Union in London and lived. Some of the canals in Yorkshire, whose names evoke the industrial past (the Huddersfield Narrow, the Aire & Calder), pass through impossible-looking gradients on their way across the Pennines. Between Hebden Bridge and Todmorden, the Rochdale Canal has thirteen locks in six and a half miles, and the annual sum of human labour involved in opening and shutting lock gates on the Calder and Hebble canal between Halifax and Wakefield must be enormous.

It was over tea at Bernie's Caving Café in Ingleton, after a swim in the village pool the miners built, that I heard of Hell Gill. Gavin Edwards, an Aysgarth potholer, described a hidden canyon, a deep gash in the limestone filled with white water dropping steeply for two hundred feet, on the remote moors near Garsdale Head, just beyond the top of Wensleydale. Not many people knew of it, he said, but it was possible, given the right conditions, to descend the gorge through the water. The way Gavin described the place immediately seized my imagination and I resolved to go and find it. I didn't realise at the time quite how much the experience would take over my dreams in the weeks to come.

I was sharing a table with a group of potholers, all regulars, tucking into big plates of chip butties and sausages. Considering that in potholing your life can depend on the ability to squeeze through a letterbox crack or a hosepipe cave, I was mildly shocked. It was interesting how many were first-generation descendants of miners. They agreed that the instinct to go underground was probably in their blood; it didn't seem so frightening to them because they had grown up amongst miners. The café was the HQ of the local caving mafia, full of equipment for sale and decorated with posters and photographs of the insides of immense caverns festooned with stalactites, or cavers hanging upside-down over raging underground torrents. There were ropes, harnesses, helmets, lamps, and big maps on the wall showing the astonishing labyrinth of interconnecting caves and potholes that surround Ingleton, like the London tube map. You could plan your route for the day, setting off down the Wormway, perhaps, to Bloody Thigh Rift, through Monster Cavern to the Wurlitzer via the Keel Hauler, nip down Ramsden's Crawl, change at Sausage Junction and resurface through Ratbag Inlet. The place had something of the atmosphere of the warren, with dozens of tough, skinny, burrowing people busy exchanging notes and tall stories of the Underground. Potholing discoveries are earnestly discussed and christened like new strategies in chess: The Doctor's Dilemma, The Squeeze Box. The need to communicate detailed directions in this twilight world has sparked off the inventive patois you always find in sub-cultures. The 'New Routes' book hangs on the wall full of improbable instructions for climbing rocks or navigating potholes:

SWINDALE: THE CAT'S KNACKERS 6a (easy). Wall right of Castration Crack. Start right of above – pull through roof easily on left to small ledges, place wires in Castration Crack (yes, I am a coward) and step right immediately above the roof into the centre of the wall and climb delicately up to the faint crack of First Cut – up this and Right to finish.

Jan and Andy. Aug '97.

That evening, I swam alone at nightfall in one of the village swimming holes: the black pool below the Beezley Falls on the River Doe. The falls drop twenty feet down rock walls to a deep pool, with wooded cliffs rising perpendicular either side of it for forty feet. I undressed on a ledge by the pool, noticing all the right signs; the worn, precarious bough of an old stag-headed oak at the cliff-top stretching high over the water like a gibbet, dangling a frayed and weather-beaten rope. The air had cooled suddenly under a clear sky and the water felt thick with mystery when I climbed down the shadowed rocks, dived, and swam across the eddy to the waterfall, circling the boiling epicentre. In the night, the place was that much noisier, with a sound like continuous wild applause; at once beautiful and menacing. It seemed to swell and die, then redouble, then fade again, as though a ghostly audience were all about the rocks. Swimming through invisible force-fields of turbulence, I rolled over on my back and looked up at the night sky past the brooding rock and the canopy of oak. The sleek, black water tasted fresh and peaty as I leant into the shuddering current with each new stroke in the deep, high-sided cauldron. It brimmed over a slender lip of rock into a second waterfall that in turn sent others dashing down the steep ravine, winding darkly out of sight towards Ingleton, echoing through the lichened oaks. I felt acutely alone, not so much lonely as a rank outsider to this adventurous place, one of the 'offcumden', as Ingleton people still say; literally 'people who have come from afar'.

Curious to witness the daytime comings and goings in this theatre of seething water, I returned at noon next day to an astonishing scene. Swimmers thronged the banks, above the waterfall, in the pool, on every rock. Some even launched themselves recklessly into the falls themselves, tumbling

220

helter-skelter into the pool below. Before a gallery of admiring teenage girls across the water, the boys queued up by the worn oak bough I had noticed the night before. It seemed to have no life in it at all, yet was springy enough to bear the weight of the average Ingleton daredevil. Boys teetered out along the touch-and-go springboard to a point directly above the centre of the pool, poised themselves, and jumped. They seemed to hang suspended for an age, treading the air, before hitting the water. I half-expected the crack of the tired branch snapping, but it never came. Some swung out on the rope, judging the moment to let go and sail on into the void, rising before falling. Once you kicked off, you had to let go else you would be dashed against the cliff. The informal air-traffic control was too haphazard for swimming under the waterfall, so I swam in the river pools above the falls, grappling my way upstream from pool to pool, pausing to cool in the eddies in rocky bays along the banks.

I had made my camp two miles away in Kingsdale the night before, in the lee of the Cheese Press Stone, overlooking the single-track road from Ingleton to Dent. Beneath me, hidden under the limestone, ran a seven-mile system of underground rivers, submerged passages and flooded caves. A group of skilled and daring cave-divers, centred around Ingleton and Dent, have dived and swum through miles of these sub-terranean streams, exploring and mapping them for the first time. I had naively enquired in Bernie's Café whether I, too, might swim underground. 'It all depends how long you plan to stay alive,' was the reply.

In the morning, a swaddling of white mist hung over the rivers that converge on Ingleton as I breakfasted in my camp. A pair of rabbiters came downhill off the moor, out with their guns for some early sport. They were from Oldham and had set out in the middle of Saturday night in a battered red Ford GT Manta to be on the moor by four o'clock. They were both short, wiry and moustachioed, dressed in camouflage fatigues and black woollen bobble-hats, each with several rabbits slung jauntily over one shoulder. Describing their previous week-end's expedition to a field on a farm across the dale, they said, 'There were that many rabbits, it were like a shag-pile carpet.'

At Kirkby Lonsdale that afternoon, a hot wind ruffled the blanket of Virginia creeper on the walls of the Royal Hotel by the town square. I walked down through the churchyard to the elevated viewpoint known as Church Brow, and got into the River Lune, a hundred feet below, down a steep, wooded bank. I swept along with it in a great bend past the water meadows below the town. This was the landscape of woods, river and meadows Turner painted. It was described by Ruskin in *Fors Clavigera*, as 'one of the loveliest scenes in England'. The river was broad and often shallow as I swam down past the town parkland, then in faster water that surged through giant dark-grey boulders towards the stone-arched Devil's Bridge.

The river ran down into a deep pool fifty feet beneath the highest point on the bridge, and I found myself suddenly surrounded by fellow bathers. Groups of them sat about the banks, waded about the shallows, and swam. Most were bikers, out for a Sunday ride. There must have been a thousand motorbikes parked up by the bridge, so there were probably nearly 2,000 bikers, including a chapter or two of Hell's Angels, leaning over the vertiginous parapet, besieging the hot-dog van, or crowding the banks. A blinding aura of chrome heightened the scene. Everything glistened and scintillated in the sun: leathers, studs, Raybans, and the river, snaking off beyond the old stone arches.

What I witnessed on the bridge stopped me in my tracks. A Byronic young biker, stripped to the waist, stood poised on the parapet as if to leap to his death. There was a big commotion and a lot of shouting, which I assumed was fellow bikers trying to talk him down. One false move and he might jump. A series of images flashed up in quick succession; Harold Lloyd up a skyscraper, James Dean, Evil Knievel. The youth kept poising himself to leap, raising his arms into the swallow-dive position, stretching out his fingertips, and going up on to the balls of his toes. The crowd would hush. Then his resolve would waver, and he would step back an inch or two for a moment. The shouting would begin again. Swimming closer, I realised to my horror that the crowd was *egging him on.* 'Go on, yer bugger! Yer've bottled it seven times now, mon.' I had heard of Hell's Angels' initiation rituals, but wasn't this going a bit far? Just then, it all went quiet again and this time he jumped, sailing down in the silence for what seemed like an eternity into the pool between two massive rocks. Deafening cheers and mingled obscenities rang round the gorge as the jumper shot back up like a yo-yo, apparently none the worse, and hauled himself on to the bank. In no time at all another kamikaze candidate was up on the parapet at a point at the centre of the bridge, which I later examined and fancied was distinctly toe-worn. A chorus of chicken mimicry instantly ensued, punctuated by such encouragements as: 'Wanker!' 'Get 'em off!' 'Get on with it!'

A more or less continuous procession of lemming leapers continued to hurl themselves off the bridge all afternoon, sometimes in pairs like Paul Newman and Robert Redford in *Butch Cassidy and the Sundance Kid*. It was a time-honoured custom, they told me, and the Devil's Bridge has long been a rendezvous for daring young men on flying machines from all over the North of England on summer Sundays. The chief peril of the Devil's Bridge leap lay in the necessity of targeting the deepest part of a pool that looked relatively small from such a height, and in keeping well balanced for a streamlined entry at high velocity. Meanwhile, a break-away chapter of rope-swingers diverted the audience with Tarzan leaps (with matching vocals) from the official Kirkby Lonsdale Dangling Rope. There were Janes too, although heavily outnumbered by the Tarzans. They queued on one of the big rock slabs beneath the bridge, swinging off a sycamore branch into the same pool. One proud biker-father even launched his little son swinging into the river off the rope. The boy was barely four years old, and still without tattoos. Steep banks formed a natural amphitheatre to the afternoon's drama, and the huge audience showed its appreciation. A group of wags even yelled marks out of ten, holding up flattened paper cups like score cards at the Olympics. In the foreground were the usual notices forbidding bathing or canoeing, draped with wet trunks drying out in the sun.

Such a display of anarchy and sheer *joie de vivre* was

inspiring; and miraculously, no one seemed to come to any harm at all. Nobody dived; everyone jumped, and when I asked about this I was told the pool was 'deep, but not *that* deep'. The entire scene was straight out of the pages of *Three Men in a Boat*, and Jerome K. Jerome's description of the Sandford lasher on the Thames:

> The pool under Sandford lasher is a very good place to drown yourself in. The undercurrent is terribly strong and if you once get down into it you are all right. An obelisk marks the spot two men have already been drowned, while bathing there; and the steps of the obelisk are generally used as a diving board by young men who wish to see if the place really *is* dangerous.

Diving is a declining art in Britain. Few pools even allow it, and the boards have mostly been dismantled. The minimum safe depth recommended by the ASA for diving off the poolside is your height with your arms outstretched above your head. There are plenty of swimmers over six feet, so the minimum has to be eight or nine feet. Many pools are not even this deep, and diving boards would logically require yet greater depths.

I still remember the first time I went off the top board at the Watford Baths and, that same summer, at the Kenilworth Baths. Such moments were important rites of passage, climbing that extra set of steps, holding on to the rails with shaky hands you hoped no one would notice. An even greater day was when instead of jumping, you dived. Once you had taken that fateful walk along the coconut matting to the edge, you knew all eyes were on you; there was no going back. If your nerve failed, you would jump instead of diving. In the school swimming pool, the top board was close enough to the roof to reach up and grasp a girder, dripping with condensation, and go out swinging hand over hand, then let go. I still dream of such moments.

Samuel Beckett would have been at home in Kirkby Lonsdale. As a child it was his habit to fling himself out of trees; he once climbed to the top of a sixty-foot fir and launched himself to the ground, relying on the lower branches to break his fall. He became obsessively keen on perilous diving, in pools, off cliffs and in dreams.

Richard Hoseason Smith, a sea-swimmer and diver born and raised in the Shetland Islands, wrote and described to me how generations of Shetlanders have learnt to dive off a rock called the 'Giant's Leg'. It is 150 feet high and there are ledges all the way up to the summit. As children, they simply graduated one notch higher up the rock as their confidence, or bravado, grew. There was no swimming pool in the Shetlands at all until 1969, so everyone swam in the sea. Richard used to spend part of his summer holiday in Norfolk, and swam in what was once the largest open-air pool in the country at Great Yarmouth. High-diving displays were held at the pool every afternoon during the season, and a £5 prize was offered to anyone who would dive off the high board. It was thirty metres high and the pool was twenty-four feet deep. Richard was eleven or twelve years old at the time and already a skilful Shetland rock-diver. Volunteers were first invited to dive from the eight-metre board to demonstrate their competence. Richard passed the test and went on up to the high board. A hundred feet up, all you see are the tiles on the bottom, but you need to aim for the surface; and above all you want to be certain it is there. So Richard got a friend to sit at the side of the pool and splash his feet to disturb the water. He took so much prize money off the Yarmouth pool with his spectacular dives that he was eventually banned from entering the display. On his farewell appearance, he dived from another man's shoulders. Another swimmer there used to execute swallow dives wrapped in flaming hessian. Yet another dived off a ladder he had lashed to the high board.

During the 1920s there was a wild gang of boys and market-traders in Norwich who used to swim in the River Wensum and dive off the bridges for small change. The painter Edward Seago, then in his mid-teens and always fascinated by gypsies or wild outsiders of any kind, knew them, and used to go and watch. Like the boys at Ely, the daring ones used to go higher, off a crane that unloaded the barges. But the craziest of them all was Sonny Goodson, grandson of the famous Norwich poacher Billy 'Pitler' Goodson. Sonny would climb to the roof of a tall dye-works in the St George's district and dive into the river from the parapet. Then one afternoon in 1924 Sonny attempted the most astonishing feat of his diving career. No doubt the bet of a pound by a couple of the local traders seemed attractive to the fifteen-year-old, and there was a family daredevil tradition to honour. He climbed over the roof of the Norwich Art School just downstream from St George's bridge, on to a brick ledge below the copper dome of the tower, sixty-nine feet above the pavement. Then, instead of diving straight down into the river below, he launched out in a great arc upstream, taking an outward trajectory that would clear the bridge and land him in the river *beyond* it. His feet are said to have missed the parapet by inches as he shot down. The distance he had to travel through the horizontal was some forty feet. Goodson later said that he thought there was about twelve feet of water in the river at the time, although it has silted up a good deal since. The little crowd who watched Sonny's dive took up a collection and gave him the two shillings and fourpence on top of his bet money. He took a group of them to Yarmouth on the proceeds for the day. The police got to hear of the incident and gave Sonny a ticking off. And that was all the recognition he received.

It was too warm not to be in the river, and the bridge-jumping was strictly a spectator sport for me, so I set off back up the cooling Lune as the bikers saddled up and rode away in little swarms. Some had lit barbecues and small wood fires on the rocks, and smoke hung over the water in the reddening evening. What I liked about this river was the way it combined the play of wild life with the play of human life. Wild salmon still run up the Lune each year from Lancaster, and the egrets and herons that fished along the banks had been quite unruffled by the angels on the bridge not far away. I swam, waded and walked back to my rucksack, hidden by the bank, and repaired to the public bar of the Sun to plan my Monday morning expedition to Hell Gill. Dropping off to sleep up Barbondale in the tent that night, the limpid cadences of remembered Cumbrian speech from the pub mixed with the song of the running beck as I lay trying to imagine Hell Gill, and feeling some apprehension about my total lack of potholing experience.

21

A DESCENT INTO HELL GILL

Yorkshire/Cumbria border, 18 August

BACK IN BERNIE'S Café at Ingleton, they had told me to expect an experience somewhere between potholing, swimming, surfing and rock-climbing if I ever ventured down the inside of Hell Gill. To find it, I was going to have to trek over the wild moorland of Abbotside Common beyond Wensleydale and Garsdale Head. After an indolent morning in the wilds of Barbondale, I drove up through Garsdale, took the road towards Kirkby Stephen, and parked the car half in Yorkshire, half in Cumbria, astride the county boundary. To walk up the Hell Gill beck on a sunny afternoon out of the vale of the River Eden (of which it is the headwater) was my idea of heaven. There were foxgloves and trout, and a buzzard sailing lazily aloft. From here, the Eden runs north through Appleby to Carlisle, and something odd must have happened in the upheaval of the Ice Age, because Hell Gill is only yards away from the source of the River Ure, which flows the opposite way, to the Humber.

I had packed a rope and wetsuit boots in the rucksack and followed a track over the Settle to Carlisle railway line and uphill past Hell Gill Farm, following the beck to a bridge and a small wood that grows around the precipitous gorge that brought me here. I skirted past it uphill, and there, suddenly, was the entrance to the canyon. The beck just funnelled between four rocks and disappeared into the hillside in a steep, concealed cleft. Even from a few yards away, you wouldn't know it was there, and the hidden character of the beck is one possible origin of its name, from the old Teutonic *Hala*, 'the coverer up, or hider', and the verb *hel*, to hide. Looking down into the chasm, listening to the wild clamour of the hissing water pressing forward over the brink, I felt like a child at the top of the helter-skelter, or some equally dubious fairground ride: not at all sure this was such a good idea.

The Hell Gill gorge is like a pothole whose roof has cracked open sixty feet or more above. It plunges almost vertically down the hillside for four hundred yards in a continuous series of waterfalls dropping into overflowing pools of hollowed limestone. Geologically, the tunnelling of the limestone probably began at the end of the last Ice Age, 11,000 years ago, when the melt-water from above, finding no other way out, flowed down through alternate strata of limestone, shale and sandstone higher up the hill, and, still trapped by the glacier overhead, burst down a weakness in the limestone layer it encountered here, and bored out the gorge by dissolving the rock.

My temporary state of funk took the form of an impromptu exploration of the upstream beck in the afternoon sun. It forms the county boundary here, and with all the energy of the serious procrastinator, I waded and swam my way upstream, criss-crossing from Yorkshire to Cumbria between huge slabs of grey limestone crammed with fossils. Trout lay in the riffles and darted into shadows. I wallowed in a five-foot-deep waterfall pool, and found vast water-slides, twenty- and thirty-foot tablets of the smoothed limestone that was once coral reefs rising out of a tropical seabed 280 million years ago. Here you could bathe all day without meeting a soul, and better still, know in your heart that you would be undisturbed. A hawk had been killing pigeons, butchering them on the rock beside the water here and there. The black stains on the limestone, and stuck feathers, accentuated the desolation of the moor.

Courage up, I returned to the turbulent rim of the gorge and did what I knew might be an unwise thing. I couldn't help it. I began to slide into the mouth of the abyss itself. I found myself in the first of a series of smooth limestone cups four or five feet in diameter and anything between three and five feet deep, stepped at an acute angle down a flooded gulley of hollowed limestone that spiralled into the unknown. In the low light, the smooth, wet walls were a beautiful aquamarine, their shining surface intricately pock-marked like the surface of the moon. All my instincts were to hold on, but to what? The ice and the water had polished everything perfectly. The torrent continually sought to sweep me with it, and so I slithered and climbed down Hell Gill's dim, glistening insides, through a succession of cold baths, in one long primal scream.

There is something atavistic about all swimming, but this was so intensely primitive it was visceral. I felt like Jonah inside the whale. Each time I dropped, or was swept, into a new cauldron, I thought it would be bottomless; the turbulence made the water opaque. Borne down this magical uterus, deafened by the rushing and boiling of the flood, with the sheer rock and just a crack of sky high above me, I felt at once apprehensive and exhilarated. Water was cupped, jugged, saucered, spooned, decanted, stirred and boiled. It was thrown up in a fine spray so you breathed it in, it splashed in your face, it got in your ears, it stung you with its force, it bounced back off every curving surface, it worked unremittingly to sculpt the yielding limestone into the forms of its own well-ordered movement. Beneath the apparent chaos, all this sound and fury conformed to the strict laws of fluid dynamics.

So steep and labyrinthine was the descent that it was impossible to know or see what was to come next. The slippery blue-green wetness and smoothness of everything, and my near-nakedness, only made me more helpless, more like a baby. It was like a dream of being born. Unnamed thunderings like deep, booming heartbeats rose from somewhere below. It was exactly as Frederick Leboyer said in *Birth Without Violence*: 'The horror of being born is the intensity, the immensity of the experience, its variety, its suffocating richness . . . It is a sensory experience so huge, it is beyond our comprehension.'

Everyone I had talked to about this descent had said that once you're in, you must keep on going down, because you can't climb up. I was glad of the rubber boots and the grip of their soles, but the rope was no use at all because every surface was so perfectly smoothed there was nothing to loop it round. I was conscious that I shouldn't really be doing this alone. I had impetuously broken the first rule of potholing or climbing: that you let somebody know where you're heading before you set out. The feeling became acute as I reached a waterfall that sounded as if it dropped to Australia, and might be the source of the thundering Pink Floyd 'Atom Heart Mother' effects. They were becoming louder and more insistent.

Suddenly I found myself beneath an overhang of rock. A rope was bolted in here and there, and stretched off into a gloomy void beyond. It was impossible to see where it led, how deep the pool below might be, or how far down. I had no idea where the next foothold was. The torrent just shot over a rocky lip and disappeared from view, into a gothic emptiness. One option was to plunge blindly towards the waterfall and hope to drop into the pool, which might be deep enough for a safe landing. But the voices of reason shouted above the din that I stood an equal chance of being dashed into a rock face. The dilemma, and the stark solitude of my predicament, set my mind racing feverishly. I considered that for all I knew I might find myself, like the climber in H. G. Wells's story 'The Country of the Blind', marooned in a subterranean land full of people like myself who had strayed optimistically down the Hell Gill chasm and stranded themselves beyond the waterfall. I also recalled that in the story, the sightless majority propose to put out the eyes of the newcomer.

I pondered my position carefully, still thinking fast because every minute I spent immobile I was getting wetter and colder. Normally, you would clip on to an overhead rope, but I had no harness. I had met a pair of potholers down by the road and spoken to them briefly. They were accoutred in harnesses, buckles and steel clips like door-to-door ironmongers, and I now cursed my failure to ask them about Hell Gill. Once over the edge and dangling from the rope there was no going back. I would have to go hand over hand down it with fingers that

230

were by now half-numb. But how far? I didn't fancy being stuck in a freezing beck all night in swimming trunks. On the other hand I had been told it was impossible to climb back up. Was it really? I wondered. I spent what seemed an eternity fighting my reluctance to turn back and accepting a growing conviction of the logic of at least attempting the ascent. The slight fading of the afternoon light filtering down led me to my decision. I would try going up through the cascading water, and, if I failed, then I would just have to risk going down instead. With the help of strung nerves, the rubber boots, and liberal helpings of adrenalin, I managed to heave myself up the narrow chimney from pool to pool, waterfall to waterfall, against the water. It was slow going, making my way up like a salmon, and I resolved to return some day with a companion, a little more local knowledge, and the right kit.

Emerging at last at the mouth of the gorge, I glanced back at it with faint disbelief and greeted the sky. Then, having dressed, I wandered a little way up the beck in the warm evening and fell asleep on the grass like a new-born babe. I was woken with a jolt by the searing rush of a buzzard stooping on an unwary pigeon. There was a silent explosion of pale grey feathers, like a distant shell. I felt a breath of wind in the grass that could have been a white rabbit hurrying by. 'I've had such a curious dream!' I said to myself, and went off for my tea.

22

HOT & COLD

Argyll, 20 August

WHATEVER HAD HAPPENED to me in Hell Gill, I felt
profoundly changed and cleansed by the long slide and the
deep drenching. I had never delved so far into the earth
before, so alone, or so naked. It could have swallowed me up,
but here I was, the other side of it. Like every boy of five, I had
begun digging a hole to Australia, and abandoned it at six.
Now I felt I had completed something; that my sliding and
struggling had fulfilled some purpose quite unknown to me. It
was the same feeling that comes after I've struggled and
grappled through a big dream. I awaken from it, but the
essential feeling of it may stay with me for days, so that I
know it has been important without knowing why and I half
inhabit both the waking and the dreaming worlds at once.

It was in this freewheeling state that I decided to abandon
the route I had originally planned, missing out the Lakes and
the crowds of hikers, and going straight to Scotland in the
warm, dry spell. Inspired and elated by my descent into Hell
Gill, my one desire was for the beauty and silence of the West
Coast of Scotland and the Hebrides. I longed to swim the
lochs and the wild islands, and at last I felt ready to cross over
the sea to Jura, and to meet the Corryvreckan whirlpool.

I took my first Scottish swim two days later on the Argyll
coast at Ardpatrick. I had stayed here before, in the lovely old
estate house beside West Loch Tarbert, and it was from the
Point Hut, as they call it, a solitary wooden cabin perched on
the rocks at Ardpatrick Point, that I had first looked across

232

the sea to Jura. I was immediately fascinated. In the distance, the island looks like Saint-Exupéry's drawing in *Le Petit Prince*, of the snake that's just eaten an elephant. The humps are the three Paps, rising off the sea to over 2,000 feet. The light reflected off the sea before the island gives it the appearance of floating, airborne, like Laputa in *Gulliver's Travels*. The optical illusion is intensified by a luminescence that stems from the tendency of cloud to hang over the main-land, while over the Hebridean islands the weather is clear and sunny, like a halo. As soon as I saw Jura, I knew I had to go there, and I have returned to this rugged paradise several times since.

Before attempting the Gulf of Corryvreckan, I wanted to swim across the loch at Ardpatrick, almost the same distance, but without the whirlpool. My bedroom at Ardpatrick House looked over this lovely expanse of water (between half and three-quarters of a mile wide, depending on the state of tide) beyond wide, sloping lawns, a field of rough-coated cattle, and the chimney smoke from the old ferry cottage where they bake the local bread. The Caledonian Macbrayne ferry sails past the window each morning to Islay, and the Islands. Seals, cormorants and otters swim off the rocks, and on the far side a single white house stands on the hill, with its own jetty. I had talked about crossing the loch with friends on earlier visits, but we had never actually done it.

We waited until the evening to catch the top of the spring tide when the loch would be at its deepest and the currents slack. The plan was to row across from the ferry cottage to the quay on the opposite shore. I would then swim back, escorted by the boat. We had also timed things to avoid meeting the ferry from Islay sailing back up the loch. It was a crimson evening as we crossed over and picnicked on the little quay, my companions thoughtfully saving enough hot tea in the flasks to warm me after the swim. There were four of us in the boat: Caroline, Ruth, Neil and I, and a pair of spaniels, Louis and Nelly.

I went in off the stone jetty at six o'clock. The loch was clear and cold, and during the early part of the swim I had to pass through the beautiful kelp forest that grows in the shallower waters. Beautiful, that is, to all but swimmers; kelp tends to wrap itself round your neck and arms as you swim, so I soon felt like Isadora Duncan out for a drive, or like the Houdini who used to jump off Southend pier, bound in a weighted sack. Untangling myself broke the rhythm of things. But I wasn't long gaining deeper water, sensing its coolness and swimming free. Caroline rowed beside me, and Ruth and Neil peered ahead for jellyfish, dolphins, or other items of interest, liberally dispensing encouragement from the boat. Neil talked about Belnahua, one of the Black Isles, where the light changes every half-hour, and you can swim in the deep lagoons of its flooded, long-deserted quarries. He also told a story of how his sister was locked in the aquarium at Brighton for the night. We discussed swimming across Jura, which they say has a loch for every day of the year, and weighed the chances of swimming the Corryvreckan whirlpool.

Killer whales had recently been spotted in the loch, but none appeared. Louis was concerned for my safety, returning again and again to the stern and whimpering in my direction. The picnic baskets, and the dog standing alert on the thwarts, gave our little flotilla the authentic look of a Famous Five adventure. A curious mixture of vertigo and exhilaration at the miracle of the sheer mass of water bearing you up from beneath overtakes the swimmer in deep water. I was crossing the main channel of the ferry route, and a slight swell drove in up the loch from the open sea. A seal appeared and swam some of the way across with us, all whiskers and openly inquisitive, coming up from below at every point of the compass in turn. We could only guess where it was swimming underwater, and it never came up where we expected it to. It was quite harmless, and a useful bearing in the water: on the wide horizon of a longish swim, anything that can help convince you you're actually moving is a help. It was at about this point that Caroline mentioned the possibility of a hot bath up at the house, and I swam with redoubled energy for the shore. Some yellow mooring buoys marked the three-quarter point of the swim, at which moment, as usual, I was just beginning to relax into the rhythm of the breaststroke. The final stretch of a swim always seems quickest, and I reached the beach in about half an hour through moored boats and buoys.

Up at the house, I now proceeded straight from the frigidarium to the caldarium, and took a second, equally memorable dip in one of the Ardpatrick bathrooms. The bath itself was an immense lion-clawed seven-foot wallow with a column of white porcelain pipe at one end leading to an orchestrated arrangement of levers and brass valves operating the plug. Its white enamelled cast-iron and moulded porcelain formed a shrine of scalloped soap-dishes at one end. Soft, pale brown water from springs in the hill now gushed like mulled whisky from two of the three giant taps. Steam splashed and billowed to the high ceiling and fogged the tall windows that looked over the walled garden. The plumbing was magnificent and ponderous. Pipes wandered about everywhere, as if part of a great musical instrument, and four different taps filled the washbasin. The lavatory was panelled and caparisoned in the original mahogany of earlier times, long before rainforest crises put it out of reach for responsible citizens. Even the cistern was casked in deeply polished panels, like something in a church.

Following a prolonged immersion in cold water, the wise swimmer will always enter a bath lukewarm, having recruited a reliable friend (preferably lacking too keen a sense of humour) to test the water first. What with 'endolphins', cold sensors, adrenalin, thyroxine and the hypothalamus, the body has a hundred ways of protecting itself from the cold, and will anaesthetise itself from the discomfort of prolonged exposure. The prudent bather knows that numb fingers and toes are no judges of water temperature. What greater pleasure than to come out of the sea aglow from your swim and then gently to raise the temperature of your hands and feet by trickling the hot tap as you soak? Your lukewarm bath will feel deliciously hot by contrast with the cold water of the swim. To enter it thus as a prelude to later excesses is to practise what the psychoanalysts call 'deferred gratification'. It is the ante-room of the hammam to which you now proceed, opening the hot tap, letting rip with a scalding waterfall that reduces visibility to zero and raises the bath to new levels of pleasure. You lie and soak your chilled chops, feeling the warmth, the softness, the intoxication of guiltless indulgence permeating every cell, floating your toes up towards the steamy ceiling with sounds of dinner underway somewhere below. The boat-shaped tub was so generously proportioned I fancied I could almost swim a stroke or two from end to end, and I wallowed for some time, doing imaginary lengths, melting away the numbness and the pins and needles, topping up with hot water now and again like a man on a veranda augmenting his sundowner.

That hot baths are now two a penny for many of us may not be such a boon as it seems. G. M. Trevelyan's house-master at Harrow, Edward Bowen, an ascetic bachelor who once walked the eighty miles from Cambridge to Oxford within twenty-four hours, told him, 'O boy, you oughtn't to have a hot bath twice a week; you'll get like the later Romans.' T. H. White thought once a fortnight was probably about right, arguing that, 'The true voluptuary wears sackcloth nearly all the time, so that when he does put on his sheer silk pants he can get full satisfaction out of rolling in the hay.' Our cossetted, over-heated way of life may have robbed us of a natural ability, evident in most mammals, to enjoy both extremes of the spectrum of warm and cold. I have always had a special affection for François Truffaut's film *L'Enfant Sauvage*, in which he plays Jean Itard, the anthropologist-teacher of Victor, the feral boy raised by wolves and found in the Aveyron region of France, in the woods near St-Affrique, in 1800. Before he came under the tutelage of Itard, Victor was looked after by Monsieur Bonnaterre, the natural history teacher at the St-Affrique school, who wrote careful notes about his behaviour, and noticed how he loved the cold as well as the warmth of a fire:

> One evening, when the temperature was well below freezing, I undressed him completely, and he seemed delighted to get out of his clothes. Then I made believe I was going to take him outdoors. I led him by the hand down the long corridors to the main door of the Central School. Instead of showing the slightest hesitation about going out, he kept tugging me through the door. From all this, I concluded that the two

things are not incompatible. He can both be indifferent to the cold and take pleasure in warming himself by the fire, for one notices that cats and dogs have the same habits.

Like fires, hot baths engender meditation, and I dreamed happily in mine almost until dinner time, imagining cooler dips ahead.

The following afternoon, under a blue sky fringed white with distant clouds on the horizon, four of us swam in 360 feet of turquoise water in a sheer-sided quarry on Belnahua. The island encircled a huge natural swimming pool, raised above sea level, whose waters were so utterly transparent that when we swam, we saw our shadows far down, swimming ahead of us along the bottom. All around, only yards away, was the deeper blue of the open sea, and the Hebrides: Fladda, Scarba, Jura, Lunga, the Garvellachs (the 'Islands of the Sea', St Columba's favourite place), Luing, Mull and Colonsay. The light and the skies kept changing all afternoon: from bright blue with distant dazzling clouds to deepening red and gold. Diving from the rocks into the immensely deep, clear, brackish water, intensified the giddy feeling of aquatic flying. There was a curious absence of water plants, and absurdly crystalline underwater views down the sheer faces of hewn slate. The only signs of life in the water were aimless three-inch fish grazing the apparently barren rocks. It was so still and silent that as we swam, we could hear the trickling of the racing tides beyond the strip of land and the black beach.

We had come up the Sound of Luing in a beautiful aluminium motorboat, steering for a dot on the horizon that was Belnahua, a tiny, almost square island not much more than a quarter-mile along each side. The island is now uninhabited, but was once home to a hundred people, whose menfolk worked the slate quarries. The slates from Belnahua, and Easdale island, across the water towards Mull, roofed most of Glasgow, Edinburgh, Dundee, Belfast, and even New York, because cargo boats would often carry slates back over the Atlantic as ballast.

The tide runs fast through the Sound of Luing, and

although there was plenty of power in the boat's twin engines, they had to work hard to make headway over a sea that was calm but alive with cross-currents, eddies and the polished smoothness that belies great turbulence below. Jura was off to the south-west and our course lay close to Scarba, passing within two miles of the Gulf of Corryvreckan and its whirlpool. I looked across at the channel I would have to swim between Jura and Scarba, then gazed at the warring currents, wrestling each other beneath the surface. Their unease had a palpable effect on us all, and we fell silent for a while.

After Scarba, we skirted another notorious tide-race to its north known as the Grey Dog and headed for Belnahua, leaving the white lighthouse on the tiny island of Fladda a few hundred yards to starboard. We landed and anchored on the southern shore by a ruined jetty, then waded in over a bed of slate pebbles like loose change. Getting the anchor to bite on them was not easy.

Everything on Belnahua was ruined, except its wild beauty. There were two rows of dilapidated slate cottages carpeted in long grass with just their walls and fireplaces left. Holed and half-demolished by the winter storms, what was left of their windows framed dramatic views of the Garvellachs and the distant Paps of Jura across the sea. Bits of derelict machinery lay everywhere: cogs and pulleys, shafts, spindles, wheels, gears, cranes, pitted bollards and rusting fragments of narrow-gauge track. The beaches were all silver, black and grey, with fine black sand and all denominations of the island's slate coinage, some flecked with a starry night sky of fool's gold, others striated with the finest random white pencil lines of quartz, the doodling of mermaids. The tides had sorted and screened them by size, stacking them like books end-on in flowing lines and whorls that traced the eddies and turbulence that clamoured over them.

We swam the length of the quarry in relatively warm, sheltered water, whose utter calm was a complete contrast to the inner turmoil of the surrounding sea. Entered down a shelving beach of slates, the enormous pool was about 300 yards long, with two narrow grey-green islands almost dividing it in two. At the far end, we reached a big black sun-soaked radiator of hot slate. Little spiders, their fine webs spun across the fissures, greeted us, and the hot rock felt delicious to my chilled hands as I climbed in and out diving. Then I went exploring. I stood before the hearth in one of the quarrymen's cottages, under a roof of sky, and climbed to the top of the island, where the views were unsurpassed. The central ridge, shaped like an old concrete air-raid shelter, must have afforded some natural protection from the westerly weather to the Belnahuans at work in the quarries, or on what little land there is. The houses all stood on the south coast of the island. It must have been a bleak life quarrying slates in winter.

Belnahua's black beaches are rendered nearly unswim-mable by the subtle ferocity of the running tides, except perhaps at slack water. There are several beaches, separated by black rocks, each with a distinct character: one a mass of warm, black paperweights; another, a hoard of the slate money combed into watery patterns, clustered around rocks. I bathed in the shelter of a rocky inlet. It was colder than the sheltered quarry pool, but startlingly clear, magnifying every detail below. Beyond the rocks, the rising tide was running fast enough to snatch away even the strongest swimmer. It rose rapidly up the shore, continually dragging and sifting the island, every grain of black sand, in its anxious, restless tugging. It sucked and rattled the teeth-chattering pebbles in rhythms and counter-rhythms. We listened to it as we picnicked in the grass beside the quarry pool, and looked across to the white lighthouse tower on Fladda, less than half a mile away, with an overgrown walled garden the keepers used to tend. When we put out in the boat, the tide was running our way, and we sped home to the mainland, like a skimmed ducks-and-drakes pebble. Looking back at Belnahua in the sunset, I thought how like a desert island atoll it was, set incongruously in the Hebrides. And I have some-thing to declare: a tiny cargo of slate pebbles slipped into my rucksack, that now sit, like small islands, on my desk.

23

ORWELL'S WHIRLPOOL

Jura, Hebrides, 22 August

PORING OVER THE map of Jura in the library back in Cambridge, with its bewildering choice of swimmable water, I had nearly resorted to planning my journey by throwing darts blindfold at the map. To know the island as I do is only to realise how much more there will always be to discover of its beauties and difficulties. It resists you at every step. For a swimmer, it combines heaven and hell. It has delicious water and dramatic beaches, but also a menacing whirlpool and some of the fiercest tidal currents in the British Isles. There is only one road, almost no footpaths (just deer-tracks), it rains a good deal, and in summer there are midges. It is really a tawny desert, with less than 250 people on 160 square miles of island. This is why you can wander on the face of Jura for days without meeting a living soul, and it is probably why George Orwell came to live here in April 1946.

Orwell had first visited Jura in September 1945, at the suggestion of his friend David Astor, whose family owned an estate on the island. It hadn't occurred to anyone that the trip was more than a holiday, but when the writer heard that a remote farmhouse near the north coast was available, he decided to move in. His wife, Eileen, died suddenly that winter, and he temporarily abandoned the plan, but by April 1946 he was moving into Barnhill. The house was twenty-five miles from the nearest shop. It had no electricity and no telephone, and only the roughest of tracks leading up to it for the last five miles, but Orwell was anxious to get out of

London, and wanted his three-year-old son Richard to grow up in the country. What could be better for a small boy than a wild island? He set about farming and gardening in a small way, went fishing, planted fruit trees, bought a rowing boat with an outboard engine, and began writing *Nineteen Eighty-Four*. The hardship and the adventure of the place must have appealed to him. But as desert places, the Western Isles were also where the Celtic saints retreated to hear the voice of God in the silence. Orwell, writing his prophetic novel about politics and the human soul, needed somewhere silent to hear himself think his own special brand of common sense.

It was late afternoon by the time I arrived on the remote white sand beach of Glenbatrick Bay on the far west coast of Jura. On the neighbouring island of Islay I had enquired amongst the fishermen on the quayside for a boatman and was told, 'If it's Glenbatrick you want, that's your man.' They pointed out a commanding figure loading up a sleek rubber-hulled powerboat who turned out to be the laird himself, Lord Astor, the nephew of Orwell's friend, fetching provisions for his solitary island cottage. He had readily agreed to take me over the Sound of Islay with him and entertained me to tea when we landed.

I dived into the loch in the calm, clear sand-warmed water of Glenbatrick Bay. It is a wild, enchanted shore fortified by a succession of steep rocky ridges running out from the high ground like breakwaters to the sea, each sheltering a sand or a pebble beach. I swam on the rising tide, keeping an eye on my rucksack, like a milestone on the beach, as I drifted perceptibly up the loch. Two seals watched me idly from one of the rocks that stand out everywhere like crocodiles' teeth until the tide conceals them. There were otters here too. The dazzling sun burnt a furrow straight down the loch, and shone on the heathery pelt of the island, which looked easy walking from out in the sea, although I knew it wasn't. I turned and struck back towards the beach, with the white stone cottage at its edge, and a backdrop of the three rounded summits of the Paps, curiously striped with streaks of white quartzite as though gigantic prehistoric birds have roosted and shat on them for millions of years. The tallest of them always seems to have a white cloud hovering just above it, like Kilimanjaro.

I made my camp in good time, about six o'clock, before the midges came out to play, choosing a heathery level patch near one of the raised beaches that abound along this coast. When I had first seen the words 'Raised Beaches' on the map, recurring like an incantation, forming a ribbon along the western shores of Jura, I immediately wanted to tramp over to this wilderness and explore them. These ridges of big, smooth, pale-grey, purple-veined pebbles, like curling stones or loaves, rise to between ten and thirty feet above the seashore along most of the windward side of the island. They are a monument to centuries of giant waves roughing up the island, trying to flip it over like a pancake. The island responded by throwing up huge wet-stone ramparts. On top of them, generations of ants founded ant-hills that grew to the size of small tumuli as they built on the ruins of their forebears. Heather, moss and bilberries took root in the fertile soil, and deer nibbled them to a close-cropped topiary, like green thatched roofs.

As the sun began to sink, I lit a small fire of flotsam and dead heather between two rocks to keep away the midges that come out of nowhere and can make life unbearable for all but the most leather-skinned. By piling on handfuls of dead bracken, I found I could make it smoke in their faces, and mine. Meditating on the sea, I remembered the best solution to the problem, slid stealthily into the cool loch, and circled about in the pink and purple wavelets. Midges respond to the heat of the body, so cooling it is a sound strategy. It is only the female of the species that bites, and only when she is carrying eggs and in need of protein. The males are innocent, and vegetarian, and during most of the year midges keep themselves to themselves, eating decayed plants and nectar. *Culicoides impunctatus* has probably done as much as anything for nature conservation in the Highlands and Islands, by deterring the holiday hordes. It must cost the country millions in lost tourist revenue. When I came out I made a dash for the towel and my clothes, piled more bracken on the fire, and sat drying off in the smoke like a kipper. I dined on bread and sardines, watching the smooth lanes and tracks of subtle turbulence beneath the surface of the sea. From inside the tent

I could gaze straight across to Colonsay on the horizon and I watched a small boat emerging out of the dusk as, at ten to nine, the sun touched down on the little island.

There was an immense silence, with only the sound of the sea breaking gently on the pebble beach just below, and the throb of the boat's engine. As night fell I heard an anchor drop in the bay, and the splash of dinghy oars, voices, and the crackle of a beach fire a few hundred yards away. All I could see was the boat riding at anchor. A breeze got up and the midges evaporated. I lay with my head out of the tent gazing wakefully at the full moon silvering the sea, heart thumping in the sheer elemental drama of this island.

I woke in the first light to the sound of a fishing boat setting lobster pots in the loch. When I put my head out of the tent, deer were watching me from the hillside. Red deer are the island's prime population; they say there are 5,000. Theirs are the only tracks through the rough terrain, and there is not a moment when you are not being watched by them, usually from high ground. 'Jura' is said to be a Chinese-whispers version of the words for 'Deer Island' in Old Norse: *Dyr Oe*.

After a spartan breakfast of burn water, biscuits and an orange, I packed up and lurched up and down the steep sides of a series of ferny, bracken-filled ravines that run down to a thousand hidden coves along the shore. Loch Tarbert almost cuts the slender island in two at this halfway point, pinching it like a wasp's waist. I veered inland on the switchback deer tracks and climbed steadily until I was level with the first of a string of swims that winked in the sun, stretching in an imaginary ley-line across the island. Feeling no modesty before the deer, I entered the ineffable softness of Lochan Mic-a-phi and crossed straight over it. If some of the Fen rivers were gin clear, this was like swimming through single malt whisky. It was deep and refreshing, but by no means cold; somewhere in the mid-sixties fahrenheit. The loch turned my body to the dull gold of a carp, and bore me up as if in water-wings, as I returned across two hundred yards of the finest water in the world, tasting it at intervals. To feel its balmy softness in every limb, at every stroke, was a kind of heaven.

An hour later, the combined effects of loch swimming and hard walking were going to my head. For many people, parboiled and half-dissolved in daily hot baths, the ecstasies of cold water or hill-walking must seem a long way off, probably bracketed with S&M, but I was getting hot, and searching for the Liundale River on its way to the loch. Suddenly, round a bend in the deer track, I found what I was looking for. An eighteen-foot waterfall tumbled off the moorland into a deep peat-brown basin just above the beach. Filtered through moorland moss, the river turned my body back to amber as I pushed out into deep water twenty or thirty feet across. The pool was walled round three sides with perpendicular rock. It was probably jumpable from above, but thankfully there were no members of the Kirkby Lonsdale Flying Corps here to try. I swam under the waterfall, dived through its deafening turbulence, and came up behind the curtain of white water. It was gaspingly, shockingly, ridiculously cold. This was water straight from the mountain that sends your blood surging and crams every capillary with a belt of adrenalin, despatching endorphins to seep into the seats of pleasure in body and brain, so that your soul goes soaring, and never quite settles all day.

Swimming in the deepest part of the pool, I felt the updraught of cool air drawn across the surface and up the rock chimney by the falling water. There were dozens of rainbows in the spray, in that misty aura in which the waterfall atomises and evaporates into the surrounding air, a border territory between the elements where naiads play. And indeed I swam in the company of a tame water ousel. These dainty incognito river spirits are usually quite timorous, flying nervously from rock to rock, always keeping to the limit of your field of vision, so you sometimes wonder if they're really there at all. But this one just carried on minding its own business, hunting amongst the wet stones for aquatic insects or snails like the robin by my compost heap. Perhaps it was more used to the company of saints; St Columba must have known this shore, not so far from Iona. Not much has changed here since the eighth century, when it was easier to travel by water than by land, and probably safer. People here still talk about being *joined* by the sea to the other isles, and to Ireland, not separated.

Two minutes' scramble down the steep river gorge to the sea, and I was swimming out in a cleft between two walls of rock. But the tide had turned and was racing out alarmingly fast, like a river, so I returned to the waterfall and sat tingling with elation, drying off in a sunny corner on a grassy ledge, observing the comings and goings of dragonflies and butter-flies. The dipper curtseyed and flew off.

The deer-paths led me up a steep incline to a point where I could soon see a much larger sheet of water, Maol-ant-Sornaich, dammed forty feet above the sea by a spectacular wall of pebbles perfectly graded in a wide curving sweep of bay from the size and shape of eggs at one end to rounded loaves at the other. The grey- and purple-striped stone was polished smoother than skin and still glistened from the receding tide that now raced down Loch Tarbert like mountain rapids. I made my way across this great, dazzling, pale-grey, ankle-challenging desert. In the sunshine each pebble cast a dramatic, sharp shadow on the next. I plunged in and crossed the lochan, now ruffled by a gathering breeze, to some cliffs on the other side. Sunshine and clouds chased each other across the surface, and I soon hastened back, feeling uneasy at the scale of things – the looming cliffs and the giant natural dam – after the intimacy of the waterfall pool.

The next swim, from the wooden landing-stage of a boat-house on a little trout loch nestling in a purple bowl of hills, was a sheer delight. This loch had a shallow end, where the burn flowed in, and a deep end where it was dammed by a stone wall and flowed down a salmon ladder into the sea. Each time the wind blew a wavelet in my face I gulped it happily. Trout jumped four feet out of the water as I sat reading outside a fishing bothy, propped against an upturned boat. Perhaps this was one of the places Orwell had in mind when he wrote in a letter to his friend Celia Paget:

We went for some wonderful picnics on the other side of the island, which is quite uninhabited but where there is an empty shepherd's cottage one can sleep in. It is a beautiful coast, green water and white sand, and a few miles inland lochs full of trout which never get fished because they're too far from anywhere.

I crossed the giant mantrap that constitutes the majority of the land surface of Jura, sidestepping off the deer-paths to avoid disturbing fat mother-spiders in their webs. Walking on Jura is not for the faint-hearted. You really need hooves, not boots. And always there are the deer on the skyline, watching, with their ears up like leaves. I swam in two more lochs, one with white waterlilies, before I eventually reached the road at four o'clock, just in time for the post-bus on its afternoon run, delivering provisions and gossip, schoolchildren and the mail, up and down the island. Alex, the driver, took me north to Ardlussa, where Orwell's neighbours, Mr and Mrs Nelson, used to live. Having cooled off in the sea, swimming from the tiny bay there with a seal, I set out to walk the seven miles up the track to Barnhill and the two more on to the Gulf of Corryvreckan.

It was a testing journey for Orwell to make contact with the outside world. But then he liked hardship, and had always enjoyed testing himself, posing as a tramp in the Kentish hop-fields, down and out in Paris and London, fighting in Catalonia, running a village store in Wallington, keeping goats in the outskirts of Marrakesh, or farming on Jura. He tried a variety of transport on this track. First there was a motorbike, which constantly broke down. He would often carry a scythe on the back to cut down the rushes which sprang up in the middle of the road – and still do – and spent many hours sitting beside it, tinkering with the engine, hoping someone might come by who could help. Although practical in other ways, he was no mechanic. Later there was an unreliable lorry, a temperamental pony, an old Austin truck and a fishing boat to collect visitors and supplies from Ardlussa in good weather.

As I walked the last few miles, beginning to feel the weight of my rucksack, I imagined Orwell's life here: collecting wood, lighting a peat fire, rolling a cigarette, planting potatoes, typing in an upstairs room above the kitchen, swimming in a clear, green, sandy bay on the wild side of the island. He was certainly a swimmer. At Eton he swam in the Thames with his friend Bobbie Longden, the great love of Cyril Connolly's youth, and, later, headmaster at Wellington College. In a radio interview in 1960, Orwell's friend Denys King-Farlow said he loved swimming, 'but never bothered about swimming or diving with any style'.

It was on a bathing and camping expedition to Glengarrisdale Bay, on the uninhabited side of the island, that Orwell's natural taste for adventure nearly ended in tragedy. It was the long, hot August of 1947, and Orwell set out in his boat accompanied by Avril, his sister, his little son Richard, two teenage nieces, and a nephew in his early twenties, who had come for a holiday. The trip round the coast was uneventful, and after two days' swimming, fishing and hiking, camping by the bay, they headed back for Barnhill in the boat. Avril and one of the nieces elected to walk home.

But Orwell had miscalculated the tides, and, as they entered the Gulf of Corryvreckan, the whirlpool dragged the outboard engine off the boat. They were only saved by Orwell's nephew Henry Dakin, a young army officer, who had the strength to row them out of the whirlpool before they were too far in, but they capsized near one of the little islands in the Gulf. Richard went under the boat and had to be dragged out by Orwell. They lost everything, even their shoes. The party managed to get on to the rocky island safely, and stayed there until they were picked up by a passing fishing boat a few hours later.

I approached Barnhill, a surprisingly extensive slate-roofed stone house, with single-storey additions at both ends, commanding a view of the Sound of Jura towards the mainland. Its beauty lies in its extreme remoteness. Orwell had recruited a young Scotsman, Bill Dunn, to come and help him and his friend Richard Rees run the farm in 1947. At one time, they had fifty sheep, ten cows and a pig. It was hard to imagine, looking at the wet, rushy ground, how they could have succeeded.

Bill ended up marrying Orwell's sister, Avril, who was also

living up there. He had lost a leg in the war in Italy, and he was in the habit of nailing a piece of wood to the bottom of his wooden leg to stop it sinking into the bog. Some time in the early eighties, Bill Dunn swam the Corryvreckan. I have met people who saw him do it. He took off his wooden leg and smeared himself in sheep's fat. It was a flat calm day, and a whole flotilla of small boats turned out to accompany him. He had been practising for weeks in the bays along the island. Dunn was powerfully built in the chest and shoulders, and crossed the Gulf from Jura to Scarba, swimming the crawl, in not much more than half an hour. By now, the distance between the two islands was imprinted in my mind: 1,466 yards.

Pressing on north towards the Corryvreckan, I passed a second isolated farm, and the track became a path wandering over the hills. The sun was going down, and the midges were becoming impossible, so I looked for a level, heathery ridge for my camp. It is surprising how delicious a supper of bread and sardines can taste after a long day's swimming, and a walk. It was the explorer Sir Richard Burton who said, 'In the desert there is a keen enjoyment of mere animal existence.' I zipped the midges out of the tent, and slept in the sweet repose of weariness that comes like spring to the body, so you can almost feel it renewing itself in every cell. But my sleep was tempered by apprehension about the next stage of the journey and I dreamed comprehensively of the Corryvreckan all night.

The morning began unexpectedly grey, with a sprinkling of fine rain driving in off the sea as I set off up the last two miles of dilapidated path to the gulf itself. Obeying some inescapable impulse to confront my nocturnal fear, I trudged on north like a lemming. There was no telling which of us was in greater turmoil: myself or the whirlpool. I heard the commotion of water before I saw it, a low-pitched, continuous seething of brawling waves. The unnerving sound carried vividly on the damp drizzle. These were not the wide blue skies I had imagined; the scene before me was mostly muted shades of grey. The shore was a fortified steep escarpment, with no beaches, only fissured rock, indented by narrow clefts, alternately filled and sucked dry by the Atlantic swell with the awful gurgling I associate with the dentist's chair. This was it. The Gulf of Corryvreckan. One of the most notorious stretches of water anywhere around the British Isles. Standing before it, at the extremity of the island, I felt like The Last Man in Europe, Orwell's original working title for *Nineteen Eighty-Four*.

The sea all round this part of the Western Isles is so full of warring tiderips, sluicing through narrow gaps between islands in deep channels, that it is rarely still. Enormous volumes of water have to find their way in and out of the islands that stand in their way. So serious is the danger of the Gulf of Corryvreckan that it is officially classed by the Royal Navy as 'unnavigable'. It is not much over half a mile wide, yet it is more than 300 feet deep over most of its width, except in one significant spot, where a huge conical rock is sunk only ninety feet beneath the surface. It is called *Cailleach*, 'The Hag'. The special menace of the Corryvreckan is created by the sheer force of the Atlantic tidal wave, which sometimes races through the passage at the rate of fifteen knots. The effect of the pyramidal rock is to create a standing wave up to thirty feet high which combines with a welter of eddying turbulence along both shores to create the Corryvreckan whirlpool.

What no navigation guide could communicate is the deeply unsettling atmosphere of the place, the intense physical presence of the whirlpool and the scale of the turbulence. Wind and tide were herding the waves into the narrow gulf, and they stretched away, falling over themselves, for a mile across the sea beyond the outer coast of Scarba.

The whirlpool was clearly visible, three hundred yards offshore towards the western end of the gulf. Inside its circumference was a mêlée of struggling white breakers, charging about in every direction, head-butting one another. Outside, the surface was deadly smooth. The neatly-folded swimming trunks in my rucksack felt somehow irrelevant as I stood by the shore, feeling a very tiny figure, unable to take my eyes away from the epicentre of the vortex. It seemed scarcely credible that a swimmer could have made this crossing from Jura to Scarba.

Bill Dunn's swim was true to a tradition of derring-do in the face of the maelstrom that began with Bhreachan, an early Norse king who gave the gulf its name – Coire Bhreachain. In love, and out to prove it, he vowed to anchor his galley in the gulf for three days and three nights with three specially-made anchor lines of wool, hemp and virgins' hair. The first two parted, but the virgins' hair held fast until the last hour of the last night. The ship was dragged into the whirlpool and Bhreachan's dead body was later hauled ashore by his own black dog. He was buried in Uamh Bhreacain, a cave on the north shore a mile from where I stood.

I had to face the fact that I wasn't going to swim the Corryvreckan, at least not on this occasion. It would be madness to swim alone, and suicidal in these conditions. But even given the right tide and weather, would I have done it? And why? I would certainly have attempted it with an escort boat and a navigator with local experience. It would be a test, a way of facing out a risk in order to feel more fully alive, like climbing a tree or a mountain. I feared the whirlpool, therefore it fascinated me and dominated my dreams. But there was another thing. I longed for the heightened experience of somehow physically sharing in the Corryvreckan's excess of mad energy. Perhaps this is what a wolf feels when it bays at the moon, and perhaps it was quite as impractical a desire. Nevertheless, I felt that the whirlpool, in league with the moon, and renewing itself at every tide, could likewise renew the swimmer bold enough to seize the moment and cross it in a moment of repose. It would be like tiptoeing past a sleeping tiger. Keats wrote in a letter to his friend Bailey, 'If a sparrow come before my window, I take part in its existence and pick about in the gravel.' By swimming the Corryvreckan, I wanted to 'take part in its existence', to feel part of it, to swim *with* it, not against it, in one of its gentler moods.

The whirlpool and the gulf were the quintessence of the wildness of Jura, and just the kind of thing Orwell's police state in *Nineteen Eighty-Four* had abolished, because they knew such wilderness nourished freedom of thought and action. When Winston and Julia go into the country and make love in the apparent solitude of an ash glade, they hardly dare to speak because they know there are microphones hidden in the trees. Whirlpools and wild places are inextricably linked with our capacity for creativity, as Orwell demonstrated when he chose to come to Jura to write his last novel.

Only the deer saw me turn away from the Corryvreckan and make my way slowly back up the hillside. I would go instead, I decided, to the far coast in search of Bhreachan's cave, then follow the coast south to Glengarrisdale Bay, one of Orwell's favourite places. The map was thick with caves along that untrodden shore, and I wanted to see Maclean's Skull Cave. Its occupant, so the story goes, had been murdered in clan warfare, probably by the ruling Donalds. Until recently, there were still people on Jura who remembered playing with the skull of Maclean as children, fitting the broken pieces back together like a jigsaw puzzle. The dead of the island were always carried to these caves to rest on their journey to Iona, where they were buried.

I was halfway across the hills when the rain closed in. It came in thick curtains driven by a strengthening west wind, and I began to get really wet. So did the boggy moor. My boots filled up with water because I had stupidly left my waterproof trousers behind in the tent. Each time I struggled with the sodden map in the wind, I got more lost. Rain even drove into the rucksack like water-cannon. Just as my feelings of fine solitude were turning to self-pitying loneliness I met a toad coming the other way along the peaty deer-path. She stood up, straightening her hind legs like a runner on starting blocks and stood glaring at me with a defiant 'don't mess with me, chum' look. I stepped aside. But the encounter with another living being somehow rallied my spirits. So did the beautiful jet-black slugs, and the plentiful insectivorous sundews, one of my favourite plants ever since I first encountered them in the New Forest on school botanical field-camps. Here, they are a friend to man, snaring midges on their honeyed tendrils. I tried humming to myself in the curiously private world of sound that exists inside the clammy hood of an anorak. I did my best to convince myself of George Meredith's idea that we should 'love all changes of weather', and his assertion in *The Egoist* that 'rain, the heaviest you can meet, is a lively companion when the resolute pacer scorns discomfort of wet clothes and squealing boots'. I lurched on, strafed by the gusting rain, half-walking, half-paddling, scorning the discomfort with all my might. The weather was worsening all the time.

I decided to abandon the caves and turn back. Dense mists swilled from hill to hill and I was by now 'mokado', a Romany word meaning 'soaked to the skin' that George Borrow once casually threw into conversation to establish his credentials as he sought shelter from a downpour in a Cornish gypsy encampment above Rosewarne. My feet, by this time, had been for a distance swim in my boots. I sensed the imminent onset of trench foot under the composting socks, and incipient blisters boiling up like party balloons. Somehow, I found my way back to the only shelter for miles, my tent, and lay in it nibbling chocolate like an adolescent, contemplating the eight-mile walk back to Ardlussa and the post-bus, and thinking wistfully of the Ardpatrick bath.

24

A CASTLE IN THE AIR

Northumberland, 28 August

THE LONG ROAD south from Jura afforded me plenty of time to reflect on my failure to swim the Corryvreckan. My spirits were more than a little dashed, but I resolved to return and try again. I was on my way south from Edinburgh along the Northumbrian coast, where I came to the sands of Bamburgh beach, once trodden by the early Celtic Christians from Iona. In a flat calm sea I took a long cold-water swim straight out towards the Farne Islands, almost hidden in the lead-grey mist. The lighthouse there stood out like the white snick of an otter's bib. I was alone on this great horizon except for two lovers lying out like seals in the gentle surf of the outgoing tide. Mist flowed in like cigar smoke, wafting into a second surface hanging just above me as I swam.

Behind me, Bamburgh castle stood out like a cloud in a sky that continually changed. It took a long time for the water to deepen, but then I was cutting through the oily calm in a soundless dream of swimming. I kept on striking further out towards the lighthouse, and the island where Cuthbert, who succeeded Aidan, the first Bishop of Lindisfarne, spent the last years of his life in retreat. He used to like to pray standing up to his arms and neck in the sea at dead of night. Emerging on to the beach at daybreak, he would kneel down on the sand and resume his prayers. The *Lives of the Saints* relates how one of his brother monks saw two otters run out of the water to warm his feet with their breath and dry him with their fur.

As the mist thickened, I turned and swam back towards the

castle, spotlit in a shaft of sunlight, too romantic to be true. The lovers were walking back, picking their way across rivulets in the sand where starfish and small jellyfish sidled back to sea. Two runners splashed past along the sea's retreating edge, and there was a distant rumble of thunder inland. As I crossed the wide, puddled sands, the sunlight fell from the castle and it looked suddenly grey and forbidding. Beyond it all was distant golden evening. Gulls floating on the sea looked airborne, lifted on the mist that painted out the horizon in pale grey. Then the rain came, just as I was getting dressed, and I felt suddenly lonely and ridiculous on this huge expanse of magnificent beach. I threw the rucksack over one shoulder and ran hard, barefoot through deep sand under the tall sand-dunes, until I reached a natural gap between them and a path through marram grass that stung my wet calves as I ran, slowed down by the cloying sand. This halving of each stride by the sand made the running dream-like, as the swim had been.

The Farne Islands still hovered like planets suspended in the mist. I felt far wetter than in the sea. Then the car itself was misted up inside. I felt miserable. But when I dived through the deluge into a phone box in deserted Bamburgh a rainbow appeared over the heavenly castle. It was all absurdly magnificent and sad. I drove on in my own mist to Lindisfarne, spinning across the causeway, not caring whether I were cut off by the tide or not. In the seventh century, King Oswald of Northumbria had commissioned Aidan to come down from the monastery on Iona and convert his people to Christianity. Aidan had chosen to live on Lindisfarne because it reminded him of Iona, and because twice a day the tide covered its causeway and closed it for prayer. Seals lowed somewhere in the gloom as I walked round the curve of the strand by the harbour at dusk, past some of the best buildings in England: black rows of fishermen's sheds improvised from the tarred hulls of upturned boats.

25

THE OXBOW

River Windrush, 29 August

I TOOK A HIGH swallow dive south out of the mists of Lindisfarne and Bamburgh all the way down into the head-waters of the Thames in the Cotswolds (not 'the Cotswold hills', which, as William Cobbett pointed out, is tautologous because wolds *are* hills). I drove through rainstorms over glistening roads most of the night, and slept in the car some-where near Oxford, rain drumming on the roof incessantly, feeling seedy and exhausted, disgusted with myself for having fallen from my state of grace in the Northumbrian sea and devoured an 'all-day breakfast' on some oily motorway or other. I crept into the sleeping bag, grateful for the one luxury of the trip: my goose-down pillow. I was due at the birthday party of an architect friend at Coleshill, close to the upper Thames, and so pathetically eager for company that I was a day early and had the whole of a rainy Friday to kill in the Cotswolds. The truth of it was, I hated coming south and I loathed the unending straightness of the desolate, black motorways. How I had longed for a bend in the road – even just a bit of a kink – for some relief from the relentless efficiency of travelling in a continual bee-line. Even with the radio for company, there is nothing so lonely as a long, straight road. And besides, there was so much more water in Scotland and the North, so many shores still to tread, such unknown swims.

What an irony that with the sleep still in my eyes, and straight lines on the brain, this should be the day I discovered a whole new way of swimming rivers. A Third Way of swimming so blindingly simple, nobody had noticed it. It happened in a Cotswold tributary of the Thames, the Windrush, whose beauty to me that day was that it still winds, and still rushes.

About a mile downstream from Burford on the meandering footpath to Widford, I found the finest oxbow bend I have ever seen. Sheep grazed the meadows, and the cropped grass was in wonderful condition, springy and deep green. At the narrow turkey-neck of the oxbow were two old pollard willows. One of them masqueraded as a hybrid, with dog-roses, hawthorn and elder growing from the marsupial recesses of its anguished trunk. Each was an independent world, with whole cities of insect life in the grimy wrinkles of its bark, and generations of birds-nests in its dense topknot. I slid into the upstream side of the oxbow, and swam all round it almost back to where I had begun, climbing out by the twin willows again. Two hops across the grass, and I was back in the river where I began, swimming the next power-assisted lap around the grassy peninsula.

The Windrush flowed strong and fast, swollen by the rains, sweeping me along and flinging me ever outwards with its centrifugal force. It was only two or three feet deep, often less, and very clear, with a gravel bed under dark bunches of water crowfoot waving in the current. All down this valley the river snaked joyfully, unconstrained by anyone who might have thought they could put it straight on its exuberant, doodling course to join the Thames. It went its own way, like Shakespeare's dawdling schoolboy on his way to school. Like all running water, it wanted to turn everything into the image of its constantly undulating form. It worried at the river banks, hollowing them, rounding them into oxbows. If you made a very slow-motion stop-frame aerial film of a river's history, it would look like a swimming snake, or a writhing garden hose when water is run through it. Left to itself, a river will always meander. This is how rivers grow longer, and slow themselves down, and hold more water, and make them-selves more interesting and pleasing to the human eye, as well as to the creatures that live in them. By increasing the total length and capacity of the Windrush, these natural meanders, oxbows and flood meadows slow and diminish the impact of sudden storms by storing the floodwater. They also provide a far richer natural habitat for all the river creatures that crave the shelter of uneven places and all that is haphazard about the river's whimsical progress.

Despite the gloominess of the afternoon, these boomerang swims were highly satisfying, because they solved the river-swimmer's eternal problem of returning to your towel and clothes. It was like tobogganing endlessly downhill without having the fag of trudging back uphill. I was so absurdly delighted with my discovery that I swam round and round until I was dizzy. Fortunately no one appeared on the foot-path to witness this excess except a few unimpressed sheep.

Upstream, there had been a herd of black-and-white cattle, more appreciative spectators who kept galloping to the next bend of the bank opposite to watch, bandy-legged with amazement, as I sped past them, urged on by the swollen water, having leapt in through a gap in the rushes for a dash downriver. The Windrush is a coot river, so there wasn't a moorhen in sight. Some early and probably dastardly form of gang warfare must have carved out the territory between these two species, and the coots had triumphed.

My cyclical swims were very like the repeated bike-rides I take round the local lanes in Suffolk. The whole quality of cycling is akin to swimming; the economy of effort, the defiance of gravity, the dancing rhythm, and the general need to keep moving, lest you sink or topple. As modes of pro-pulsion, both could safely be classified as environmentally friendly. I enjoy the gliding, swooping motion of the bike as I enjoy the grace of swimming. And the steep plunge in top gear down a hill with the hedges dividing before you sends the air whipping your face as it does in a high dive. You are flying, as you fly and glide when you swim. There is also a governing of the body's motion on a bike as in water, where no sudden movements are possible and even a stone sinks slowly. So it is hard to overstrain your muscles by swimming or cycling; both are essentially benign forms of exercise. Completing the circle of the bike-ride is always satisfying, landing back in the world of ordinary gravity, as I did when I clambered out of the Windrush for the last time by the pollard willow.

At the birthday party at Coleshill the following afternoon, the sun had come out and there were architects with cantilevered glasses of champagne all over the lawn. I wandered off with a friend to explore Coleshill Park for signs of the false acacias imported from America and marketed as 'locust trees' (the American name) by William Cobbett. He sold no less than 13,600 of them to Lord Folkestone in 1822, to be planted in clumps of 200 in the park. 'They are the most beautiful clumps of trees that I ever saw in my life,' Cobbett says modestly in *Rural Rides* when he comes to Coleshill and sees his trees, already sixteen feet high only two years after they were planted. 'If men want woods, beautiful woods, and *in a hurry*, let them go and see the clumps at Coleshill.' Cobbett would cheerfully have replaced all the elms in Wiltshire with a plague of 'locusts' given half a chance. We should be thankful he never got his hands on *Cupressus lawsonii*. My companion and I failed to find even the single craggy old specimen, full of nesting owls, that is said to remain. It is curious that Cobbett should visit Coleshill and advertise his trees so volubly in *Rural Rides*, yet omit to mention the greatest agricultural building in England – the Great Coxhill Barn – only two miles down the road. I went and stood inside it in the late afternoon sunshine. The enormous wooden doors were open like lock gates, flooding the place with golden light. When he lived nearby at Kelmscott Manor, William Morris loved to visit the building, which he thought as beautiful and dignified as a cathedral.

The evening was warm and tender, and after the party I took a long swim in the pool below Buscott Lock, in what Morris used to call 'the Baby Thames', upstream from Kelmscott. The river is still quite a modest affair up here on the borders of Oxfordshire, and the water was clear enough just above the lock to see the dark shapes of tench weaving lazily amongst the lily stalks. I entered the water down a steep bank, slithering over a well-worn muddy shute in the grass; the sort of thing known to opponents of wild swimming as bank erosion. This was obviously a popular bathing place. Swimming in a big circle round the pool, I was observed by several swans and surrounded by tall, untidy old crack willows. These were the very trees that inspired Morris, on his daily fishing trips aboard his punt, to design his 'Willow Boughs' wallpaper. I wondered what he would have made of the assortment of big, ugly notices proclaiming the danger of deep water. A smell of fish and duckweed hung in the air.

At Kelmscott, I visited Morris's grave. I found it in the south-eastern corner of the churchyard beneath a laureate bay between five and six feet tall and nearly spherical, like Morris himself. This quiet corner is a miniature arboretum, with a mature box hedge, two yews, a syringa bush, hawthorn and ivy. It also contains the initialled headstones of Janey and May Morris. Morris's tomb was designed by his friend and partner in the Firm, Philip Webb, and is said to have been inspired by a piece of early stonework he found in the churchyard. Morris loved the church for its simplicity, and his gravestone is decorated with just two delicate stone carvings, often interpreted as trees. I like to see them as umbellifers; single stalks of cowparsley, or lady's lace, one of the commonest and most beautiful of wayside flowers. In spring this exquisite plant must flower all around the tomb in clouds of white, echoing the unassuming stone carving. The gravestone lies horizontally, laid a foot or so above the ground on two supporting blocks, like an upturned rowing boat laid keel up for the winter.

The raised tomb suggests levitation, and the flight of the soul from the body. There is something American Indian or Icelandic about it. It brought to mind a moment in Thoreau's *Week on the Concord and Merrimac Rivers*, when he discovers the graveyard of the extinct village of Dunstable near the banks of the Merrimac, and reflects how remarkable it is that the dead should lie everywhere under stones. Like Morris, he deplores the oppressive effect of 'all large monuments over men's bodies, from the pyramids down'. A monument, he suggests, 'should at least be "star-y-pointing", to indicate whither the spirit is gone, and not prostrate, like the body it has deserted'. Thoreau despairs that we are always writing 'Here lies', when we might put 'There rises'.

I couldn't help thinking that it was in his boat on the river that Morris was probably most at home, and that it is just what he would have chosen to row him over to the Other Side. Writing to Janey Morris in 1888, he described the river here as:

> Altogether a very pleasant river to travel on, the bank being still very beautiful with flowers; the long purples and willow-herb, and that strong-coloured yellow flower very close and buttony are the great show: but there is a very pretty dark blue flower, I think mug-wort, mixed with all that besides the purple blossom of the horse-mint and mouse-ear and here and there a bit of meadow-sweet belated.

Morris lived most of his life by water; by the moat at Water House, Walthamstow, as a boy and then at the two Kelmscott houses, here and by the same river at Hammersmith. It would be quite natural for him to be buried in a boat, floating above the ground.

26

Swallow Dives

Suffolk, 5 September
MY NEXT DESTINATION being the coast of Essex, I took the opportunity to make the detour to Suffolk, and the moat. Returning to my village past the familiar, centuries-old Neighbourhood Watch sign always makes me smile. Some wit has emptied a shotgun through it at close range, turning it into a colander which whistles eerily on windy days; an aeolian burglar alarm. It hadn't deterred the squirrels from pilfering my walnuts. When I arrived, they hardly paused in the serious business of walking their booty off the tree, along the barn roof, down the big crack willow and off to some subterranean vault to be laid down in date order for later on. I see them in winter, wandering the lawn disconsolately, trying to remember where the secret hiding places are.

The moat still maintained a steady sixty degrees fahrenheit, in spite of the weather, which was suddenly turning cool and briskly autumnal. The usually pristine clarity of the water was obscured by a surface oily with pollen dust from the fields. When I swam, it rippled before me into viscous rainbows, streaking and curling itself about in animated marbling, leaving a clear, black wake a yard wide that reflected the inverted heavens and the trees. By the time I had turned and was on my way back, it was already closing together again like curtains, and I came out like a bee from a flower, dusted in pollen. Most of the adult amphibians had left the water by now, and the weed had stopped growing. Dead leaves floated down underwater and settled belly-up on the bed of the moat.

I was prevented from lighting an autumn fire by the swallows that had arrived from Africa in April and were still occupying their nests in the chimney. Swallows are really cave birds, so it is easy to understand the attractions of a massive thirty-foot-deep brick flue easily big enough to fly up and down. The chimney is over 400 years old, and it is tempting to think that this particular family of birds, by now a dynasty, has been returning here to nest over all those summers. The last of the second clutch of fledglings, now fledged, was still roosting in the nest. Even after they have begun to fly they still return to the chimney nests each night, chattering long after dark, like children in a dormitory. Of all birdsong, the happy talk of swallows is my favourite. Theirs is a language I almost begin to understand as I stand by the fireplace eavesdropping on them in the chimney. They call to each other continually as they dip and wheel after insects, or swoop down, dapping the surface of the moat. But in the chimney their conversation is different, more intimate, more expressive and varied, some-times bickering, often simply a cascade of delight. Their maiden flight is the most heroic feat. On their very first attempt, the fledglings must rise vertically like harrier jump-jets some twenty-five feet up the sooty chasm before they reach daylight and the open air. Once there, their delight in the novelty of flying is expressed in great swoopings and soarings and flutterings above the house. I watch their earliest arcs of ascent with heart-stopped parental joy.

Now the weather had worsened, I was itching to get a fire going. I caught myself for a moment wishing the birds would hurry up and leave, as you sometimes do when a guest lingers that bit too long after dinner. Thomas De Quincey says that people often felt this way about Coleridge, who could be relied upon to arrive for lunch and stay for a week. However, whenever such selfish sentiments creep up, I remind myself that I'm a mere newcomer to this ancient dynasty of nomads, who settled here centuries before I ever appeared on the scene and will, I sincerely hope, long outlast me here.

27

THE JAYWICK PAPERS

Essex, 17 September

JAYWICK SANDS IS the first place I ever went on holiday. It was only two or three years after the war and I was probably about four. It must have made a big impression, because I remember aspects of it quite clearly. Most of my uncles, aunts and cousins seem to have been there, and we had rented one of the wooden houses on stilts by the bay. I remember being lifted up to touch the ceiling by an uncle, and paddling about in the sandy pools beneath the forest of soused crutches that propped up the houses. The smell of sea and seaweed permeated everything, and my cousins and I spent a lot of time running up and down the wooden steps that led to other houses, jumping off into the soft wet sand. It was like living in our own sandcastle. I was enchanted with this shack city, and have been in love with the shed life ever since. To this day I am never happier than in my tool shed, or in someone's beach hut.

My most vivid memory of the Jaywick holiday was of catching my first fish. Uncle Laddie, the prankster in the family who later taught me to swim in the Kenilworth swimming pool, fixed me a simple fishing rod with a bent-pin hook and took me down to the beach, where I landed an enormous plaice almost instantly. This was borne back to our shack villa in triumph, and enjoyed by one and all for lunch. It was some years before I learnt the truth; how Laddie had bought the biggest plaice at the fishmonger's and attached it to my hook by sleight of hand. The benevolent conspiracy was the high point of the holiday.

This was the first time I had returned to the place since that early taste of the beach-bum life. My Essex friends had often spoken of Jaywick as a hippie holiday home where people squatted the wooden houses, lived on apples from a bucket, and had dogs on bits of string. Such tales only fed my desire to return there. Because of its low-lying position on reclaimed marshy ground near the mouth of the Blackwater estuary, it isn't just time that passes Jaywick by. It is a cul-de-sac on the map too, secluded from the mainstream of visitors who stray out of Colchester on summer days to Clacton, Frinton and Walton on the Naze, windsurfers strapped to the roof-rack. Nobody has spent much money on Jaywick, with the result that you can still feel some of its original atmosphere and character. The deserted Jaywick Drug Stores has somehow survived, with a dusty display of Ex-Lax chocolate in the window, and over the road, the Model Farm Restaurant is still going, even though the model farm isn't.

I took the small grey German army-surplus rucksack I use for my swimming gear down to the far end of the beach, by the big boulders of a breakwater that protects one end of the bay. There were pools in the fine sand full of whelk-, oyster- and cockle-shells, and limp bladderwrack on the concrete. These were the shells of the best oysters in England, Colchester oysters from Mersea Island twenty miles away up the estuary of the Blackwater and the Colne in Arthur Ransome country. Around the rim of the bay people were settling down for the evening. A woman was taking in her washing off a line rigged on poles in the sand. I heard the pips for the six o'clock news on somebody's radio.

The swim was icy but wonderful, with the sun setting behind the nuclear power station at Bradwell across the huge waters of the estuary beyond St Osyth and Brightlingsea. The sea was so bright that two suns were setting. One in the sky, hovering under a thin cloudbank and one in the water, melting down the nuclear power station. It is rare to watch a sunset over the sea on the east coast, and I had the perfect viewpoint from water level. I swam in brown, deep water in a ripple-sanded lagoon to the west of the man-made spit of rock that forms a tiny harbour for what's left of Jaywick's fishing fleet; two or three little boats, with tiny cabins like allotment sheds, tugging at their moorings in the whizzing tide-race.

I turned and looked back towards the shore and the curious collection of bungalows that lined the seafront, lit by the dying reflected sunlight, their wooden clapboarding picked out in garish colours. At one end of the little curved sandy bay was the Jaywick Beach Bar, with a fifteen-foot square of concrete jutting out into the water, and beyond it, further off, a Martello tower. A fishing smack rode at anchor, trailing a wake that ploughed the smooth surface of the tide-stream. The bungalows were tiny, with much brightly-coloured picket fencing around them. A light plane flew in over the bay and came in to land behind the houses on a tiny airfield that had a windsock and a board advertising pleasure flights along the coast. The ancient gnarled remains of a groyne heaved out of the sand, the concrete slabs thrown together like dice by storms. The defiantly anachronistic spirit of Jaywick was distilled in a sign on the miniature promenade advertising the pub: NEVER SAY DIE – LIVE ENTERTAINMENT. The promenade was tiny, more of a sea path squeezed in behind the sea wall, and the bungalows, with their stilts and verandas, crammed together facing out to sea like punters at a racecourse trying to get a view. On the skyline of low sand-dunes a horse and rider trotted round and round.

I swam in the shelter of the breakwater, parallel with the racing tide, straight into the eye of the sun, watching seagulls bobbing past at a terrific rate, and a pair of canoeists leaning on their paddles to make headway. An unusual stillness often comes over the sea at this time of day, and the voices and the rhythmic splash of wood on water carried a long way to me with absolute clarity. Dogs barked in the marram grass, chafing their string leashes, the horse snorted, and the strains of Status Quo floated across the bay from one of the dimly-lit verandas. I tried to imagine what it must have sounded like here in the 1930s, when people spent their evenings dancing to a band in the Brooklands Club or a gramophone in the Morocco Café. I kept on swimming towards the subsiding sun, down its fiery wake, as if this were the last I would see of it before winter. I wanted to retrieve it like an elusive beachball. I was sunbathing.

Like a lot of makeshift landscapes, Jaywick grew up as plotlands, sold off in the 1930s by a developer from Dulwich, F. C. 'Foff' Steadman, with ambitions for the place as a holiday resort. In 1928, Steadman paid £7,500 for the reclaimed marshland, dunes and dykes, but Clacton Town Council refused him planning permission for houses because they were unhappy about the sewerage arrangements on such low-lying land. Undeterred, Steadman got permission instead for 'Beach Chalets' and 'Bathing Houses'. By 1929, he was offering beach chalets in the London papers for £20 to £100, and plots with land for car-parking or a garden for anything from £25 to £200. The chalets caught on with East Enders and by 1931 there were 200 of them at Jaywick. They drew water from a standpipe and had Elsan toilets, emptied by contractors, known locally as 'The Bisto Kids', with a tank on wheels – the 'Honey Cart' – pulled by a pair of horses known to all as 'Bugger and Sod'. In the same year, over 200 citizens crowded into the Beach Café for the first meeting of the Jaywick Freeholders' Association.

You can catch the cockney flavour in their genius for naming things. When they were flooded in 1948, one of the locals, Adrian Wolfe, built the first sea defence, instantly christened 'Adrian's Wall'. There were no street numbers, but every chalet had a name: *Lazy Days*, *Windy Way*, *Whoopee*, *Spindrift*. Like the street names, they speak volumes about the romantic aspirations of the plotlanders. The little streets of Jaywick are all grandly called this or that 'Way', and named after the flowers of the sea shore: 'Sea Lavender', 'Sea Thistle', 'Sea Holly', 'Sea Cornflower', 'Sea Pink'. In truth, every one of these plants is now extinct in Jaywick, so their names evoke a cumulative melancholy as you wander the potholed streets. There is even a Snakes Lane in Jaywick, named after the long-departed grass snakes that lived in the rushes in that part of town. Later, in homage to the motor cars which made Jaywick possible, they christened another twenty-five avenues after a litany of extinct manufacturers from Humber to Alvis, with the happy result that you could holiday in Sunbeam Avenue.

The romantic Jaywickians built their own wooden jetty and had a lifeboat called 'Beryl'. They had been promised 1,600 hours of annual sunshine in the promotional literature when they first moved in, and they meant to enjoy it. There had even been a Jaywick beach chalet at the 1935 Ideal Home Exhibition. But in the east-coast floods of 1953, Jaywick suddenly looked like Bangladesh. Five hundred had to be rescued by boat from their vulnerable homes, and thirty-five died.

I had lingered in the water to see the last of the sun, and was considerably chilled when I swam back up my Sunbeam Avenue into the warm shallows and slid out on to the rocks to get dry. Despite some natural east-coast turbulence, the sea had been clear. Towelling myself vigorously, I reflected that the Blackwater and the Colne are both listed as Class One rivers by the Environment Agency, and that their estuary waters would need good care too, flowing over some of the most highly-prized oyster beds in the world. Half a dozen Colchesters can set you back twelve or fifteen pounds in Wheelers, Bentleys or Bibendum. But then I looked again at Bradwell, shut down yet again because of some cracked pipe or faulty duct, and wondered.

Sauntering along the beach, I tried to imagine the exact spot where I caught my first fish. The sand shelves gently, so the inanimate plaice would have slid ashore easily enough. For all I know, it was already gutted and filleted too. Further up, there were scars of driftwood fires, horse manure where they tether the beach ponies, and a dense ribbon of dry seaweed, oyster-shells, plastic bottles and oily blue nylon rope. It added to the general air of unselfconsciousness I liked so much about the place. So many seaside towns have joined in the mania for tidy beaches, it made a welcome change. Seaweed and flotsam can actually be really useful, forming the nuclei of future sand-dunes as beach sandstorms pile up round them, and homes for the sandhoppers and other delicacies that form the diet of so many shoreline birds like sandpipers and dunlin.

Rows of wooden pegs danced on the washing lines along the sea wall and on the scuffed sands above the high-water line as I strolled back along the miniature promenade.

Someone had just painted a final coat of pungent orange on *Why Worry*, and *Happy Returns* was for sale. A black cat chased mosquitoes on the beach. All along the seafront was an ice-cream feast of pinks, creams, oranges and blues, as though the houses were in pyjamas. No one drew their curtains, in fact no one seemed to mind very much about anything. Everything in Jaywick looked outwards and pretty well the only things to look in would be the sea and the weather. Porches and planked verandas were jumbled with windsurfers, fibreglass boats, deckchairs and picnic tables. The whole place had the far-off feeling of my childhood. It looked absurdly insubstantial, as though it might just float away one day on the face of the rising North Sea.

28

GREAT EXPECTATIONS

Kent, 18 September

MY FIRST SIGHT of the Medway on my journey out of Essex into Kent next morning was from a great height, crossing the bridge that speeds the M2 towards Dover and France. The river sparkled from beneath a blanket of mist hastily thrown back by a burst of early sunshine, and the boats riding at anchor looked like Pooh-sticks on the mightiness of the river. I went to Chatham, where I browsed round the magnificent half-deserted, half-asleep dockyard, and climbed into the whispering roof-beams of a gigantic wood-framed, mud-bottomed, dry-dock shed, clinker-built in clapboarding and whitewashed like a Shaker barn. Then on alongside the river to Gillingham and down Water Lane to a boatyard behind the gasometers.

'Denis is on board. Just give him a shout,' said a man cradling an outboard motor. A hatch cover went up and Denis waved from the deck of the *Doris*, a handsome wooden fishing yawl moored near the quay with a plume of dense coal smoke rising from her stove chimney. He came over in the dinghy to fetch me. Denis had the bearded, philosophical look of a seafarer, and twinkling eyes. On board, we had a cup of tea together in the cabin by the bubbling stove, and planned the course we would take across the Medway to Hoo Salt Marsh Island and the Folly Fort.

Denis, who has spent his entire life on boats in and out of the Medway, had generously agreed to escort me in his rowing boat. I was glad of it because, to tell the truth, I was really quite nervous about this swim. This was my first big industrial river, running right through the heart of the most densely populated part of Kent; some 400,000 people live in the Medway towns of Chatham, Rochester and Gillingham. I was scared of the pollution mostly; there were rumours of Hepatitis B, polio and bacteria in such rivers. But there would also be strong currents out in the deep shipping channel, not to mention ships. Hoo Salt Marsh Island is a mile long and lies nearly a mile across the river towards the north bank. At its eastern end lies a ruined naval fort, one of two built in the river in 1860 to defend Chatham Dockyard and our navy from invasion. My plan was to swim across to the island on the last forty-five minutes of the rising tide and visit Steve, an artist camping in Folly Fort, and working on the island.

My Jaywick dip had taught me that there was too much of a chill in the late September water for a long swim in the skin alone. I donned the wetsuit on board the *Doris*, and we set off in the dinghy for Gillingham Strand past banks of eel grass submerging in the rising tide. The sun was now eclipsed by the leaden cloud that reached right down to the long black horizontal line of the marsh and the river. As I waded in down the shingle bank, a melancholy north-westerly began to sweep towards us across the mud-green river.

I struck out for the first objective, a green boat bobbing at a mooring a few hundred yards out, and swallowed my first mouthful of brackish Medway water. My breaststroke was made awkward by the waves, cutting at me diagonally from the left and catching me unawares just as I was breathing in. This was exactly the sort of thing that had kept me awake at night. Snorting and spitting out the unpalatable draughts or trying to hold my head in the air only broke up the rhythm of my swimming even more, so I either had to learn to love Medway water or, almost too embarrassing to contemplate, abandon the swim. Denis called out the course from the boat: 'Go for the orange buoy, then the green one.' I passed the last of the moored boats, a beautiful forty-four-foot Whitstable yawl, and a pair of antique West Country luggers whose rigging rapped a tattoo against their masts in the breeze. I now kept my eye on a pair of distant pylons at a point just to one side of the Kingsnorth power station chimney, the one vertical feature in the horizontal world before me.

The river was the colour of verdigris, the island was still a blur, and so far there had been no big ships or tugs to worry about. We were carrying a canvas harness on a length of rope just in case I should need to be towed at speed out of the path of anything. I became conscious of the giddy depth of the river as I reached the fairway, the main shipping channel. The tide seized me as I swam out past the line of boats, like a thermal lifting a glider, and I instinctively lengthened my stroke to swim with as much power and economy as I could summon.

We had set off at a quarter to two, and high tide was at half-past two, so I was being carried upriver, which on the whole is a better thing than to be carried out to sea. Halfway across, we realised that neither Denis nor I had a watch, so we had no idea how close we were running to the turn of the tide. I just kept on gazing at the power station chimney, with the island and the fort now coming into focus in the foreground, and swimming somewhat crabwise across the current. Curious things happen in the mouths of rivers as they reach the sea. The fresh river-water runs out over the top of the sea-water, which in turn slides in underneath it as the tide rises, because it is denser and heavier. Curious things were also happening in my own mouth; from now on 'Medway' would for ever mean the taste of khaki water.

Sometimes Denis rowed ahead of me, sometimes to one side, and sometimes behind. Both of us had settled into the zen of rhythm by now. His great-grandfather had been the last man to live on Hoo Salt Marsh Island. It belonged to the dockyard and has always been used as a dumping ground for the dredgings from the river. Denis's great-grandpa was the keeper of the island, and kept an eye on the moored lighters and machinery out there. The coastguards often met him as he loomed out of the fog in the early morning, rowing his two daughters to school in Gillingham. In the end, his single-storey house was buried under the mud they dredged and tipped on the island. The family bred black rabbits, and set some free. The local poachers still bag the occasional descendant with a patch of black in its coat. There are foxes there too, living on rats and rabbits, or crabs from the foreshore.

Until 1858, two years before the fort was built, the floating prison hulks familiar to readers of *Great Expectations* were moored in the deep water of the estuary along here. They were crudely converted decommissioned naval vessels where prisoners were consigned to await transportation to Australia. Although Dickens locates the hulks in the Thames Estuary in his novel, they were in fact in the Medway. He was certainly familiar with the prison ships and the Medway marshes from his own childhood in Chatham, where he lived between the ages of four and ten. He returned, too, in 1854, to live by this river, six years before he published *Great Expectations*. The imaginative landscape of the book is surely the one in which I was now literally immersed; I might well have been following the same course as Magwitch when he dived from his floating Alcatraz and escaped. Once on the Hoo Salt Marshes he could have made his way across the muddy creeks at low tide and ended up on shore in the churchyard at Hoo village for the dramatic meeting with Pip that begins the story. Of course, Magwitch could never really have swum the distance fully dressed, in freezing water, with the heavy prison iron locked on his leg.

The river in the lee of the island was calmer and the swimming easier as Denis called out from the boat that he could now see the grass quite clearly, and Steve appeared like Prospero coming along the shore to meet us. I swam in through a confusion of submerged timbers and slimy wooden stakes standing up from the water, which I afterwards discovered once constituted a landing-stage. We landed on a strip of shingle beach and I climbed out, steadying myself on the boat, trying to find my land legs again, looking back at the infinite, gunmetal-grey line of the other shore.

I walked up through a squat forest of elder, bramble and a wilding pear tree to the fort with Steve, while Denis went back across the river, having arranged to return later and ferry me back. I was feeling quite as ravenous as Magwitch in the graveyard and had experienced several mirages of cups of tea on the way over, probably as a reaction to swallowing several gallons of the dubious Medway. So I was delighted to find that Steve had a driftwood fire crackling in one of the fort's original fireplaces and a kettle on the hob. We had entered via an overgrown earthwork rampart and across a plank, set like a token drawbridge over a puddle, then through a massive creaking fortified doorway with a six-foot iron bar for a latch (which Steve secured at night). We then crept in darkness through an arched brick tunnel (the gunpowder magazine) and up a stone staircase winding through a buddleia bush on to the circular upper gallery, in one bay of which Steve had set out his camp. He lives and works here for days at a time.

I was wide-eyed with astonishment at this building, a massive eleven-sided polygon built of granite, brick, steel and wood to house eleven nine-inch rifled guns, each weighing twelve tons. Its walls were of four-and-a-half-foot granite blocks bedded on lead-plate joints, and each artillery bay had its own fireplace and looked out through a casemate, where the deafening gun would have been, to views of the river, marshes, Kingsnorth power station or Darnet Fort, an identical twin built at the same time on another island three-quarters-of-a-mile away. A steel boom could be slung between the two forts across the shipping channel as an additional defence for Chatham Dockyard. The navy were understandably anxious to avoid a repeat of the successful raid on Chatham and the English fleet by the Dutch in the previous century. This is one of the most impressive historic buildings in England, and certainly one of the most neglected.

Steve's canvases were propped up around the walls or hung from a washing line like dried cod. They were a kind of collaboration between the man and the river. When we had finished our lunch and I had changed, we set off over the marsh to explore the island and see some of his work in progress. The tide was by now receding to reveal a number of canvases pegged out on the shore or in the mud channels that wind through the marsh. The action of the tide had drawn the subtle pigments of the mud across the spreadeagled canvas in beautiful striated sweeps of greys, browns and black that looked uncannily like the very landscape in which we stood.

273

Steve would dry the canvases, take them back in Denis's boat to his studio in Chatham Dockyard, and add to the river's painting himself, using his own pigments made from the mud, natural materials and found objects of the island. One of his greens, for example, would be made from verdigris scraped from copper nails and other boat scrap found on the shore. He was working towards an installation work, to be called 'Time and Tide', in which he would hang a canvas in each of the eleven casemates of the nearby Darnet Fort and bring people over to see it by boat.

We walked along the eastern shore past the wooden hulks of several scuttled trawlers, sunken concrete lighters and a tramp steamer, the *Moonlit Water*. She had belonged to a drug-runner who had abandoned her and disappeared. The island has been a rubbish tip and a dump for the river dredgers for centuries, and its shores are a mass of Roman pottery shards, coins, old bottles and bones. Denis had shown me when we landed how the shingle is full of sea coal, a barnacled legacy of the estuary's industrial past. He collects it to burn on his stove. Steve has a ready supply of fresh tomatoes from a self-seeded forest of them growing wild on the dumped rubbish and mud of the island. Along the north shore we even found a broken burial urn and the tide-washed cremated bones of a Roman, recently revealed by the constant erosion of the oozing mudbanks.

I returned to the Gillingham shore with Denis, leaving Steve on his island. As we retraced the course of my swim, I pondered what he had told me as we stood over the Roman bones; that I was by no means the first to have made this crossing. In the year 43, the Emperor Claudius had sent an invading army of 35,000 men under the command of Aulus Plautius to land on the Kent coast and subdue the Britons. When they reached the Medway, they were confronted by 60,000 Britons on the far bank under the command of Caractacus and Togodumnus. At that time the estuary was fordable at low tide, but the Britons had sabotaged the ford by digging deep channels. Aulus had with him a regiment of Batavians, members of a German tribe living on an island in the mouth of the Rhine, who were renowned as swimmers. At high tide, just before dawn on the third day of a tense stand-off, Aulus sent the 3,000 Batavians swimming silently across the water with their weapons tied on their backs. They took the sleeping Britons by surprise and ran straight to the lines of chariot-ponies, ruthlessly disabling several thousand of them. Meanwhile, two battalions of the Ninth Regiment crossed the river on an assortment of rafts, inflated wineskins and captured coracles, to be followed later by the elephants and camels they had brought with them. The defending forces were put to flight and the amphibious regiment marched on to the Thames, which they also swam, since the Britons had not by then perfected the ultimate deterrent to river swimmers, pollution.

29

CHANNEL SWIMMING

Kent, 19 September

THE FOLLOWING MORNING I took my first steps into the nearest thing in England to a desert: Dungeness. The sea has dumped millions upon millions of pebbles here in a gigantic raised beach that juts out into the sea beyond the Romney Marshes like Cyrano de Bergerac's nose. In aerial photographs, you can see how the pebbles are arranged in whorls reminiscent of the 600 species of wild flowers that are found on this unpromising terrain. Somehow or other, nearly one-third of all the flowering plants in Britain grow naturally here, and it is for a garden, Derek Jarman's, that Dungeness is now known as much as for its nuclear power station. The whole thing is a living organism, like Blakeney Point, Orford Ness, or Chesil Bank, and it is constantly changing shape, growing out into the sea.

On my way across Kent, after the high-sided scrap lorries, animal sanctuaries and lay-by mobile cafés of the arterial roads through Maidstone and Ashford, I had driven through the misty wastes of Romney Marsh, a landscape out of time. Three miles away, I had passed a farmer on an old grey Ferguson tractor followed by a gang of women harvesting potatoes and leeks by hand, much as the Land Girls did. The dykes all had quaint names, like Jury's Gap Sewer, and wandered aimlessly about the flatness as though they were lost. My road, too, looped absent-mindedly along the courses of past and present waterways until I eventually arrived at the first few pebbles of the Denge Beach. I parked the car at the edge of this spartan wilderness and set off to hike across its scrubby undulations and stone-dunes for two-and-a-half miles to the Britannia, a pub at the uttermost extremity of Dungeness, under the lighthouse. I sat talking to the landlord and drinking tea, wondering if the sea-fret would ever clear. It hid the horizon and removed all sense of perspective in this outback, with its isolated fishing huts and wooden bunga-lows planted at random on the pebbles. An empty No. 12 bus from Dymchurch bumped along the concrete road and stopped opposite, where the Grand Hotel once stood, then moved off again after five minutes, still empty. The few figures in this landscape moved deliberately, slowed by the shingle.

The mist showed no signs of lifting, but I thought I would go down to the shore anyway. The fishermen's creosoted huts were named after their boats: *Oasis*, *Seapatch*, *Celebrity*. Sunshine had melted the tar off their roofs, and sparrows and starlings strutted along the ridges, puffing themselves up against the mist. House martins gathered impatiently on the telegraph wires over an old railway coach that was once Queen Victoria's, now somebody's home.

Thirty feet below the raised beach, down a steep bank of pebbles, this stretch of the English Channel looked calm but a long way off, like water at the bottom of a well. I clattered down several tiers of stones and, quite alone in the mist, dived out into deep water. There were no shallows here. No horizon either, just the enveloping greyness, and the mesmeric, searching glint of the lighthouse overhead. As I swam out, I felt dwarfed by the immensity of the beach behind me, the great depth of the quiet water as it lapped at the steep shelf of submerged shingle. If I felt out of my depth and further than far out, it was because I was swimming off the end of a natural pier; the sensation you get when you bathe off a sailing boat far out to sea. It led me to a deeper feeling for Keats's lines, in his sonnet 'Bright Star': 'The moving waters at their priestlike task/ Of pure ablution round earth's human shores.'

It is only by swimming in deep water that you really sense the motion of the tides as a cosmic event, as one with the moon and stars. This was indeed some of the purest bathing to be had anywhere on the south coast, and I was busy wallowing in its freshness, laving my limbs and, I hoped, not polluting it with too much Medway mud. The sea was cool, but I soon grew used to it and breaststroked round in wide circles, conscious of the longshore currents that I knew must flow around the outcrop that has wrecked so many ships. After a wetsuit swim the day before, swimming-costume nakedness was blissful, my pale hands showing in sharp focus through the clear water before me. How ironic that a few hundred yards away a nuclear power station should be cooling its eternal fever in such crystal waters like some fated monster of the *Odyssey*. The thought sent me swimming back inshore towards the daunting wall of shingle and my solitary rucksack perched above the tideline. Everything here was larger than life, except me and my rucksack. The dim shape of the latest of the Dungeness lighthouses loomed above the scene. This is the fifth one to be built at the point since 1615 because the shingle keeps accumulating and pushing the beach further out, leaving the beacons misleadingly far inland.

Glowing inwardly after the swim, I explored the upper beach and discovered comfort food: smoked cod's roe and extra big kippers in Jim's Smokehouse at Pearl Cottage, just along from Jarman's Prospect Cottage. He told me that in springtime carloads of Greeks come down from London to pick the tender young shoots of the seakale. It used to be enjoyed as a delicacy by the locals, who would kick up the shingle round the plants to blanch the leaves. Now this is one of the few wild colonies of a plant that was once common on our shifting coasts. Jim showed me his garden, a vigorous Manhattan skyline of seeding mullein and other native flowers, plagued by earwigs. His ponds were all wired over to protect the goldfish from herons, and another was full of common frog tadpoles, which he releases as adults on the marsh to compensate for the recent dominance of the vociferous bullfrog around Dungeness. Like the wild boar which roam other parts of Kent, they have been introduced.

Jim's garden had no fences. It just melted into the wider

natural garden that is Denge Beach. This is the local way of things, but Jim pointed sadly to a neighbouring property that had recently changed hands and been fenced. The meanness of it amongst all these free-thinking desert gardeners with their undefined patches shading into the wilderness was striking. 'If there's one thing that gets me really titty,' said Jim, 'it's fences.' Fishing communities, especially net-fishing people, are essentially communal. Most of the work is shared and co-operative. There is trust and interdependence. So who would need fences?

Jim's friend still goes fishing for a living in the last wooden boat in Dungeness. There is something profoundly sad about the place that Derek Jarman must have felt and expressed in his garden full of relics of the fishing industry. Prospect Cottage, where Jarman and Keith Collins lived, is a simple, black clapboard fisherman's house with yellow windows and doors and matching burglar alarm. A set of yellow oilskins hung, motionless, on the washing line that day. The cottage is a place of pilgrimage for Jarmanites, the film buffs and gardeners who turn up from all over the world to admire the highly original natural garden, often without an appointment. The place is so unassuming, and so obviously a retreat, that I decided it should be left in peace, and skirted it well to the west along the abandoned narrow-gauge Romney, Hythe and Dymchurch Railway line that used to bring holidaymakers out here and is still used occasionally by steam enthusiasts.

Trudging through the pebbles past clumps of plantains, seakale, sage, toadflax, yarrow, yellow lady's bedstraw and dwarf broom, I reached another set of narrow-gauge rails that led from the concrete roadway down the beachhead. Lying about in the shingle were some small rusting wagons that were used to run the catch up to a waiting lorry on the first stage of its journey to Billingsgate. The ruins of our fishing industry lay everywhere. The entire beach was an industrial graveyard of derelict huts, rusty anchors, makeshift boat winches with taxi engines and gearboxes, hopelessly tangled nets, oil tanks leaking on to whelk shells, the dented torso of a tank engine, a deserted net-drying tower, a sunken bulldozer drowned in shingle, and dormant Dormobiles. The shabby grey mass of the half-spent nuclear power station in the background looked perfectly in keeping with all this dereliction. Every now and again through the fog came the garbled monotones of announcements over its tannoy.

Fourteen full-time fishing-boats still work out of Dungeness, but the nature of the fishing has changed dramatically since the decline of the herring and mackerel, and a scattered pile of parched, lanky wooden stakes was the last remnant of a great tradition of net fishing off the shore from Dungeness along to Greatstone-on-Sea. The kettlenet-fishing along these sands was dominated by certain families: the Southerdens, the Tarts and the Gilletts. Each family had its stands, areas of shore 900 yards long and 210 yards wide, where they set up their nets on tall wooden poles like those you see in Kentish hop-fields. Each stand would have about ninety wooden poles sixteen feet long, dug three feet into the sand. The fishermen would go out on the sands with a horse and cart at low tide and hang the netting on the poles like cricket nets. The configuration of the nets was a huge trap, which ensnared whole shoals of fish in the 'kettle', a circle of net in the centre, which sometimes boiled with panicking fish when the tide receded.

About eight men would stand by on shore with the horse and cart as the tide went out. When there was still three feet of water in the kettle, they would wade into the sea in their oilskins with hand nets and shovel the live fish into the cart. Others would go round the standing nets filling baskets with the gasping fish that had been left hanging by the gills. Sometimes there were just too many of the creatures to be gathered before the tide exposed the sand, and the nets would be lifted to let them escape. In the event of a bumper catch, the fishermen would put a number of baskets on top of a pole and hoist it up on the sea wall. Lookouts with telescopes were posted back in town at Romney, and they would send out the appropriate number of relief horses and carts to bring in the fish. Mackerel was the main catch, and they would be packed by the women and sent up to Billingsgate by the evening train from Lydd. They sold the smaller sprats and mackerel locally and kept the herrings for smoking as bloaters or kippers. This kind of fishing had its heyday in the early part of the century, but Ed Gillett and his brothers carried on until 1953.

I decided to drive round to Camber Sands, eight miles down the coast, for a late lunch, as the sea mist was beginning to clear to reveal a gloriously mild and sunny afternoon. By two o'clock I was seated outside the Kit Kat Café on the seafront in my shorts. The first thing I saw as I stared out upon the vast expanse of gleaming sand was an old man with a metal detector and a trowel. He was clutching his headphones excitedly, as though receiving news of a lottery win. He burrowed feverishly into a tiny fraction of the billions of silicon grains that constitute Camber Sands, but found nothing worth keeping.

At the first bite of my sandwich, I heard sand echoing through my jaw like tinnitus. The sea breeze was blowing it off the dunes towards the café. Here we all were at the tail end of September on a Friday afternoon enjoying an Indian summer holiday. There must have been two hundred people on the beach, yet it is so enormous it looked empty. They were mostly local Kentish mums and children seizing the chance sunny afternoon. I seemed to be the only person lacking a dog, and the only man without a bunch of keys dangling from my belt. What with the dogs and the keys, it looked and sounded like a Securicor outing. Kent appeared to favour little dogs: cairn terriers, poodles, dachshunds, the occasional Jack Russell.

As the tide receded, Camber was all sand-pools, lagoons and impromptu sand rivers snaking to the tideline. At the café, all the mums sat out at white plastic tables smoking cigarettes that lasted about fifteen seconds in the breeze. The group at the nearest table had put their trainers on it to weigh down their napkins. Mine had already disappeared in a small tornado. A crocodile of little blonde girls in black wellingtons, shepherded by an older sister also in black wellies, stood out as reassuringly old-fashioned amongst all the Nikes and Oasis T-shirts. There must have been at least a dozen kites aloft. A tough-looking youth made straight towards me with a Dobermann, yanking its lead every four paces and shouting, 'Come 'ere!' Looking down, I realised I was posted right beside a Tupperware container labelled 'Dog Water'. I had come here expecting to find some peace, and was struck by the complexity of the soundtrack – the shouting men, the frantic barking of a tethered Labrador, the roar of the Gaggia espresso machine inside the café, the whine of a nosediving Peter Powell stunt kite, and the steady, seductive whisper of the distant sea.

I took off my shoes and set out for a two-and-a-half-hour barefoot hike along the shoreline, paddling most of the way ankle- to knee-deep in the receding tide. As if unsure of the immense freedom before them, most people seemed to stay within range of the café, and I had gone only a few hundred yards when I found myself entirely alone. The Battle of Britain had been fought in the skies reflected on the gleaming, lugwormed flats. I thought of the wounded planes that limped back over the Channel, only to nosedive into these sands in desperate attempts to crash-land, twisting their steel propellers like the petals of giant daisies. I had found some of the old aircraft engines and propellers rescued from this beach leant up against a hut on Romney Marsh like wilted crucifixes; monuments to their unknown pilots and crew.

Choosing a low tumulus of drier sand, I changed into my swimming trunks and left my rucksack and shoes there to wade out and investigate what looked from a distance like a half-submerged tank, but turned out to be a wrecked steel fishing trawler. The beach at this point is four or five hundred yards wide, and at low tide you have to wade through yards more shallows before reaching water deep enough for swimming. The sea, brown with churned sand, was marginally warmer than at Dungeness, but still cold. I waded in up to my waist and swam out to inspect the rusting hulk. It was festooned with ragged seaweed and pimpled all over with barnacles. A solitary cormorant perched atop the bridge, and white-capped waves broke over the sandbar that must have grounded the boat.

I swam beyond it into the open sea. When I turned back towards land I spotted two construction workers who had been operating a pile-driver on the sea defences hurrying down the beach towards me. As I swam back towards them, they hesitated, then turned and walked away again when I emerged from the sea and returned to my towel and clothes. I was embarrassed to realise they thought I was doing the same as John Stonehouse, or the fictional Reginald Perrin: leaving a pile of clothes behind and disappearing for good. I went up to where they were resuming work to apologise and thank them. I had guessed right, although they had also worried about my swimming in the riptides out there and the remoteness of the spot, and besides, they said, they were curious.

Stonehouse's story is amongst the best and worst of modern sleaze. The Labour MP for Walsall disappeared on 22 November 1974, a month or so before Lord Lucan, and the two lives became strangely connected. Stonehouse was reported missing, feared drowned, in the waters off Miami, where he had gone on a dubious business trip to try and save various ailing banking enterprises from imminent collapse. He had last been seen going swimming, and his clothes had been found by police at the beach. Stories began to appear in the papers that he had been murdered by the Mafia, and a mysteriously empty 'concrete overcoat' was discovered on Miami Beach. He was said to have been part of a Czech spy-ring, and it was confirmed that Harold Wilson, with his ready sense of humour, had had Stonehouse's telephone tapped while he was Minister of Posts and Telecommunications. The MP's wife, Barbara, said he was in the habit of swimming far out to sea on his own, and she was convinced he was drowned.

Then, just before Christmas, Stonehouse was arrested in Australia by the Melbourne police, travelling on two pass-ports in the names of Markam and Muldoon, who turned out to be two of his deceased Walsall constituents. Using Markham's passport, and living as Muldoon in a flat in the suburbs, Stonehouse had been in the habit of visiting the main Melbourne post office to check its poste restante for mail.

Meanwhile, another tall, distinguished-looking Englishman with black hair and money worries had also disappeared. Every police force in the world had been alerted to keep an eye open for Lucan, especially in Australia. The Melbourne police simply did what any police force would do in the circum-stances: they staked out the poste restante desk at the post office. When a tall, distinguished-looking Brylcreemed English smoothie strolled in, they couldn't believe their luck. They arrested him. Down at the station, Markham/Muldoon/Lucan/Stonehouse found himself in some difficulty. Faced with explaining a passport in one false name and a flat in another, Stonehouse's predicament was pure Kafka. Only by confessing he was the fugitive MP could he convince the police he was not Lord Lucan.

The wreck was marked by a totem pole, and three more deathly cormorants had returned to perch symmetrically on it, two on each side of the triangular 'Danger' sign and one on top. If these birds looked wizened, it was because they probably were; they can live to be as old as fifty. As sunset arrived, and low tide, I was joined on the great deserted beach by two figures, the first apparently carrying a double bed into the sea, the second digging lugworms with a tiny-bladed spade with the rapidity of a bird. 'They move like lightning,' he told me. 'You need skill.' I asked him what he fished for, and he said he didn't fish at all himself. He preferred the challenge of lugworm hunting, and gave them away to his friends. The double bed turned out to be an enormous shrimping net with which its owner hoovered the sandy bottom, pausing after each flurry of passes to empty it into a plastic washing-up bowl, pick out any shrimps, and pop them over his shoulder into a plastic bucket strapped to his back. He was joined by a second shrimper, also accoutred like a one-man band, who appeared from nowhere and kept a respectful distance.

Across the glistening sands, small questing Lowry figures now began springing up everywhere, curious to see what the low tide had deposited on the beach. On its big blank canvas someone had etched a beautiful looping line with a stick. I picked up a hunk of solid mahogany, almost petrified by the salt-water and worn smooth by the sand. It sat dense and cold in my hands, nearly black as coal and flecked with ginger from iron salts in the mud or sand it must have been buried in. Perhaps it had been part of a breakwater or a pier. Carrying it two or three miles in my rucksack before drying it slowly in my workshop back in Suffolk somehow gave it more weight in other ways. Such driftwood survivors are signs of hope. I turned it into a lamp for a friend who loves to write late at night, adrift in a sea of papers; a small desk lighthouse to help steer her course.

The ribbed sand was hard work on the feet, like walking on a tin roof for miles on end. I came back towards the Kit Kat past a row of beach houses nestling in the dunes, several of them empty or derelict. One clapboarded bungalow caught my eye, with a wood-shingle roof, bay window, and french windows facing the beach. Its garden was boarded up and overgrown with yellow sea poppies, sea cabbage and sea pinks, the local seaside weeds. I stepped through a gap and looked in through a hole in the boarded french window. The scene was like Miss Havisham's. The place must have been abandoned for thirty years, but when I parted the curtains there were tennis rackets laid out on the table, and an open cupboard door revealed early mark-one Marmite and Robertson's marmalade jars. Next door but one, the influence of Derek Jarman had spread along the coast and there was a full-scale Jarmanite garden complete with pebble cairns, massive balks of sea-bashed timber standing on end like megaliths; various oddments of rusting iron, bits of boat, fat, tarry lengths of hawser laid out like serpents, and the wild plants of this shore in pebble bunkers. Its playful spirit perfectly suited the atmosphere of this limitless desert playground. On a summer's day you wouldn't be surprised to meet Saint-Exupéry and the Little Prince stepping out of a light plane in a mirage over the hot sands.

30
WATER LEVELS

Somerset, 14 October

BOB'S BIKE WAS leant against the gate. I saw his bent figure on the far side of the orchard gathering windfall cider apples into sacks. As I approached the door of the wooden shed, a flurry of sparrows flew out of the cider press. Over the winter, Bob was going to sweep the dust off the wooden trays and oil the massive corkscrew shafts of the press to get it going again. During the war, the farm's cider shed had been an unofficial pub dispensing Dutch courage to the Spitfire pilots from the aerodrome across the fields. Cider and bread and butter was all they served. Bob said he always lets the apples fall before he harvests them. These were Kingston Blacks, just what he wanted for a chap down the road in Dowlish Wake. Nineteen sacks would fill a barrel.

The fine spell of October weather had enticed me west again, into the watery Somerset Levels, where some friends have one of the small, traditional farm orchards that were once common all over the county. People hurry past the Levels on the motorways, hardly registering the flat meadows, serried pollard willows, ancient church towers, osier beds, oozing marshland, small orchards, winding rivers, and cows. It is still a medieval landscape. They call it 'the land of shaking trees' because they float on a fenland raft of peat, so when a heavy load passes down the road, everything moves.

In a wild stretch of the River Isle, a mile upstream from Ilford bridge, I stumbled on the perfect swimming hole. It was marked as a fishing spot by a little wooden square pegged in the bank. This was No. 38. Someone had sculpted the sheltered hollow into a natural armchair of reeds and hardened earth. A fast-flowing gravelly rill poured into a sudden pool ten feet wide, causing the fallen willow leaves in the river to rise like pike spinners out of the depth, twisting and flashing in the light.

The intimacy of this unexpected place was a pleasing contrast to the wide open spaces of Camber Sands, and I decided on a dip. I had seen fresh otter prints in a mudbank further downstream. If the river was good enough for otters, it was good enough for me. After some gardening of the nettles around the point of entry, I sat down to get into my wetsuit boots, and was stung. I spread out a few burdock leaves and had another go. I plunged straight into the deep pool. It was too startlingly cold to do more than rocket round it several times, gasping, and shoot out again. Then came the exaltation, mingled with relief to be warm again, as I stood in the sun getting dry. Everything looked suddenly very clear and sharp. White granules of fertiliser gleamed in the freshly-harrowed deep-brown loam. A latticed frieze of brittle umbellifer heads shone against the bright blue sky.

I discovered afterwards why the water was so cold. The river flowed through shady woodland upstream. I followed a rhyne back over the fields through willows and alders, puzzling how it could be running at a lower level than the river. With their pumps and sluices, the Levels are full of such mysteries; water is everywhere. Bob had said they used to go swimming all over the Levels; he bathed at the Red Bridge at Isle Abbots, and by the pump house at Ilton. Every village here has a Frog Lane, and a sign that says 'Road Liable to Flooding'. I met a woman by the Westport Canal who told me that when she was a child in the village, there were so many frogs in the meadows that the men would tie string round their ankles to stop them jumping up their trousers.

This veiled landscape is full of medieval paths and ancient droves. At dusk, I walked out of Fivehead down Swale Drove towards the misty fen. Swale is an old word meaning 'turbulent water', and it is the root of 'swallow', the bird of swooping flight. All I saw in the fading light was the dull sheen of newly-turned plough sods. Blackberry lianas hung in my path off the hedge banks, either side of a ten-foot holloway driving downhill to the moor and river. The fields were above the level of my head. There had been a pink and purple sunset like a bruise, then the orange glow of Taunton in the distance. The only sound was the clickety-clack of a water pump a mile away. It was already dark enough to get lost. The wooden signposts were beautifully carved, but you needed a brass-rubbing kit to read them. Outside Swell Court Farm, a sign pointing up a path said: ANCIENT CHURCH. BE WARNED. WE HAVE TWO PLAYFUL ALSATIANS. The poplars here all held giant hanging-baskets of mistletoe that could have been bee-swarms in the dark. Looking across at the Levels, I could still make out the pattern of rivers and drains, silver under a lid of hanging mist.

On Wednesday morning, I woke to more mist flooding the land, floating the church towers and trees. Then it evaporated into a brilliant, shining blue morning, and I swam just outside Hambridge in one of the long, straight drains crossing the flat grazing meadows on West Moor like tall mirrors. It was about fifteen feet wide and four feet deep. This was a more leisurely swim; the black water, exposed to the sun, was less cold than the river. My breaststroking sent a bow-wave wobbling the reeds along the banks, and the eels shifting in the mud. From the water, I could see Burrow Hill rising steeply to a single tree at its summit. A tiny figure was sitting on a swing under one of its branches, silhouetted against the blue.

In the afterburn of the swim, I raced to the top of the dramatic hill, where the man on the swing, who owned a pair of white goats grazing nearby, politely offered me a turn. The view from this swing is one of the finest in England, across the Levels for miles in every direction until the fields and rivers disappear in mist. Being airborne, and already high from a cold dip, it was like floating above the world as you sometimes do in dreams.

Immediately below Burrow Hill is Pass Vale Farm, where Julian Temperley makes cider and distils it into Apple Brandy, as he calls it, because the French won't let him call it

Calvados. I called in on him, and we stood drinking cider and apple brandy in the cool barn, looking out at a sunlit doorway framing the farmyard sheepdog, orchards, mistletoe and chickens stretching out their wings and baking themselves in the sun. Julian said cider-makers don't talk to each other much. They keep their secrets.

It is no secret that we have lost an enormous proportion of our orchards in this country, and that orchards are still disappearing at an alarming rate. In the last thirty years the total area has declined nationally by about two-thirds. In Somerset, more than half the small traditional farm orchards have gone since 1945. In Auberon Waugh's village, Combe Florey, the old pear orchards succumbed to the plough ten years ago. Across the border, Devon has lost ninety per cent of its orchards in twenty years. Most of this is because of agricultural conversion; farmers finding that there is more money to be made out of other crops. On top of that, until 1988 the Ministry of Agriculture actually paid them grants as an incentive to grub them up. But a great many small orchards are now being destroyed to make way for development. The sites are usually in villages or towns, and just the right size for a house or two. Ironically, such places often end up being called 'Orchard Close'.

The character and diversity of the old fruit trees in a place are a vital part of its identity. In response to the crisis, people are now beginning to plant community orchards, and demanding a greater variety of local fruit from their shops. As Julian Temperley pointed out, we are nowhere near as loyal to our own local apples as the French. When he sees French apples on sale in Somerset towns and villages, he imagines how the French would react to English apples in their local store. 'They'd burn the shop down,' he said. Things may be changing. Near Dowlish Wake, a farmer has planted twenty-five acres of cider apples and signed a twenty-year contract with Bulmer's to supply them. Kingston Blacks, the best of the cider apples, are now so scarce that their value has climbed from £40 to £150 per ton. There's a man in Herefordshire growing 200 tons a year and doing very nicely. Meanwhile, great debates rage amongst the apple-growers between those who prune to create hollow-centred trees, and those who favour the shape of a Christmas tree, like the Bigendians and Smallendians in *Gulliver's Travels*.

Two miles down the road, the other side of Kingsbury Episcopi, I met Brian Lock, who cultivates twenty acres of osier beds on the marshes. The withies of Belgian Red and Black Maul were stacked in neat bundles of different lengths in his shed. He learnt to swim in the River Parrett in a mill-pool just across the fields. Everyone used to swim in the river. 'All the parents and children would be there in summer. There would be dozens of us,' he said. They would dive off the paddles of the mill-wheel, and float on the surface watching the eels on the bottom of the pool. 'We used to lower down baited hooks, watch for them to bite, then swim away with an eel on the line.' A couple of years ago, he was out with his dog on a hot day on the marsh. He stripped off and swam naked as he had done as a boy. 'We used to swim out here in the drains as well,' he said. 'All over everywhere we swam.'

At the village school in Charlton Mackrell, six miles away, boys and girls were given swimming lessons in the River Cary on alternate days of the week in the summer term during the 1930s. A farmer dammed the river with wooden boards to create a deep enough pool, and once he had dipped his sheep, the swimming season began. The pupils thought nothing of finding a leech or two clinging to them when they emerged, but every child in the village could swim. Walter Long, the head teacher, awarded beautifully-drawn certificates and small sums of money to his young swimmers.

I had arranged with Bob to drive him over to Dowlish Wake in the afternoon, to see his friend about collecting the cider apples. Peter Hansford has been making cider on Oxenford Farm for years, and used to supply eighteen gallons a day to the New Inn in the village. A blue tractor stood in the yard, with a length of belt running off a flywheel into the shed to drive the apple-chopper. We stepped inside.

There was an almost religious atmosphere in Mr Hansford's cider shed. We stood between rows of gloomy tuns with just a sixty-watt lightbulb hanging from the cob-webbed rafters and the bit of daylight that crept in by the door. Each barrel held forty or fifty gallons. A row of nine stood just beside us, raised off the floor on wooden beams. Mr Hansford drew off some of the dark nectar out of a tap in one of the barrels, and offered us a half-pint each. It was viscous, cool and sharp, then the taste of the fruit came through. It was probably vicious too, but I liked it and was soon on a second glass. I asked what kind of apples went to make it. 'Oh, we call this one Liquorice Allsorts,' said Mr Hansford. The shed used to be a milking parlour. Now it was dominated by a giant cider press at one end, with a big half-barrel set by it to carry the juice to the barrels. This press was a replacement for the original, which once had two drums of paraffin set down on it. One must have leaked, because ever after that they could never seem to get the smell of paraffin out of the cider. The tainted press had to be burned in the end. In the other half of the shed were stacked-up chairs and trestle-tables and a big carnival mask on the wall. Bacchus was sleeping somewhere in the shadows.

3 1
A MILL-RACE

Norfolk, 23 October
BACK IN EAST Anglia, a bonus autumn day of clear skies
brought me to Norfolk for the afternoon, with the bike on the
car. I parked in Aylsham and set off on two wheels in quest of
a pool on the River Bure. I had received intriguing intelligence
about it as a favourite bathing hole of the family of George
Barker, so hidden away down snaking lanes that if I found it,
I would certainly bathe undisturbed. It was called John's
Water, although no one knew why. The late October sunshine, bowled underarm down the lanes, threw my pedalling
shadow many yards ahead.

Towards dusk, I was bicycling along the valley of the Bure
where it passes between the estates of Blickling and Wolterton
Hall. A layer of mist veiled the water meadows a few feet
above the ground and suffused the alder copses. It flowed
down the valley through the trees and hedges just at the level
of my crossbar. I followed the meandering road for several
miles, fording the mist, until I reached a solitary mill cottage
by a twin-arched red brick bridge. A vigorous mill-race sped
through one of the arches, darting its turbulence far out into
a wide black pool which whirled evenly between dense banks
of reeds and watercress. It could have been a scene from
Constable. I had arrived at John's Water.

I leant the bike in an open-fronted cart shed, stripped off,
eschewing the wetsuit but glad of the trunks and the boots,
and waded into the icy water. The fine gravel bed was shallow
at first, then shelved deeper into the mill-pond. I plunged in

and was soon out of my depth, swimming with the eddy up towards the mill-race where it spouted from the bridge. Then I launched myself into it and shot downriver into the weed-carpeted shallows. I swam on, in water that reached halfway up my thighs if I stood up, much as ice reaches halfway up a champagne bottle in a bucket. The river was embroidered with such vivid green braids of water buttercup that I half expected to meet Ophelia lying on the bottom, garlanded unseasonably in its white flowers. I was swimming down an ice-floe, but it was so clear, so sweet, so lush that I soon warmed to the cold and paddled and waded back up through the eddies, gathering watercress as I went. This was one of the best crops of wild, untutored cress I had ever seen, let alone picked. It banked up along the dusky river like green cumulus clouds. I circled the pool twice more, shooting the rapids of the mill-race, crazed with the opiate cocktail the brain and body must have sluiced into my frozen veins.

As darkness fell, I sat on one of the old carts in the shed drinking the hot chocolate I had brought with me in a flask, listening to the moorhens' falsetto croaking in the rushes, the tut-tutting of an anxious wren, and the steady surf of the mill-race.

I had come back to stay in Suffolk to make ready for winter in the house: to saw logs, receive a delivery of heating oil, and write up my notes in front of the fire. The forecast was for the first cold spell, and like everyone else in the countryside that night, I panicked when I returned home, and went stumbling about outside in the dark throwing blankets over the tractor bonnet, running the car into the barn to keep cosy, and giving the cats extra rations. The kitchen door was like a sieve. The cold night air raced in through every crack and rotten hole. At midnight I found myself struggling with a roll of gaffer tape, patching the worn old door until it ended up looking like Just William after he's been in a scrap and had his face seen to by his big sister.

By the following morning it had begun to rain hard, and an oil lorry appeared in the yard. Its driver hopped out and berated me for the state of the bumpy track that leads across the common to my house. 'This is no road for a lorry, mate. Just look at that! I've lost a light off the top and the mirrors are all bent to buggery.' I hadn't finished apologising and promising to lop all the trees when he began a tirade against my oil tank. 'Plumber who put that there wants shooting an' all.' I began to feel a deep sense of inadequacy. Only the day before his employers had laid off two drivers because of a shortage of orders. 'Then today we get thousands.' Fixing me with a meaning glare through the pouring rain he continued. 'The buggers all wait until the first frost to order. Then they panic. They all tell you it's desperately urgent and they've nearly run out. You get there and there's a hundred gallon or more in the tank. There was one week in the summer when we all sat about in the yard and not a single order. It's a joke.'

His firm, once a small and friendly local one, has recently been taken over by a national conglomerate. 'Pigs they are; they've got the manners of pigs. You walk past them in the yard and they won't look at you. And if you do anything not quite right they put you on remand, so next time you're out. What is the point of running a business like that? I'm too old to care but it riles me all the same.' He drove away, still furious, and tore off his wing-mirror on a tree beside the track. The lorry lurched ominously to a halt. When I reached him he had picked up the bits and was standing in a puddle. 'I don't believe this,' he said, looking at himself in the shattered mirror like Richard II, with job prospects to match. I took him inside for a cup of tea.

It was too wet for digging, so I found myself turning the compost. The best view of the moat is from behind the heap, and turning it made a change from sitting inside at my desk watching raindrops on the windowpane. Compost-making is like a strenuous version of cooking, and it often steams satisfyingly. I had taken to decomposing newspapers, and had a big pile of them, left out to soak in the rain. They are much easier to tear into strips when they're wet, and of course you must always tear down the grain of the paper. In this respect, newspapers behave just like trees.

The work was held up every now and again by an interesting story: CBI COSTS POLLUTION CLEAN-UP AT £40

BILLION; IN THE SPACE OF JUST ONE YEAR, WHERE DID OUR RIVER GO?; 'COMMON' BIRDS IN DANGER; BLAIR PUTS BRAKE ON LEGAL RIGHT TO RAMBLE. It felt good to be tearing up news of environmental disasters and composting it. Curing bad news. The secret of rotting down newspapers is to keep them wet and layer them with plenty of succulent nettles, comfrey, grass-cuttings and manure. The moat benefits directly from my composting: I don't use any artificial fertilisers on my garden, so there is no leaching of nitrates or phosphates to pollute its waters. The compost also benefits from the moat. The summer waterweeds I dragged out with the crome were rotting down well. The compost is a composite living being that needs to breathe and be watered. Even at the dead of winter, it can be full of symbolic heat. It is central to the ecology of an organic garden, and I am deeply involved with mine.

Having worked up a sweat, I took an incandescent plunge in the rainswept moat, swam as far as the hazel halfway along and back, then pranced indoors across the lawn and stood, steaming pinkly, before the open fire. Listening to the rain outside I dreamed, into the flames, of a steam cabin I would one day build by the moat, a village caldarium. All you would need is a small, well-insulated wooden shed with a boiler beside it, heated by a wood-burning furnace, and a 'Natando Virtus' sign over the door. By European or Roman standards this is not so eccentric a notion. I stayed with a perfectly respectable family of German friends in Austria recently who piled out of the sauna every afternoon before tea and rolled naked in the snow.

32
PENGUIN POOLS

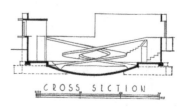

CROSS SECTION

London, 2 November

I HAD NEVER SET out to make this a comprehensive tour of the nation's swimming holes, but sitting before the fire reviewing my notes and maps, one very obvious omission became quite clear: I had hardly swum in any of our cities and I had barely dipped a toe in London. It made sense to make amends straight away and sample some urban swimming during the winter months. So I migrated to my perch in the big city, a flat in Chalk Farm, to swim round the capital, beginning in the famous ponds on Hampstead Heath, and moving on to the lidos at Parliament Hill Fields and Tooting Bec; the club pool of the RAC in Pall Mall; the Ironmonger Row Turkish Baths; the Marshall Street Baths; and the Oasis in Covent Garden. The Thames has changed since an intrepid friend of mine swam alone in it at night amongst the moored barges off Butler's Wharf. Swimming is now forbidden by the Port of London Authority's bye-laws. Apart from the danger from constant river traffic, the water itself, although not as polluted as it used to be, can still seriously damage your health. On the walls of the authority's offices they still have photographs of bathing beauties on what was once the Tower Bridge Beach, and at Greenwich Beach there were swimmers and ice-cream stalls until the 1940s. Bargeloads of sand were brought up to the beaches by the council.

I travelled as often as possible by bike, the natural complement to swimming, and my selection of pools was highly random, although admittedly biased towards the open air. The opportunities to swim outdoors in London are getting increasingly rare. There are now only three lidos left, at Tooting Bec, Parliament Hill Fields and Brockwell Park. The only access to wild swimming is at the Highgate Men's, Ladies' and Mixed Ponds on Hampstead Heath, and the Serpentine in Hyde Park. Apart from three or four remaining outdoor public baths, that's about it – unless you're lucky enough to be invited to swim in somebody's private pool as I had been, in Highgate, a month earlier.

My friend Lucy had recently moved from a sixteenth-century house in Walberswick to an elegant flat high up on the fourth floor of one of the great buildings of the 1930s: Berthold Lubetkin's celebrated High Point in Highgate. Lucy is a serious swimmer and I had wondered how she was going to cope with the sudden loss of the sea. Earlier in the year I had secretly marvelled at her courage and dash as she led the way off Walberswick Beach, swimming fast out to sea in a straight line towards the horizon. I did my best to keep up, mistakenly imagining she would pause and turn back at any moment. We were some way out in the grander swells of Sole Bay before Lucy, cool as a cucumber, enquired if I thought we should head home for tea. 'Might as well carry on to Amsterdam,' I gulped, feeling grateful to have a distant, intermittent view of the beach in my sights, just visible over the tops of the breakers. How on earth was she going to survive four floors up in Highgate?

I had found my answer when I peered gingerly from the vertiginous balcony. Looking down into the gardens I caught sight of the ripple and glint of a swimming pool over in one corner beyond the tennis courts. Lubetkin, who also designed the Penguin Pool at London Zoo, had strong views on the civilising influence of swimming, and the pool was central to the whole novel concept of High Point. Consistent with the modernist ideas espousing open-air recreation and exposure to the life-giving properties of the sun, the inhabitants of the three white towers of flats were to have their own heated open-air pool where they might meet and mingle with their neighbours in an informal, even playful atmosphere, much like the penguins at the zoo. An outdoor pool on the doorstep is such a perfect antidote to the enclosed, even claustrophobic, interior of a flat: in an ideal world every block or estate would have one. I've noticed that a lot of the regular swimmers at the Parliament Hill Fields Lido live in the red-brick blocks of flats whose richly floral balconies overlook the pool from the edge of the Heath. Many of them swim between the hours of seven and nine in the morning, when entrance is free.

After dinner we had taken our towels and walked down through the giant ocean liner foyer, crossing lawns down curving concrete paths similar to the spiralling penguin promenades at the zoo, and ducking weeping willows. The pool lay hushed and steaming in the night air, dimly lit by a single floodlight at one end.

By the time we were into the black water it was just after midnight. There would have been a moon, but there was too much cloud. Nosing through the luxurious water, we swam under a faint curtain of rising steam that hung just an inch or two above the surface. The pool is heated by the same boilers that supply central heating to the flats and is simply one of the basic services supplied to leaseholders. It opens on 1 May, and this was a last chance to swim before it was closed for the winter the next day. It is about forty-five feet long, and the same rectangular shape as everything else in Lubetkin's design: the rooms, doors, windows, even the counter of the Porter's Lodge. Overlooking it is the perfect flat for a swimmer, upstairs above the changing rooms. The High Point residents hold their pool very dear, and can swim at any hour of the day or night.

The pool is surrounded by herbaceous borders and trees, and York-stone paving stones that are kinder to the feet than the regulation concrete slabs. Nearly all the High Point people swim in here. The Jewish ladies in red jackets with big gold buttons come down in the afternoons, and so does the successful architect who owns a Lubetkin flat much as other people might own a Stubbs or Hockney. There is a modest list of rules: 'No ball games, no dogs . . .' I can think of no greater luxury than swimming outdoors at night in gently mulled water when there's a chill on the air. It is like being tucked up in bed on a frosty night with the window ajar. The effect intensified as a light drizzle began to pock the surface. We stole up and down, only the slap of our bow-waves in the plug hole at the deep end betraying our presence. I suppose the people in the upstairs flat are used to swimmers, like living next to a railway and not noticing the trains.

Lubetkin's Penguin Pool, built three years earlier in 1934, was not only the first piece of modern architecture in Britain to hit the headlines and capture the popular imagination; it is still probably by far the most exciting swimming pool anyone has ever built. More than that, it is a bold experiment in community housing for a little society of birds that look and behave very much like people. I had left High Point that night determined to go and see it for myself.

On Sunday afternoon, I biked through Regent's Park to the zoo and made my way to the Penguin Pool past a gorilla having a think inside a plastic barrel, like Diogenes. There was the famous elliptical enclosure, its delicate bands of curving concrete gleaming white in the sun. I squeezed through the crowds to look in through the proscenium arch of this living theatre at the penguins, sunning themselves in their dinner suits on the twin cantilevered spiral ramps that caused such a sensation in the architectural world when they were built in 1934. They were engineered by Ove Arup, and indicate his close involvement in the project with Lubetkin. They dramatically demonstrated the potential of reinforced concrete as a new and poetic way of building that could flow and spiral like water. Each tapered ramp is between only 3 and 6 inches thick, with no intermediate support over a 46-foot span, yet it will stand the weight of 24 people evenly spaced along it. Such dramatic technical innovations, and the elegance of the Penguin Pool, must have had a tremendous impact on the public at the time. The clean lines, open plan and abstract simplicity of the construction afforded a glimpse of the possibilities of life for people as well as penguins in a new modern environment.

This was architectural showmanship on several levels. Lubetkin's partnership, Tecton, had only just been formed, and the Penguin Pool and Gorilla House were their first two commissions. They were keen to show how their new ideas could work. But on another level, Lubetkin's design expressed his conviction that a zoo should recreate 'the atmosphere of the circus'. Like Sir Peter Chalmers-Mitchell, Secretary of the Zoological Society at the time, Lubetkin saw the relationship between the zoo animals and the public in terms of performers and audience. The ramps and steps, and the central pool, were meant to show off the two contrasting aspects of penguin behaviour that Lubetkin thought people would most appreciate: their comical walk, and their skilful swimming.

The enclosure is a stage set, and an abstract, surrealist one at that. Lubetkin had lived in Paris and knew Picasso, Braque and Cocteau. One of his commissions there, in 1927, had been to design a nightclub, the Club Trapèze Volant, for the circus artist, trick cyclist and cinema actor Roland Tutin. The club, with its climbing pole, suspended rings and flying trapeze, was a great favourite with the surrealist hoorays, and the equipment was in nightly use. It is long demolished, but the photographs immediately make you think of the circus, or the monkey houses in the modern zoo. The parallels between Lubetkin's ideas of the zoo as spectacle and the subsequent evolution of 'wildlife' television need hardly be underlined.

A great deal has been written about the architecture of this pioneering pool, but amid all the talk of Euclidean geometry, double helixes and Constructivism, there is hardly a mention of the actual penguins. Lubetkin was a Marxist rationalist, schooled in pre-revolutionary Russia, and you would not expect him to entertain any romantic notions about animals. He had completed his original design for the Gorilla House at London Zoo in 1933 within the astonishing deadline of four days, without the time to find out as much about gorillas as his perfectionism must have demanded. Apart from the pool's status as a listed building and an undisputed miniature masterpiece, how did it suit the swimmers?

There were thirty-eight penguins in residence when I went to see them. It was two o'clock, and apart from a few serious swimmers most were sunbathing on the ramps or pottering about outside their nesting boxes. In their smart suits, the birds themselves could have been architect-designed. Their swimming is best described as underwater flying. They topple into the water (diving would be an exaggeration), and row themselves at speed with their flippers, using their feet as rudders. The elliptical pool only comes up to the keepers' knees at its deepest and is only six inches at the two shallow ends. In the wild, penguins will dive to thirty metres. But as one of the keepers observed, that would be 'a heck of a lot of water to clean out'. Penguins are torpedo-shaped, and are said to have inspired the design of modern submarines. With their black-and-white stripes, they look like dolphins when they swim. The gentoo penguins in Edinburgh Zoo are the best swimmers, leaping out of the water like porpoises to catch their breath without losing momentum at high speed.

The penguins in London Zoo are not king or emperor penguins as many people expect them to be. They are relatively short black-footed South African penguins, and most are hand-reared. One of their keepers, Paul, said life around the pool can be something of a soap opera. He knows them all by name; 'Some you say hello to; some are your mates. Others aren't so friendly; Ulrika can sometimes get a bit pecky, Jessica and Roy wouldn't hurt a fly.' They generally mate for life and live in established pairs with their own nesting boxes round the pool: Arnold and Vicky in Box 2, Kojak and Felicity in Box 3, Spikey and Wanda in Box 4. Wanda was named by Michael Palin, who adopted her and pays for her keep. Spikey is twenty-seven, a great age for a penguin. Twelve to fifteen would be a good age in the wild, but here they live longer. Beatrice is the oldest at thirty-three. Blind Pugh, who was Paul's favourite, died a week before his twenty-eighth birthday. 'He lived in Box 6,' Paul told me, 'and he was found lying by Box 5. He was on his way home and his heart just stopped. He'd had a really good innings. It was a sudden cardiac arrest, so he wouldn't have known anything about it.'

There are occasional exceptions to monogamy amongst the poolside penguins. Like a man talking about his family, Paul revealed that: 'We did have a female who wasn't monogamous, bless her. Hookbill was a floozie; she was playing the field, and even ended up helping with the incubation of another bird's eggs.' Another penguin, Bog, was paired with Jodie, who got a fungal infection and had to go off to the zoo hospital. Bog thought she had died, went into mourning, then began courting a pair of widows, Heidi and Gabriella. He had picked up a penguin. As an available male, several of the younger unattached females also became interested in him. When Jodie returned from hospital, poor Bog didn't know what to do. He would spend his afternoons sunbathing on the ramp with Heidi, then go down to the poolside to look in on Gabriella, who was by that time incubating a pair of eggs. Then he would return uncertainly to Jodie at the other end of the pool. As Paul said, 'It was quite confusing for him.'

Another of the keepers, David, said all the penguins like to take an early-morning swim together, and another late at night or during the evening when there's nobody about. He thinks they behave differently when they're alone. Apart from going in the water to get fish at feeding time, they do seem to swim up and down the pool quite happily for exercise and enjoyment, just like us.

Penguin nests are even more modernist than Lubetkin. They have a nouvelle cuisine approach to nest building, constructing careful arrangements of three pebbles and a stick. The architect was very keen that the Tree of Heaven should be retained on the site beside the pool. He was right, because it stands beautifully for nature against the cool lines of his rationalist art. But as the keepers pointed out, it is also an invaluable source of that vital twig each penguin couple needs for its nest. They will spend hours underneath it, like shoppers in John Lewis, choosing the right one. The rate of fertility amongst penguins is naturally low, but the zoo usually manages to hatch two or three chicks each year. Some recent additions have been Rudolph, Tinsel and Noel. I suspect Paula Yates must be naming them. (Lubetkin would have opposed such sentiment. When he went off to farm in Gloucestershire in 1939, he refused to give his pigs names, calling them instead by numbers.)

The Penguin Pool is such an irresistible architectural metaphor that the magazine *Mother and Child* couldn't help making the connections in November 1938:

How many citizens of London have brooded over the railings of that pool, envying the penguins as they streak through the blue water or plod up the exquisite incline of the ramp – and have wondered sadly why human beings cannot be provided, like the penguins, with an environment so well adapted to their needs.

The deep, natural water of the Highgate Men's Pond the following day was considerably colder than the cosseted High Point pool had been at the end of September. It is a marvellous second-best to Highgate Ladies' Pond for a swim. I say this on the authority of a number of female friends who swim there regularly (FEMALES ONLY, says an imposing notice). They argue that its waters must be the purest, because their pond is the highest in a descending series, and is fed straight from the springs at the top of the hill in Kenwood. A number of impressive eighty-year-olds swim there every day; indeed the only accident at the pond in recent years was when one of the octogenarians spiked herself on the railings whilst climbing in after hours.

There has been swimming at the Men's Pond for over ninety years, and it rivals any of the London clubs for its conversation, atmosphere and conviviality. In a way, it *is* one of the London clubs, yet it is the very opposite of exclusive. Entrance is of course free, past a bench on the sunny hillside lawn inscribed in memory of a swimmer known by his friends at the Men's Pond as 'Goldfish'. In summer, this lawn is something of a gay hang-out, and all the more colourful for it. All human life may be there, but it is hardly the San Francisco Sutro Baths, where they used to advertise Friday night 'Bisexual Boogies' in the 1970s and '80s. In the fenced enclosure, where the serious swimmers and sunbathers congregate, nudity is de rigueur. A notice says 'Shuttlecock may only be played at the discretion of the lifeguards.' Some sunbathe on towels spread on the concrete floor, some read, some play chess or work out with weights. Out on the springboards and in the water, costumes are compulsory. There are no longer any high boards. The Highgate Diving Club used to meet here in the 1930s to practise swallow dives from a ten-metre board. On 16 August 1930, they and the swimmers of the Highgate Lifebuoys performed in the first Aquatic Carnival here in front of 10,000 people. The fancy diving team executed such specialities as half-screw-, straddle- and pike-jumps, haunch-jumps and dives, and the balled-up, single-front somersault.

When I arrived inside the enclosure at half-past one, the swimming university was in full session, and I couldn't help comparing the scene to the one at the Penguin Pool the day before. There were about a dozen of us altogether. Two taxi-drivers were discussing the perennial question of water temperature with some Hampstead types in their sixties. 'It feels colder *in* today because the air is so mild,' they said.

'It's really the *length* of the nights that cools off the water at this time of year,' said an old chap with a white moustache from a far corner. 'The days are too short to warm it up again.'

'The pond goes down to about forty for the winter, and stays there,' said another.

They all agreed that once it goes below fifty, you don't notice much difference anyway. This, of course, was a swimmers' version of the foundation of all civilised societies: talking about the weather.

I went out along the jetty to the pond. It is deep, up to twenty feet, and the water is green, smooth and cold. It is entirely natural, and samples are regularly tested for purity. It was icy cold, and I swam fast in a big circle round the buoys the lifeguards use to moor their rowing boat, past an unconcerned coot or two, and back to the ladder, feeling what they call here 'braced'. In summer, when the water is warm, this is a beautiful place to bathe more languidly beside the wooded banks.

Terry and Les, the two supervisors, relaxed in the window-seat of their shed overlooking the water. On the wall was a photograph of them standing on the ice in the middle of the pond, and another of swimmers splashing about in an ice-hole they had broken open. The lifeguards go in themselves at least once a week, 'to keep acclimatised', and rescue eight to ten people a year; 'proper rescues, not false alarms'. Most of the fifty to sixty regular bathers come early in the morning. A lot of them are in their eighties and look sixty. They all put it down to the cold water, dashing the fifteen yards between the pond's two jetties when the water gets really cold. Both Terry and Les agreed that 'It's the plunge that counts.'

33
STEAMING

London, 4 November

AS THE OWNER of Hampstead Heath, the City of London Corporation also owns and runs the Highgate Ponds, maintaining them for swimmers free of charge. It deserves the highest praise for this, and for sticking to its policy of keeping the Parliament Hill Fields Lido open, in winter as well as summer, for free swimming in the mornings from seven o'clock until nine. It is one of the few really great swimming pools left.

I went in next day with two or three dozen early-morning regulars, and for a glorious moment, during some lull in the proceedings, I had the entire sixty-seven yards of water to myself. The solitude lasted for a single blissful length. I was outnumbered two-to-one by lifeguards, and the magnificent pool was at its scintillating best. The great ice-cream fountain at one end sparkled in the sun, and there was an expectant air about the amphitheatre of paved terraces. I swam through the cold, polished water, each stroke cutting a perfect arc of tiny bubbles, everything in equilibrium.

When swimmers talk of fast or slow water, this is the sort of thing they mean. The absence of wavelets, or other bathers, means you can breathe and move in perfect rhythm, so the music takes over. Mind and body go off somewhere together in unselfconscious bliss, and the lengths seem to swim themselves. The blood sings, the water yields; you are in a state of grace, and every breath gets deeper and more satisfying. You hunker down and bury yourself in the water as though you have lived in it all your life, as though you were born to it, and thoughts come lightly and easily as you swing up and down in the blue. The sublime word 'swimmingly' is born of such moments: so is the Greek word *ekstasis*, root of 'ecstasy', which means simply to be outside your own body – exactly the state you achieve in a cold-water swim. If you tread on air on your way from the pool, it is because you are floating somewhere just above your corporeal self.

The beauty of a swimming pool is in its graphic simplicity, framing the contrasting, exquisite complexity of the snaking, opalescent mosaic of wave-forms projected on the bottom. What you are seeing is changing so fast your eye can never quite catch up with it. In every way you are dazzled. It is not water you perceive so much as light, and how water can play with it. We all look at pools differently since David Hockney. Where Courbet paints a wave, Hockney paints a splash, or the play of a hose on a lawn. His pools are erotic and innocent at the same time, just like real swimming pools.

There is, too, an affinity between pools and lawns. Both are simulations of nature, with the one essential ingredient – wildness – carefully filtered out. They resemble life, but they are not alive. The lawn has been reduced to a single species; the pool-water neutered. Both are great status symbols. Producers sit by 'the pool' in Los Angeles reading scripts. The President stands on the White House lawn. Pools and lawns make continual demands on labour for their maintenance. In California, once you have 'the pool', you then have to employ your pool man to fish out leaves and maintain it. Both make enormous demands on water resources and chemicals. In America, the hissing of sprinklers on summer lawns is a major environmental problem, and so is the demand for fresh pool-water. In all these respects, a lawn, or a private pool, is like a motor car.

Yet swimming pools are also deeply atavistic places. You notice it the moment you come through the turnstile. The screaming is just on the border between terror and ecstasy. You hear something like it when you let children loose with a hosepipe on the lawn. In the pool the impulse to make noise is a kind of acoustic graffiti, a response to the echoing brightness of your voice carried on the blank wall of humid air, a collective howl of relief at the casting-off of clothes, and the constraints they imply. That is why, I suppose, swimming pools are so full of arcane rules, enforced by the ear-piercing whistle of the lifeguard.

I worked as a lifeguard one summer at the Wealdstone open-air pool, just along the road from the Railway Tavern where the Who put in some of their earliest performances. The pool is still there, lying empty, as it has for the past five years since it was sold off by the council to a company called Relaxion. All the open-air pools of my youth have met the same fate. The Kingsbury pool, a few miles away, became a riding school, then a garden centre. The Mill Hill pool seemed to disappear without trace. The Finchley Road pool sank under a department store. There is no longer swimming at Ruislip Lido. At Kenilworth, where Uncle Laddie taught me to swim, there is still a small open-air pool beside the newer indoor pool, but it is a token travesty of its former glory.

The smell of bleach on damp concrete in the Parliament Hill changing cubicles took me straight back to the Wealdstone Baths. We would arrive at seven o'clock, half an hour before the early swimmers, to clean out the pool with an antique aquatic hoover, and, worst of all, scrub out the cubicles and toilets. As a low-caste lifeguard, it fell to me to spend the first hour of every day with a clanking pailful of bleach and a long-handled brush that perpetually moulted its bristles in the powerful alkali. From these dank, shadowed places, I had to remove the sputum, bubblegum, deliquescent wine-gums, and the floored wet towels and trunks. More important still to Fred, the Channel-swimming super-intendent from whom I took my orders, was my additional task: with scrubbing brush and pail, I paced the rows of gloomy cubicles on graffiti patrol. The superintendent wanted his pool to be spotless in mind, too.

Each cubicle was a cave, in whose unaccustomed privacy the occupant could give way to the same primitive urges that had caused them to scream in the pool, and regress to the cave-man inside them, inscribing the dark mahogany walls with depictions of their objects of desire just as their ancestors did at Lascaux. Where the Lascaux artists drew their animal quarry, Wealdstone Man or Boy scratched primitive versions of genitalia, both male and female. They were never whole people or bodies, always disembodied parts, like scalps or hunting trophies: the fox's tail, the otter's pad, the stag's antler. Wealdstone Woman or Girl was, if anything, more active inside her damp confessional. Many of these naive works of art were impossible for me to erase completely, so that an interesting layered effect, like a collage, had built up over the years; each cubicle a chronicle of desire, a Lonely Parts club.

Fred, the superintendent, used to train Channel swimmers, and they would arrive for an early session each day, covering miles each week, goaded on by his gruff exhortations from a kneeling position at the shallow end. He was responsible for another open pool, on the hill at Harrow, and sometimes my colleague Roy and I would be sent to work some shifts up there. It, too, is now extinct, but it was a beautiful pool, with a lawn, a candyfloss stall and high boards. Early mornings were best, when the pool was perfectly still and each click of the iron turnstile echoed across to the diving boards, while the sun made small rainbows in the fine spray as we hosed down the paving. Schoolmasters from Harrow used to come regularly for an early swim, well away from the boys, and one always paced round and round the pool reading the *Telegraph*. Fred remained in the office by the turnstile or was away at Wealdstone, and we lifeguards had our own shed, with a sunny bench outside, on which I read the whole of *Middlemarch* and most of *Dombey and Son*. I dreaded having to save somebody in case I failed, and although I think I helped a few people out of mild difficulties, I certainly didn't save any lives. But I noticed that if anyone was ever in trouble, Roy would suddenly find some grit in his eye, or just disappear into the hut. Once oiled up for sunbathing, he didn't like to get wet.

I soon discovered that our hut was the headquarters of the local underworld, where the candyfloss concessionaire and his league of gentlemen would plan crimes at the level of nocturnal cigarette robberies from the local cinema. Roy and

I would be invited politely to vacate the hut on such occasions, and never grassed on our affable underworld chums. I always thought they would have been wiser to hold their discussions in the pool. They would never have been overheard above the general din.

Visits to the swimming pool in the fifties and sixties were always accompanied by anxiety about diseases, especially polio whenever there was an outbreak, and verrucas. There were steel baskets for your clothes, a Brylcreem machine on the way out, and Wagon Wheels, Penguins and Bovril at the café. And always, everywhere, boys shivering. On swimming days at school the smell of wet togs pervaded the classroom, the dampness seeping through to smudge the ink in the exercise books in our satchels.

At least we had togs. At a friend's school, non-swimmers had to bathe in a state of nature, graduating to trunks only when they learned to swim. At Dunhurst, the Bedales prep school, it used to be compulsory for boys and girls to swim naked together up to the age of twelve, when they graduated to the upper school. Many of the girls were by that age highly nubile, and male friends who were there during the late forties and early fifties remember suffering agonies of embarrassment when the swimming lesson came to an end and it was time to climb out. To the apparent puzzlement of the PE teacher, whole rows of tumescent boys would hide in the pool while these young women, no longer girls at all, slipped back into their clothes. Daniel Defoe documented the essentially erotic nature of the swimming bath in this description of mixed bathing in the 'Cross-Bath' at Bath in 1724:

> Here the ladies and gentlemen pretend to keep some distance, and each to their proper side, but frequently mingle here too, as in the King and Queens Bath, though not so often; and the place being but narrow, they converse freely, and talk, rally, make vows, and sometimes love; and having thus amused themselves an hour, or two, they call their chairs and return to their lodgings.

I went straight from the people's pool at Parliament Hill Fields to the top people's pool in Pall Mall. The suave, silken waters I was to encounter that evening were several degrees above the lido in every sense. There is a fine pool in the orangery at Buckingham Palace, frequented mostly by Princess Margaret and members of the royal household, but my request to swim there had been politely refused. I biked down from Chalk Farm to the Royal Automobile Club at 97 Pall Mall carrying my swimming gear in my usual grey canvas rucksack. The porter lifted it slightly at arm's length when I left it at the cloakroom, and deposited it alongside rows of neat black attaché cases. The building is large and stately, and leaves no one in any doubt that the motor car stands squarely at the centre of power and influence in the land. I hiked across the palatial lobby and met my host, Michael, a lawyer with whom I had spent a chaotic few days in Brittany helping press cider a couple of years earlier. He uses the club several times a week, stopping off on his way home to Mayfair. He also plays a regular Saturday morning game of squash here.

I had heard about the magnificent swimming bath and steam rooms, and had once seen the pool on film in Paul Watson's classic documentary about the new morality under Margaret Thatcher, *The Fishing Party*. When we met the head waiter on the stairs, he insisted on taking us down into the basement to show us the club's avant-garde purification plant. The water is treated in the French way, with ozone instead of chlorine, so the pool is a far more benign environment. The system does away with the ravages of chlorine, producing water that is non-corrosive of the eyes, sinuses, hair or skin. I was impatient for the swim, but first we popped our heads round the doors of the Turkish baths. Towelled male figures, observing a rule of silence, lay reading on reclining chairs or gently perspiring on beds in mahogany-panelled cubicles.

The long, green pool was a magnificent high-ceilinged Byzantine affair, all turquoise mosaic pillars and wide terrazzo floors. The pool was edged with marble and a fine spray of tepid water played on the surface at the shallow end. The pillars sparkled with a serpentine brilliance and there was a Roman opulence about the place. We could have been in Herculaneum or one of Diocletian's spas. There were two paths of decking around the pool; green if you were in shoes, and blue for bare feet. As in the Turkish baths, the atmosphere was quiet and contemplative, and there were swimmers of both genders. There was plenty of room to swim up and down and converse. Michael and I discussed the cooking of eels, sea swims in Cornwall, mud baths in Pyrenean spas, and his early attempts to swim in the Bolton public baths. It made all the difference that the pool was brimful, overflowing at the gunwales into subtle gratings in the pool surround. This created a feeling of freedom, and a pleasing architectural unity. You felt less like a goldfish in a bowl.

The interesting thing was how quiet it was; we could talk in quite normal tones. Besides the welcome absence of chlorine, the princely water was just the right temperature. One or two of the older members sat in deckchairs by the pool watching the swimmers and nodding off. On the way out, we tossed our trunks into a miniature spin-dryer, passed through the Long Room round a huge table spread with newspapers, and made for the comfort of the Long Bar, where, on a leather sofa before an open fire, we sipped beer. I can think of worse ways to follow up a swim.

Next morning I took the Northern Line from Chalk Farm to Tooting Bec, and walked across Tooting Common to 'the Bec', the Tooting Bec Lido. Its sheer size amazed me. It is a hundred yards long and a hundred feet wide, so you only need swim seventeen lengths to cover a mile. No wonder the Channel swimmers and triathletes come here for long-distance training. This is easily the biggest pool in London. The next thing I noticed was the brightly-coloured rows of Rastafarian cubicle doors. Red, yellow, green they went, all along the poolside, and the colours danced on the water. A fountain glistened like ice at the far end in front of the pool café. I was welcomed with a cup of tea by some of the South London Swimming Club members who run the lido. The friendly, almost family feeling of the place, and everyone's dedication to it, were immediately apparent.

The club dates back to 1906, when the original pool was dug and built by 400 unemployed men. With over 500 members, including the 200 women of the Bec Mermaids, it must be one of the strongest and most enterprising bands of swimmers in the country. In 1991, when the pool was threatened with closure over the winter months, they asserted themselves passionately, and negotiated with Wandsworth Council to take over the running of the lido off-season. The South Londoners are enthusiastic cold-water swimmers, even breaking the ice if necessary to swim a width, and always racing on New Year's Day and Christmas Day. (The 1995 ladies' event was won by Yvonne Wood at the age of seventy-three.) If the pool temperature is four degrees centigrade or more, they swim two widths. If it is under four, they swim one. About 50 people a day swim all through winter, and on hot summer days there can be as many as 6,000 here.

The pool was about thirty degrees colder than at the Royal Automobile Club, and I was much impressed by the hardiness of the other swimmers, some of them obviously long-distance freestylers in training, who seemed hardly to notice the chill. I never worry too much about being outnumbered by crawl swimmers when I'm breaststroking up and down the lanes, but in Australia, as Ken Worpole relates in his book *Staying Close to the River*, it is apparently not the done thing for men to swim breaststroke. On a first visit to Australia and its swimming pools, he began to notice that he was invariably the only man doing the breaststroke, and asked why. His host, a sociologist, said, 'You should understand, Ken, that in Australia, swimming strokes are deeply gendered.'

'I need a good steam-up,' says one of the characters in Nell Dunn's play *Steaming*. Feeling the same way after the Tooting Bec dip, I emerged from the Underground at Old Street and walked over to the Ironmonger Row Turkish Baths, Dunn's original inspiration for the play. Unlike the Trappist steam rooms at the RAC Clubhouse, Ironmonger Row was a proper talking shop. We all trailed big white towels about with us, courtesy of the management, like Romans. As I entered the steam room, an invisible Irishman was holding the floor with a series of jokes. We must have looked like a strikingly cosmopolitan version of David Hockney's picture of the nude *Oz* trial defendants, Richard Neville & Co., as we sat side by side in the humid fug. There is room in the steam room for about eight people to sit, perhaps ten at a squeeze. We sat facing each other in rows, like labourers being driven to work in the back of a transit van, or nude commuters in the tube. Steam rises up from beneath, through the wooden slats. Every so often, invisible bellows puff fresh clouds of vapour into the dripping obscurity, and conversation begins, or somebody tells a joke. Then there is silence, punctuated by spontaneous utterances from out of the mists, whose precise origin is sometimes hard to determine. All you can make out are dim pink or black shapes.

The anonymity and equality of nakedness in blind steam appears to be a liberating influence. It is like a Quaker meeting, but freely hedonistic. Everyone is busy soaping themselves, or applying unguents. John, the Irishman with all the jokes, says to his neighbour, 'Try some of this; it's an exfoliant. Smoothes your skin.' A young bike-courier opposite has the kind of corrugated-iron stomach muscles you rarely see outside a jeans advertisement. John asks him, 'Is it true you can never get a six-pack if you drink, even if it's only on Saturday nights?' There follows a detailed discussion of the techniques and conditions for the acquisition of a six-pack, while in the hottest corner at the end opposite the door, a tall Tunisian soaps himself repeatedly from head to foot, muttering incantations. Nobody can tell whether it's religious or obsessive, and nobody minds.

People come and go, moving ritually between the steam, the shower, the cold plunge and the caldarium, enjoying the quite wild feelings that come with such extremes. At the RAC pool there had been giant chrome sunflower showerheads. Here, there were marble massage tables by the showers, where a group of black garage-workers stood and lounged, gossiping loudly about their friends over the hiss and splash of the hot water: 'He's got a good woman and plenty of cars, but he's still on his way to blow it all up, and he knows it, says it's his destiny. You can see it in his eyes; he's not got himself under control.'

The plunge pool is monumentally, outrageously, cold, down stone steps into a deep cauldron of pain that will turn to the sweetest pleasure in the imminent caldarium. A huge brass cold tap is turned full on, gushing an icy waterfall of mains water straight from under the cold streets of Shoreditch and Hackney over your head and shoulders. You are in one of the hidden rivers of London.

In the past, a great many people in Islington and Hackney used to rely on the public baths for their ablutions and laundry. Now, the emphasis is more on pleasure and fitness, although a fair proportion of the men in the baths were busy shaving, shampooing their hair, or getting super-clean. I have no doubt that this sort of experience should be much more widely available, simply because it is so very good for you. Water treatment in spas or health farms can be enormously beneficial as curative medicine, but surely its richest potential lies in preventative medicine. Hot-water bathing is a central part of Japanese culture, and the Sento, the bath house, used to be found in most neighbourhoods. There aren't so many left these days, but they are still highly popular, especially with working people, and, more recently, younger people. Visitors to Japan often imagine that the excessive heat of a Japanese bath – sometimes as high as fifty centigrade – is proof that the Japanese are genetically predisposed to bearing high temperatures. In fact, it is a matter of acclimatisation, and I am told it can be an exhilarating experience as you move freely between very hot and very cold baths. The culture of the bath house is about getting used to an extreme so that it becomes the norm. Whether it is worthwhile depends on whether you believe hot water can deliver a higher mental and physical pleasure. The cleansing is just as useful as the soothing and the stimulation for the renewal of the urban soul.

Most of the people who come to Ironmonger Row do so regularly, simply because, for a few pounds, the experience gives them an enormous amount of pleasure. They are what Josie in *Steaming* calls 'the ordinary men and women who have been coming to the baths all their lives for a swim or a laundry or to get together in a bit of steam to relax and pass the time together'. Next time you see people walking on air down Ironmonger Row, you'll know why.

*

In *Steaming*, the women bathers stage an occupation of their pool and Turkish baths in order to save them from the threat of closure. The following week, I had an early evening date to play the last game of water polo at the Marshall Street Baths in Soho before they were due to close, under a controversial plan by Westminster City Council to privatise them, and sell off the site for redevelopment into flats. The developers planned to re-open the pool as part of a private fitness club, whose members would enjoy 'preferential facilities'. The protesting swimmers had invited me to come and join them, having read a pro-swimming article I wrote in a newspaper.

Marshall Street has always been a public pool much valued by Soho people and office and shop workers from the West End. Few of the lunchtime or evening swimmers would be able to afford to join a private club. The polo players and regular swimmers had formed themselves into a pressure group to oppose the privatisation and ensure that the pool would remain open as a public baths. Wandering through Soho on a hot day, you could always look in through the wide-open doors of the baths at the elegant wide-arched roof, like a French railway station, and see the swimmers clocking up their lengths in the street-level pool. Marshall Street is one of the most beautiful indoor pools in this country. Since swimming is the most popular participation sport in Britain, it seemed astonishing to me that London could still be losing valuable and much-loved public pools like this from public ownership.

The polo began with a burst of intense training, during which we swam widths at manic speed. Then we pitched into the fastest, roughest, most demanding game in the book, a mêlée of windmilling crawl, staccato breaststroke, even butterfly, as swimmers flung themselves after the ball up and down the pool. You needed reckless courage, rocket-fuelled acceleration, and no scruples whatsoever to succeed. It was like the stock market. Goals were scored with bewildering speed in a flurry of white water designed to camouflage the flagrant fouling that was going on everywhere beneath the surface. This may sound like an all-male affair, but swimmers of both sexes played with uninhibited gusto.

The last game was over, but not the swimmers' struggle to persuade Westminster Council to re-open Marshall Street Baths as an affordable public pool open to everyone on equal terms. Something of a fiasco ensued, in which the property developer withdrew, leaving the baths shut and the swimmers high and dry. Westminster Council still refuse to vote the necessary subsidy that could guarantee a future for the building as a public pool. Perhaps the swimmers should enlist the help of the photographer Tom Merrillion, whose fine exhibition of life studies taken at the Moseley Road Baths in Birmingham, and shown at the West Midlands Arts Centre recently, helped to save the baths from closure by Birmingham City Council.

Winter had really set in, and the night was already freezing when I came out into Marshall Street and biked through the traffic for a second swim at the Oasis open-air pool in Covent Garden. My face was numb when I arrived outside at the corner of Endell Street – perfect conditions for an outdoor swim.

I walked out to the pool across a coconut rug thoughtfully laid across the frosty paving stones. The air was biting, but the water was simmering at eighty-four fahrenheit, and steaming. A dense cotton-wool mist rose off the surface, diffusing the lights and reflecting off the lifeguard's glass kiosk. But it was too cold to sit about. He or she (I couldn't see) paced up and down by the pool muffled in a thick parka with a tracksuit underneath and a bathing costume several layers in, like a Russian doll. All around, London was breathing, clicking and buzzing under an orange sky. Floating on my back in the pool and looking up, I saw the balconies of council flats and bright offices lit up with people at computers in the windows, and, up above, a black starry sky with now and again a jet. As a swimmer, I felt connected to everyday life in a way I never do in an indoor pool. I had ridden here under my own steam, and here I was in the centre of London gazing up at the stars in the utmost luxury of a heated outdoor pool. It seemed the height of civilisation. Yet this was no exclusive private pool; with a Leisure Card from

Camden Council, you could get in for £1. With Lubetkin's High Point pool in Highgate, this must be the best cold-weather pool in London. It was exhilarating to swim wild and free in the middle of the big city in November, breathing in the sharp, frosty air, limbs suffused with the warmth of the pool. Other swimmers materialised out of the mist and glided past silently. All you heard was the immediate lapping of the water and the big rumble and hum of the invisible city beyond the ramparts of flats and offices. Just a few yards away through the darkness, other bathers were visible through the glass walls of the indoor pool. It was warm in there, but there is no warmth as satisfying as heated outdoor water on a frosty night. Floating in the surreal space between extremes of hot and cold, it is so different from the physical world you are used to that you are suspended in time.

The swimming was mesmeric, and very like I imagine it is in some of the Moscow pools. Yuri Luzhkov, the Moscow mayor known as 'The Builder', rebuilt the cathedral of Christ the Saviour, levelled by Stalin in 1931, and turned it into a swimming pool whose golden domes now shine over the Moscow city centre. It would be high on my list of priorities in the depths of a Russian winter. Judith, whom I had met in the summer swimming in the Avon near Evesham, had described swimming in a heated outdoor pool in Moscow behind the Pushkin Museum. You are allotted your own changing cubicle decorated with tubs of geraniums, and emerge from it straight into the pool by diving through a kind of underwater cat-flap. When Judith swam there, the air above the pool was twenty-eight degrees below freezing. Your hair freezes, and there are icicles and snow around the edge of the pool, but the water is warm and steaming. Then you must remember the number of your cubicle and avoid swimming back through the wrong cat-flap. Surfacing inside your cabin, you return to the frozen streets.

I swam for a long time in the fog, then adjourned to a cinema.

34
THE WALBERSWICK SHIVERERS

Suffolk, 25 December
I HAD INVITED A group of friends to come and celebrate my
journey's end with a Christmas Day swim in the North Sea.
There was little enough good cheer about the weather when
we arrived in Walberswick: driving rain and breakers the
colour of dirty knickers licking up the beach. We had
arranged to meet at eleven o'clock at the Hidden Hut, a
clapboard and pebble-dash seaside bungalow with a surprisingly enormous sitting room warmed by a woozing wood
stove. My friends Lucy and Madeleine had rented it for the
week, and the sweet smell of onion soup already simmering
on the hob greeted me as I stepped in out of the horizontal
rain to join the gently steaming group in front of the stove.
Amongst them were Tim and Meg, serious year-round
bathers with a beach hut at Southwold, in a sedate row named
after the English monarchs. Theirs is called 'Karl'. Tim broke
the news to me that for the first time in years he was going to
have to forgo his Christmas North Sea dip because of a touch
of flu. Everyone else, however, already had their swimming
costumes on under their clothes, ready for a quick change by
the sea.

Apart from Tim and Meg, none of us was in the habit of
doing this sort of thing, but I had the idea of starting
something in Walberswick along the lines of the original
Hove Shiverers, who began life in the early 1920s with a
handful of winter swimmers, and still meet on Christmas Day.
I had been stirred to action by reading one of their early

annual reports, written in February 1931, which included the ringing words:

> Ten years ago there were no Shiverers. Ten years ago serious winter swimming was at a standstill in our district, and the Hove baths closed its hospitable doors in the winter evenings. People who worked all day, or children who went to school, if they wished to swim in the evening had no choice but the sea. A few swimmers, newcomers to Hove, looked at the prospect one winter's night and shivered, and that shiver has spread until nearly a thousand now join in the vibration.

With a last glance at the smug little wood stove, we set off for the beach in the slanting, stinging rain driven by a freak wind from the south-west. It was cold, yet there was a hint of mercy in this wind and it lacked the bite of the usual winter draughts that come straight from Russia to bear-hug the Walberswick dunes.

When we arrived on the beach and confronted the sea, the entire swimming party spontaneously bottled out. This was outright mutiny, a wholesale desertion by the Walberswick Shiverers, but what could I do? I was left gamely trying to balance on one leg in the wind and struggle out of a pair of long-johns and into my frozen Speedos. Trunks always seem especially sensitive to the relative humidity of the surrounding atmosphere. Like the seaweed we used to bring home from holiday to hang up by the back door and forecast the weather, costumes breathe in humidity and hold on to it. They never quite dry out, even dangling before the fire all night. The long-johns got stuck round my ankles, and wrestled me on to the wet pebbles just as more well-insulated well-wishers, Virginia and Florence, came into sight along the beach, Virginia in a massive fake ocelot coat, me in goosepimples.

Once in the trunks, I wasted no time getting rainswept, and strode with as much casual determination as I could muster straight into the khaki waves. The sea was not quite as cold as I had feared when I woke up in the night and thought about it, but it was still a case of gritting my teeth and thinking of England for that first moment or two. Having the loyal Shiverers on the beach was a big boost to the morale or, put another way, a big deterrent to copping out. I would, however, have preferred them to be in the water with me. Once fully immersed and striking out for deeper water, I experienced the intoxication of the fiery cold, and found myself splashing about and even body-surfing with manic energy. A dog spotted me and thought it would come and join in the fun. It scampered down to the shore, got one paw wet and instantly retreated. I stayed in far longer than I had intended and even received a modest round of applause when I emerged, to the outstretched towels and concerned piling-on of warm sweaters normally reserved for young children. Very welcome it was too, and my knees glowed bright purple as our party of non-playing swimmers crunched back, still snug in their bathing costumes, towards the beach huts and over the dunes, home to the Hidden Hut and Lucy's onion soup.

35
On Ice

Suffolk, 1 January

WHEN THE MOAT and ponds froze hard on New Year's Eve, I went out on the ice next morning to attend to their conservation for the coming year by cutting the overhanging branches and brambles away. If I couldn't take a swim in the moat, at least I could take a walk or a skate on it. Of course, I could have hacked a hole in the ice and taken my New Year's Day dip as they do at Highgate Ponds or Tooting Bec Lido. But it is unwise for a swimmer to do such things without help at hand. In any case, this was a rare opportunity to venture on the ice and do work that is awkward to do from a boat.

The ice was full of ripples, like the sand at low tide on Camber Sands, evidence of the Arctic wind that blew over it as it froze. Too bumpy for ice-skating. Here and there was an unexplained hole that had patched itself with clearer, blacker ice, like a window into the water below. Thoreau used to cut such holes in the ice on Walden Pond, kneeling to gaze into the 'quiet parlour of the fishes, pervaded by a softened light as through a window of ground glass'.

A few winters ago I entertained a dozen friends to lunch on the frozen moat. We carried the dining table out there, and had just begun our pudding when there was a sound of cracking ice that ran like thunder from one end to the other. I have never seen people get up so fast. Several guests screamed and dived for the bank. Others were too relaxed in their cups to worry, and indeed the ice held perfectly firm. It was like a scene on the *Titanic*. On another occasion I made

322

a bonfire on the ice, and it burned for hours without ever melting its way through into the water. Afterwards, we just swept away the ash and skated over the dark frozen patch where it had been.

The adventure of each sinuous bough, reaching out over the water in search of sunlight, had created flowing, serpentine lines that I hesitated to cut through. I had to remind myself of the trees' ability to regenerate themselves. Then I made the first incision. I worked with a small triangular bowsaw. It is surprising how much you can do with one in a day. Bowsaws have the supreme advantage of being quiet and allowing you to work at your own human pace. The manic dictatorship of the chainsaw seems to deafen you to all reason or judgement. A chainsaw is ideal for mechanical chores like cutting up logs, but it deprives you of the greatest pleasure of working in the woods: the opportunity to listen to the natural sounds around you. The knowledge that the ice may not stay for long concentrates the mind wonderfully, and by the end of the day I had produced a good pile of next year's firewood. I built it into a hollow cairn on the bank, after the fashion of the sculptor Andy Goldsworthy, who has often done his finest work in ice. In the summer it would remind me of the ice, and wild hops would clamber over it. The moat was still partially surrounded by trees but they no longer oppressed it. It could breathe more freely. I made a bonfire of the brushwood and warmed myself by it in the dusk.

36
TO THE SEA

IT WAS LATE September, just over two years after the rain-storm in the moat when I had first conceived my amphibious journey, and eighteen months after my first swims on the Scilly Isles. I had been at my desk all summer writing up my log and often swimming in the moat, which helped clear my mind, rendering the impressions and recollections of my wanderings more lucid. The more I wrote, the more I missed my adventures and longed to make one more swim across the county, beginning in my moat and ending in the sea.

I rose early in the autumn half-light, crossed the wet lawn in my nightshirt, and swam several lengths of the moat, mist rising off it from six inches above the surface. I wore goggles and plunged my face underwater at each stroke so that the clusters of duckweed looming up looked like the models of molecules built by Crick and Watson in their Cambridge laboratory in the early sixties. It was a cold, grey dawn, and the icy water jolted me awake, then settled me into an aquatic frame of mind for the journey ahead. I had drawn a sort of ley-line across the map of Suffolk, beginning in my moat and joining up all the swimmable water on the way in a 'sub-terranean stream' to the sea twenty-five miles to the east at Walberswick. This was to be my route, a kind of homage to John Cheever and 'The Swimmer'. Instead of walking or running like Ned Merrill in the story (or Burt Lancaster in the film), I would bicycle, in the hope of doing the trip in a single day under my own steam.

After breakfast, I pedalled off down our village green in a

dense fog. In spite of a promising weather forecast, here I was with both bike lamps on at half-past eight wondering what on earth I was doing. My route lay along a procession of some of the most beautiful churches in Suffolk – Mellis, Yaxley, Eye, Horham, Stradbroke, Laxfield, Ubbeston, Huntingfield, Walpole, Bramfield, Blythburgh (which is probably *the* finest, anywhere), and finally the wonderful ruins of Walberswick. If the mist would only clear, their flint towers would stand out on the horizon like milestones all the way to the sea.

I soon reached Eye, where I leant the bike beside the Abbey bridge over the River Dove and clambered down the bank to a pool almost directly below the brick arch, hidden from the road by the parapet, where the girls from the old Eye Grammar School used to come to bathe. Two frayed and much-knotted ropes still dangled from a tall Scots pine. I was mentally preparing myself for a ritual dip when a pair of loudly disputing kingfishers shot past me straight through the bridge. They shocked me into going in, and going in soon shocked me into coming straight out again into the relative warmth of the mist, now penetrated by sunbeams and beginning to lift as I went up Dragon Hill on the long haul to Stradbroke. My course passed through Horham, where Benjamin Britten used to retreat from the endless visitors at Aldeburgh and compose at his cottage. Always a keen bather, he had a plastic swimming tank in the garden.

By the time I reached Stradbroke five miles on, I was looking forward to the warmth of the village swimming pool. Here was a place that has had the good sense to build its health centre, indoor pool and village hall next door to each other as if to confirm that swimming can seriously improve your health and social life. Inside, twenty Suffolk women in grey rinses and black one-piece costumes were having a fine time doing water aerobics, like a bingo audience. I swam lengths in a lane down one side of the little twenty-metre pool, in water at eighty-two degrees, with two other local swimmers, and was struck by the easy informality of the place. This is where the citizenry of Stradbroke come to relax, take their exercise, exchange gossip, and linger in the privacy of steam under the hot shower. The infants learn to swim here almost from birth, and the older children are taught to roll like the Esquimaux in the brightly-coloured kayaks that hang upright round the walls like chrysalids.

It was mid-morning when I came out of the pool, and the sun had chased the mist away. I passed an old man in a ditch, clearing it with a sickle in the proper way, and there was home-made jam set out for sale on a little table at the roadside. At Laxfield they were selling apples outside the allotments and there was late-flowering yarrow and buttercup in the verges. From the Low House pub below the graveyard, I followed the infant River Blyth along a winding back lane down the Vale of Ubbeston for three miles, through a tunnel of ancient hornbeam, hazel, field maple and oak, bombarded as I rode by falling acorns, conkers, crab apples and, at one point, walnuts. This stretch of country is so hilly that you cycle over the crest of one dizzy eminence and you're level with the top of a church tower just peeping over the next. The tractors were all out seizing the day, attacking the pale stubble with huge ten-furrow ploughs, painting the rounded hillsides brown against the perfect blue sky.

By one o'clock I had gone through the village of Heveningham, and was speeding down Cock's Hill past venerable stag-headed parkland oaks when I at last beheld Heveningham Hall, sunlit in Palladian splendour on its grassy hillside, with an endless lake twinkling and flashing in the sun below. I made my way through the grounds along a footpath and found a quiet spot by the western shore to leave my things. There was nobody about, and the owners, who had given me permission to swim, were away. Hauling on the wetsuit, I had a moment's doubt about the wisdom of swimming nearly a mile-and-a-half of lake alone. But the weather was ideal, nobody had been available at such short notice, and in the wetsuit I would be unlikely to get cold or cramped.

I swam straight for the middle, heading for a wooded island. It felt fine. The water was green and clear. I wore goggles and gazed into the translucent sunlit mist of millions of microscopic creatures and algae, with here and there a patch of slender ribbon weed reaching up for the ceiling of the lake like an Indian rope trick. I soon fell into the trance of rhythm, the fish-like feeling that can take you a long way before you've noticed it. You lean into the water and feel its even gentleness lifting you as you steal through the surface. The secret is to respect it but never fear it, so you can relax and sense the molecules moving around you as you swim. This feeling for the water forms the basis of the training of Gennadi Touretski, who coaches the Australian Olympic swimmers. He is said to study how fish move, and believes that it is not muscular power that makes champion swimmers, but efficiency. Two of the fastest swimmers in the world, Alexander Popov and Michael Klim, are taught by Touretski to behave like fish, feeling the water for the path of least resistance. Johnny Weissmuller, the Olympic swimmer and the first film Tarzan, had noticed the importance of sensitivity to the water as he trained at the Illinois Athletic Club in the 1920s: 'I studied the purchase power I got on the water with my hands and forearms. Water is elusive, but you can get hold of it if you know how to go after it.'

As I swam past the wooded island, a heron flapped off lazily over the lake ahead and came to rest by the shore. He kept on doing this all the way, keeping such a precise 150 yards between us that you could have used him to measure distance.

When Sir Joshua Vanneck bought Heveningham Hall in 1752, he had a new classical house built around the original by Sir Robert Taylor. Two lakes, fed by the Blyth, were dug out of the marsh at the bottom of the hill below the house. The original Grand Hall had been built round six massive oaks which reputedly supported the roof as they grew. Foresters and yeomen used to hang their nets, belts, cross-bows and saddles in them. Later, in 1782, Capability Brown was employed by the Vannecks to redesign the landscape around the house. Brown's original drawings show that he planned to join up and widen the existing fish ponds, extending them into a far more extensive lake stretching one-and-a-half miles from the house all the way to the village of Walpole, following the course of the River Blyth to the east.

But six months after he submitted his plans, Brown died, and although the park was created, the new lake was never dug. By the First World War, one of the two original lakes had become known as 'the Dead Lake' because it had silted up. It later reverted to a marsh, with alder trees and sallow growing in it.

It was in this condition that Heveningham Hall was eventually purchased two or three years ago by its present owners, Mr and Mrs Hunt. The house was in a sorry state, having been sold on behalf of the nation by Michael Heseltine to a man from Dubai, during whose tenure some dreadful things happened to the exquisite original interiors designed by James Wyatt. The Wyatt library was all but destroyed in a fire which raged through the east wing, some Wyatt fireplaces were mysteriously stolen, and the owner failed to keep up the mortgage repayments to his Swiss bank. He then died bankrupt, so that this treasure of English Palladian architecture fell into the hands of the official receiver.

Fortunately, the new owners resolved to revive the noble Vanneck tradition of sparing no expense. They set out to restore the house to its former glory, and complete Capability Brown's unfinished grand plan by creating the extended lake as he had designed it two hundred years earlier. It was an enormous project. The old lake was drained and the contractors bought the conveyor belt that had been used to build the Channel Tunnel to carry away the earth and silt as they dug it out. In a classic builder's cock-up, ten men originally spent three weeks assembling the immense machine on site, only to discover it was back to front, and although it might carry mud into the lake, it would not carry it out. They then spent two more weeks dismantling and reassembling it the right way round. The resulting lake stretches very nearly to Walpole. The intention is to excavate the remaining leg to the village in the near future.

I hummed 'The Bold Navigator' to myself as I swam, an old navvies' song, imagining Capability Brown in silk breeches sketching his plans, and the immense cost in human toil of digging lakes like this at Holkham, Blickling, Blenheim or Chatsworth, or even excavating the original fish ponds here by hand. The navvies camping out in shanties, the armies of wheelbarrows and spades, wheelbarrow-bridges and viaducts over bottomless puddles of mud, the men dragged scampering after their barrows, locked between the shafts, along sprung, precarious planks. The excavated silt had been banked and planted with sapling parkland trees in the way Brown indicated on his plan. Here was a unique insight into the way great estates must have looked in the eighteenth century before reaching the maturity we see today.

I had to use the empty shell of a freshwater mussel plucked from the mud to cut open the try-your-strength plastic wrapping of a 'Power Bar' I had bought in the bike shop and tucked into my wetsuit boot. Refuelled, I swam on, plunging my face into the sweet-tasting water, my rhythmic exhalations reverberating noisily below like off-key whalesong, as though the whole lake were a sounding board. As I neared Walpole in the final stretch, submerged skyscrapers of waterweed loomed up and pale green fingers frisked me as I swam through and landed.

'It's 007,' said one of the three tractor drivers I encountered as I walked back in the dripping wetsuit. They were preparing seed drills and harrows to sow a wild-flower meadow on the excavated earth banked up beside the lake. They spoke proudly of the wild life that was already attracted to the lake and, as I walked on, an oystercatcher skittered away off the shore, complaining loudly.

After lunch by the lake, I biked to Walpole and over to Bramfield, then pressed on to the gorse heath of Westleton, and a sudden view of Blythburgh church beyond a free-range pig city of tin huts in acres and acres of mud. The foreground somehow emphasised the nobility of Blythburgh's church tower, presiding with its reflection and its church roof full of carved angels, over the Blyth estuary and marshes, now flooded by a high tide. During the Civil War, Cromwell's soldiers had lain flat on their backs in the nave, trying to shoot down the angels. They only succeeded in winging them, and the bullet holes are there to this day.

When I reached the A12, I was shocked by the sudden violence of the traffic. I had to go along a half-mile of it, then cross over and turn off. Lorries thundered by, leaving too little room, buffeting me in their slipstream. I felt suddenly vulnerable, in a way I never did in the water. I thought of Ned Merrill, trying to cross the two-lane highway in his swimming costume under gathering storm-clouds, mocked by the passing cars:

> Had you gone for a Sunday afternoon ride that day you might have seen him, close to naked, standing on the shoulders of Route 424, waiting for a chance to cross. You might have wondered if he was the victim of foul play, had his car broken down, or was he merely a fool. Standing barefoot in the deposits of the highway – beer cans, rags, and blowout patches – exposed to all kinds of ridicule, he seemed pitiful.

It is a turning point in the story, when you realise Merrill has lost everything, that he is naked right down to his trunks, that when he reaches home there will be no home. It will be boarded up, empty. It is then that he asks himself, 'At what point had this prank, this joke, this piece of horseplay become serious?' He knows he cannot go back, because 'he had covered a distance that made his return impossible.' By the standards of the A12, no doubt my journey would have seemed absurd. But it was always an entirely serious enterprise, if at times surrealist, and unlike the tragic Merrill I felt enriched by my long swim.

I turned off down a timeless sandy avenue of oaks, potholed by rabbits, to a distant farmhouse on a promontory jutting into the wide Blyth marshes. It was four-thirty. I had arrived just in time to catch the high tide and swim off a hundred-foot wooden jetty built out from the headland over the water a few years ago for the filming of Peter Greenaway's *Drowning by Numbers*. There was no need for the wetsuit because the brackish tide was warmed by the huge solar collector of black mud it had flowed over, all the way from Walberswick harbour, as it rose. I lowered myself off the jetty into a foot and a half of estuary water and propelled myself over the bed of delicate, smooth mud, out into the deeper waters of a maze of submerged drainage channels. Rows of gnarled wooden stakes, on which the unwary swimmer might impale himself, marked these channels, many of them just beneath the surface, so I embarked on a kind of maze swim which took me all the way back to that very first day's swimming on Bryher, and the 'Scilly Maze' of pebbles on the beach. But the water was astonishingly warm and delicious, and so was the sensual healing of the silky mud. I swam out into the marsh, following the deeper channels, listening to the constant chorus of the thousands of seabirds that thronged the glistening horizons of the river. This is where the mullet come up in shoals in summer to bask in the warm shallows. When I dug out a handful of mud, it was full of the blackened shells of cockles and a million invisible microscopic creatures.

Afterwards at the house, my friend Meg, one of the Walberswick Shiverers from Christmas Day, filled watering cans from the hot tap in the kitchen, and I stood in the back yard holding them one by one above my head, sluicing off the mud in a glorious hot shower. Tim came out of his workshop and joined us for tea outside the back door. There was now just time to bike on down to Walberswick across the heath before sunset.

I cycled by the woods where George Orwell made love to Eleanor Jaques, his neighbour when he lived at Southwold, and into the village past the ruined church where he used to sit and read. I passed the house of Freddy the fisherman ('The Sole Plaice for Some Fin Special'). It was a quarter past six, and the sun, which already shared the sky with the blushing new moon, was beginning to go down. I hurried out over the little wooden bridge where they hold the annual crabbing contest in summer, and printed faint tyre-tracks across the last two hundred yards of cracked saltpan desert mud on Walberswick marsh. Scaling the sand-dunes, I ran down the deserted beach, flung off my clothes and waded into the surf.

I felt the sweetness of tired limbs and fell headlong into the waves, striking towards the horizon that appeared intermittently beyond the breakers. I had left my rucksack and clothes beside a beautiful pebble starfish on the beach, another echo of the Scilly Maze. Perhaps I had at last swum my way through it. When I reached the relative calm of unbroken swell, I looked back towards the shore. A crimson mist lay over the sea as a red-hot sun dropped over the pantiled roofs behind the sand-dunes. The sea-fret shaded to a deep purple along the curve of the bay where Dunwich should have been, and obscured the giant puffball of Sizewell B. One of the beauties of this flat land of Suffolk is that when you're swimming off the shore and the waves come up, it subsides from view and you could be miles out in the North Sea. An orange sickle of new moon hung above the chimneys in a deep mauve sky. Autumn bonfires glowed in the mist and floated white smoke-rings above it. The beach shone in the gathering dusk as the tide fell and the sea grew less perturbed. I turned and swam on into the quiet waves.

ACKNOWLEDGEMENTS

I could never have made this journey, or written the book, without all the encouragement and inspiration I have received along the way. I should like to thank especially Kate Campbell and Terence Blacker for believing in the book from the beginning and fostering it so generously. Jane Turnbull, my agent, has provided endless good-humoured support, and I thank those friends whose contributions and imaginative insights on the emerging manuscript have been invaluable: Tony Barrell, Oliver Bernard, Sue Roe, Tony and Bundle Weston and Dudley Young.

David Holmes has given the book a special beauty with his subtle illustrations, and I thank him heartily. Gary Rowland, too, has been characteristically magnanimous, not only in designing these pages, but swimming through some of them too.

To those who have supported the expedition, and the book, with their ideas, hospitality, inspiration and, on occasion, guidance towards secret swimming holes, I offer my thanks. Others have swum alongside, rowed boats, provided hot baths, or ferried me to remote shores, all with the utmost goodwill. I want particularly to acknowledge: Lydia Alexander, Meg Amsden, Steve and Liz Ashley, William Astor, Tony and Teresa Axon, David Baird, Caroline Booton, Jules Cashford, Mavis Cheek, John Clarke, Sue Clifford, John Cornwell, Paul Crampin, Geraldine Daly, Clive and Jayne Davies, Mervyn Day, Andrew Edwards, Gavin Edwards, Biddy Foord, Carol Freeman, Rob Fryer, Jeremy and Erica

Hart, the late Maurice Hatton, Mike Hodges, Tim Hunkin, Carol Holloway, Jon and Lois Hunt, Robert Hutchison, Denis Johnson, J.D.F. Jones, Liz Kessler, Angela King, Caroline Kenneil, Carol Laws, Julie Llyn-Evans, Richard Mabey, Sid Merry, Tricia Mersh, Lucy Moy-Thomas, William and Alison Parente, Rob Parfitt, Megan Patterson, Brian Perman, Saranne Piccaver, Olivia Pomp, Andrew Sanders, Judith Smyth, Mark Thompson, Michael Tomlinson, Stephen Turner, Adrian and Margaret Turton, Errollyn Wallen, Mike and Kate Westbrook, David Whatley, Jules Wilkinson, John and Fleur Wilson, Ken Worpole, Sarah Young and Caroline Younger.

I am unable to acknowledge individually all the dozens of people who helped me in my search for local swimming folklore, but I am especially grateful to Mick Andrews, Jenny Davies, Pop and Pearl Day, Don Dewsbury, Ruby Hulatt, Tony Pinner, and June Shrubbs in Cambridge and the Fens; Gladys Adams in Harleston; Robert Moss in Suffolk; Amy Harvey in Chagford; Bill Mitchell in Cornwall; Evelyn Buckland in Somerset; Jenny Cavender and Elizabeth Gale in Bridport; Ailsa Wilson and Richard Hoseason Smith in Scotland. My thanks to the swimming clubs and pools who made me so welcome, especially at Diss, Farleigh Hungerford, Hathersage, Henleaze, Highgate, Ingleton, Marshall St., Parliament Hill Fields, Penzance and Tooting Bec; to Paul Kibbett and David Robinson at London Zoo; Val Russell and Robin Freeman in Winchester Library; David Beskine at the Ramblers' Association and Dr Mike Ladle of the Institute of Freshwater Ecology.

In the editorial department, I would like to thank Roger Alton for pitching me into the deep end by inviting me to write an early article on swimming for the Guardian; Jonathan Burnham at Chatto for commissioning the book and Rebecca Carter for her meticulous, patient editing of a text that often meandered and sometimes overflowed – any remaining omissions or mistakes are mine. Respect and acknowledgement are also due to Charles Sprawson, author of the modern swimming classic, *Haunts of the Black Masseur*, and, of course, I owe an obvious debt to John Cheever's short story, 'The Swimmer'.

INDEX